Our Late Great Century

1900–1999

G. Owen McGinnis
MD, FACS

HERITAGE BOOKS
2010

HERITAGE BOOKS
AN IMPRINT OF HERITAGE BOOKS, INC.

Books, CDs, and more—Worldwide

For our listing of thousands of titles see our website at www.HeritageBooks.com

Published 2010 by
HERITAGE BOOKS, INC.
Publishing Division
100 Railroad Ave. #104
Westminster, Maryland 21157

Other books by the author:
A Third Life, A Novel

International Standard Book Numbers
Paperbound: 978-0-7884-5168-3
Clothbound: 978-0-7884-8352-3

Contents

False Start

Second Chance

Life Outside the Hospital

Departures

Illustrations

Preface

The Great Century is gone, but there were days and even years when time seemed to stand still. Now that my steps are slower, my clock runs faster. I have been a witness to most of the 20th century and have talked and lived with those from the years I did not see. These stories tell of a century of change.

In my lifetime, I have seen a people without jobs, without food, and without hope. Our nation recovered only to be attacked, struggle to exist, and then gain strength to lead the world. The past century brought inconceivable changes in transportation, communication, government, medicine and personal comfort. I have seen the golden age of medicine and of my country.

We all live in history; few record what they have seen. To reflect on ourselves, we must look to the past and at those who came before to get some understanding of why we are the way we are. If we don't know where we came from, we don't know where we are and where we want to be.

Many today wonder how ordinary people lived way back in the early and mid 20th century. I would like to know about those who came before me in the 19th century and suffered untold hardships with small reward to pave the way for changes we take for granted. How did they survive those primitive days? Nothing is left of their lives, but words in a ledger, names on a tombstone and oral history, fading in time and memory. I believe my stories have importance because today we see history rewritten for political or sociological reasons by those who were not witnesses.

I make no attempt to give a day-by-day account of the 20th century. As we look to our past, memory shows vivid pictures of extraordinary events and fading images of days and sometimes years of commonplace struggles and happenings. This collection of special episodes and experiences show some of the changes in life and surgery of the century from one perspective. After the introductory chapter, it's written in rough chronological order. The Antecedents section was given to me by witnesses of years I did not see.

My stories are true, or at least mostly true.

Acknowledgements

I am indebted to my wife, Betty, for putting up with me while I wrote this book and for the final proofreading. She has always been good at pointing out my errors. My sister, Dr Carol Kay did early editing. Mrs. Sandra Ridgeway did my final editing.

New Beginning

I Didn't Go Alone

I

I again saw under the sun that the race is not to the swift and the battle is not to the warriors, and neither is bread to the wise, nor wealth to the discerning nor favor to men of ability for time and chance overtake them all.

Ecclesiastes 9:11

On a hot June day in 1954, I sat in Denny Stadium in Tuscaloosa listening to people I didn't know say words I never remembered. While I ignored the speakers, I thought of the first McGinnis in this land. He was seen as ignorant Irish, but was smart enough to fight in the American Revolution. Generations of farmers and tradesmen followed him. After four years of college, four of medical school, much sweat, some tears and scars, I was about to get my M.D. degree. As I went down the aisle and to the line going up the steps to the platform on the field, I thought to myself I had done something nobody else in the family had ever done.

But did you see those people who went with me? They weren't my parents or my wife-to-be. They were in their seats watching me. People suddenly seemed to come from everywhere. They went down the aisle and on the stage where they didn't belong. And they weren't...well, they weren't dressed for the occasion. A tall man with snow-white hair and mustache came first. He wore dark wrinkled pants held up by striped suspenders over a white shirt with no tie. Behind him a gaunt man in a torn gray uniform limped, leaning on a stick. Other men with thick stained hands wore tattered work clothes and high top shoes with mud on the sides. One had sawdust across his pants. Women wore faded print dresses with aprons. Then there's that big fellow who came all the way down from the top row. Can you believe a heavy coat with big buttons and wide lapels in this heat? And those funny looking pants--sort of like knickers--and that hat? It couldn't hide the red hair. He looked like he came from a costume party. He was laughing and talking all the way, with an accent, some sort of foreigner. Did you see those people? Of course, you didn't. There was nobody on the speakers' platform, but school officials and graduates.

If a man gains knowledge and a degree of wisdom, he originates little of this. He learned because there was a vast body of knowledge on this earth when he arrived, and teachers willing to teach.

If a man fulfills opportunities and attains success, much is not of his own doing. Untold generations before him struggled to escape persecution and poverty. They crossed oceans under unspeakable conditions. They did heavy labor with simple tools and their sweat trying to improve their own lives. When they had gone, whether by intent or accident, they had improved the life of generations to come and put opportunity in their path.

If a man both gives and receives love and happiness, he is fortunate because time and chance overtake us all. If a man has any or all of these things, then God willed it or permitted it.

I heard my name called, took two steps, reached out my hand, and the president of the University of Alabama put a rolled-up sheepskin in it. Other names brought a polite applause. After mine, I thought I heard shouts and cheers.

All those people weren't on the stage, but they should have been. Who can say they weren't there in spirit? The degree was granted to one, but earned through the efforts of many.

G.W. McGINNIS
DEALER IN GENERAL MERCHANDISE
MANUFACTURER ROUGH DRESSED LUMBER

Antecedents

Iggle
2

If you opened your eyes tomorrow morning to discover you were in the year 1910, how would you explain: computers, cell phones, television, heart transplants, antibiotics, credit cards, life in space, or a rocket ship trip to the moon? Life in the first of 20th century was simpler than the hectic pace at the beginning of 21st century. To our eyes people of those years look primitive. Other than the rich, most lived lives of subsistence. But families lived in hope their children would go farther than their parents in education and prosperity. None could have dreamed of changes, opportunities, and dangers that lay ahead in the 20th century.

George Washington McGinnis was proud of his little store and hired a traveling photographer to record it. He stood out front with his clerk, Emmett Cox, and a customer named Sheb Jones. By this time, Mr. Mac was pudgy with a round ruddy face. He had a solemn, unchanging, gruff appearance masking the man within. On this day, he invited a customer and former employee, Emma Trammell, to pose in the photograph.

"Oh, Mista 'Ginnis, I couldn't do that; I best go."

"Emma, you don't have a choice. The camera already has you in its focus. You can't leave"

"I can't?"

"No, but I'll warn you: when the camera takes your picture, it takes off all your clothes! "

So one summer day in 1916, Mr. Mac, Sheb, and Emmett stood in front of the store all in a row, solemn and stiff. Emma stood at the far side of the shed and got as much as she could behind a post. She hid her face so nobody would know who that naked woman was.

George Washington McGinnis was George to his wife and close friends, G. W. to others, and Papa to his children and to me years later as first grandson. Any man of Irish persuasion can be called Mac. He was Mr. Mac to his employees. His businesses were doing well in 1916.

His store was a plain white frame building with a sign running the width at the top of the shed-like roof sheltering the front. A window was on either side of the doorway. A bench across one side of the dirt floor under the shed was for loafers in the day and drinkers at night. Signs on the front urged people to use Coca-Cola, RyeOla or Star Tobacco. In summer, produce was clustered about the front door.

Inside rows of shelves held groceries, dry goods and a little hardware. The counter began at the front of the store and ran half way back on the right. On the counter were a cash register and a six-drawer thread box filled with spools of thread in various colors and sizes. A cast iron stove with a rail around the fat center part sat in the middle of the store. In winter, pans might be on the stove or on the railing to cook food, or put a little humidity in the air. This general merchandise store sold almost anything. Lumber could be ordered for delivery or picked up by the customer behind the store.

Will Uzzell, a meat cutter who had been butchering longer than anybody could remember, ran the market at the back of the store.

The customer came in and said, "Now Will, you know how I want my meat."

Will took the quarter of meat from the refrigerated locker, threw it on the butcher block, cut the slice and wrapped it in brown butcher paper. Old records show on one occasion Papa took a cow as

G. W. McGINNIS
DEALER IN GENERAL MERCHANDISE
MANUFACTURER OF ROUGH AND DRESSED LUMBER

partial payment of a bill for a casket. This $12.50 cow was typical supply for the meat department.

Kerosene was parceled out to customers who brought their own gallon can. People called it coal oil or just oil. The smaller cap of the cam was always lost and the spout plugged with an Irish potato. The McGinnis store sold gasoline for those automobile contraptions that might pass through town. If a customer wanted gas, he went in the store and announced his needs; the clerk walked out to an exposed hundred gallon tank near the road, pulled a lever up and down, pumped gas in a five gallon gas can and poured it through a funnel into the car. The storage tank was refilled from a tank hauled in by mule team the 12 miles from Branchville near Odenville.

When the trees are all cut, men in the lumber business move on. My Grandfather McGinnis had moved his family from Cherokee County to the little town of Springville, Alabama in 1910. The family lived in rented houses until they built their own in 1917. He bought five hundred acres of heavy timber on Blount Mountain and set up the sawmill he brought with him. His crews cut timber and sawed it in the steam driven sawmill. The boiler was fed by hand with slabs, wood scraps and sawdust. Lumber was hauled down the mountain in mule drawn wagons and sold in the rough state or finished in a planning mill near the railroad depot built a year or so later. A second mill was later started on the bank of the Coosa Rive. Logs were floated down the river to supply the mill. Lumber not sold locally was shipped by rail and sold in Chattanooga. To become part of the community, Papa joined the usual organizations. He had no formal education, but was literate. He was asked to be a member of the school board. He was a member of the Methodist Church and a Mason. He also belonged to the Klan--the Ku Klux Klan. Many merchants were members. These men were known in the community, and their membership known. But the workings of the Klan were secret, with the exception of the annual Klan picnic. Each summer Papa took his family to the crowded event at East Lake Park in the eastern side of Birmingham.

Once, he put on his robe, sash and hood and went into the night. About an hour later hooded figures burst into a small house at the edge of town. They snatched up Mose Jackson from the supper table where he was sitting with his wife and two boys. The hooded men dragged him screaming into the yard. There was no doubt about what was to happen. They tied Mose to an oak tree in his own front yard. The cloaked figures then whipped him on the back. One of these phantoms of the night told him the reason for the punishment before the whipping and again afterward. Mose abused his wife and children. His wife's face showed evidence. He commonly drank away wages while his family did without. The nightriders left him on the tree for his family to take down. His wife and children saw the beating, heard the words and promises. The riders never came back. Mose became a model husband and father.

Mose Jackson was white, as were all the other victims.

After World War I, the Klan changed in Springville. New members may have had new priorities, or the group could have become obsessed with power and changed direction. Papa never participated after that time.

Springville was typical of isolated Alabama towns in the early 20th century. People settled here for obvious reasons: a large spring gushed water from the foot of the hill on the north side of the road and poured into a lake surrounded by a walk-way, which had changed little when I saw it in the mid-thirties. The crystal clear lake was a few feet deep with a sand bottom. Huge brim, goldfish, and carp swam about attracting lookers and feeders. The lake emptied into a stream that crossed the road and was known only as "The Branch." In earlier years, there was no bridge; water spilled over the paved road to the other side. Wagons and an occasional out of town car drove through the water. People stopped to water horse or mule as they passed or even drove cattle down for a drink. Downtown Springville was paved. County roads were dirt or chert. In 1910 there was neither phone nor automobile in the county. The railroad ran through the edge of town and was the main transportation other than buggies and wagons.

With little contact with the outside world, people in small towns tended to be more introspective and at the same time more knowledgeable about their neighbor. There is a narrow line between being interested and being nosy. Sometimes this line was vague, but people tended to know everything about other people's lives in this small community, even without phones. People visited each other and stopped to talk at the stores. There was no need for soap opera characters. People saw real events with real people.

In small towns almost any event became common knowledge. Mr. Mac had his men build a small boat for 12-year-old son Gaston. The boat was great fun in the lake for him and his friends A few of the town drunks confiscated it one night, poked sticks at the fish and poured the last of their booze in the lake to try to get the fish drunk. The city fathers demanded the boat be removed.

Progress and change did come to this little town. George Byers bought the first car in the county about 1915. When he drove his aute-mo-bile back to

Springville, people came from all around to see it. The company gave him a dealership to entice him to buy the car. After that day, he did sell Fords for several years. Six months later Bob Ewing went to Birmingham and drove the second car back to Springville. When he stopped at the feed store, people gathered from the whole town. One merchant closed his store to come and see the car. They had never seen anything like this.

"It sure is purty, Bob. What kind is she?"

"I don't know. What's it say there on the side? Oh, I remember…it's a Buck. That's it, a Buck."

From that day on, he was Buck Ewing whether he drove a Buick or not.

The town of Springville was a cluster of little businesses gathered around a main highway, a railroad line, a spring and lake. Coming from the northeast down Highway 11 on the right a few feet from the road was the Herring Hotel, a large two story white frame building with a porch across the front. As transportation improved, people came from miles around, even as far as Birmingham, for Sunday brunch at the hotel.

Next was the Young livery stable, a simple square white frame building with large double doors in the center. Papa stored white and tan coffins and materials to build coffins on the second floor of the stable. Sometimes, country people could not afford the $35.00 for a coffin and built their own. They bought metal plates saying, "Our Darling Daughter" or "Rest in Peace" or "Beloved Father" and the like.

Next was a driveway, a chert covered parking area and then the McGinnis store. Next to the store was Dr. Clayton's office. This small white concrete block building had originally been a barbershop run by a black man named Fastus. Next door was the Ash Drug Store, a plain white building. Next were the Woodall Hardware, a drive with a parking area, then the Byers and Copeland and T. E. Moody stores. Byers and Copeland had a large glass front. The Moody store was plain like most of the others. Beyond T. E. Moody was a parking area and then several empty lots to the branch. This area served as a parking space for wagons, mules and horses. Long hitching posts ran along both sides. Beyond the branch were Dr. Arnold's dental office and Marshall Owen's barbershop. On the left of Highway 11, the yellow painted frame Methodist Church was across the road from the Herring Hotel; nearby was The Masonic Lodge, which G. W.'s son, Gaston, swept out once a week for 50¢, then Charley Allison's store, then the Bank of Springville with a parking area and drive, then the post office with a parking area for postal carriers in the back, Matthew's Sundries, Lee Lassater, and Porter Presley, which was on the corner of the road to Odenville. Then Bob Ewing's store came next to the branch. Bob Ewing also owned the gin and closed the feed and seed store at cotton-picking time. Beyond the branch was Scott's Blacksmith Shop. This was primarily an open shelter with glowing furnace, bellows, and anvil in the center. Clusters of tools, metal bars and rods were hanging on the walls and in piles in the corners. Old records show charges to the McGinnis business of 40¢ for shoeing a mare and 10¢ for sharpening three plow points.

These buildings were simple and drab. All had electric power, but no phones and no air conditioning. Only the $12.50 cow was cool in summer. The grade school called the Rock School and the brick high school on a hill north of the main road were the only masonry buildings in the town. Most buildings had a metal roof with varying degrees of rust. All had a chimney or stove pipe from the roof or side. Each in the main part of town was set back a few feet from the roadway. There was no sidewalk. Shoppers walked in the street from store to store. Other businesses were away from the downtown area. The McGinnis planning mill was about a mile and a half away at a railroad siding. Goodwin's gristmill was on the way toward the McGinnis sawmill on Blount Mountain. The clear water of the millpond lured boys for swimming in summer. Some rode horses, most rode bicycles.

And then, there was Jack Hatchet whose business was on Blount Mountain. Jack was a mountain man--an Alabama mountain man. He was a wiry man, always in overalls and blue shirt with a misshaped hat that had seen better days. He had a hawk-like nose, a squint to his eyes and a beard of a day or so. He was an uneducated rough looking man, but with a heart of gold. Jack Hatchet grew a large crop of corn on some of the flat areas on Blount Mountain. He claimed the occupation of trapper. He trapped raccoons and muskrats and sold the hides to T. E. Moody, who shipped them out. Jack never brought an ear of corn down the mountain because farther up the mountain beyond the McGinnis sawmill was his other business--his still. Once a week he took a load of his fresh run down the mountain to regular customers in Springville.

One busy Saturday in the summer of 1916 the usual crowd filled the stores and spilled into the street. People came in buggies, wagons, on horseback or on foot for the weekly or monthly load of supplies, cloth for a new dress, a new plow or just news and gossip. Streets and stores were filled with people. Sales were not limited to stores; things were sold or traded on the streets and parking lots. In the midst of all of the events, Porter Presley cranked up his gasoline unit and parched peanuts. After they were sacked, he was out on the street shouting, "Get 'em while they're hot--five cents!!" Men were standing three deep in Marshall Owens's barbershop to get a twenty-five cent haircut.

Emmett Cox looked at the crowd through the window of the McGinnis store and said, "Mr. Mac, yonder come ol' Jack Hatchet makin' his rounds".

Jack stopped his wagon in the lot at the side of the store and came in. "Evenin, Mr. Mac, Emmett. How's business?"

"Can't complain, how 'bout you?"

"Just finished ma route, sold ma last gallon to Mr. Moody, but I still got a little bottle if you want one.

"You mean Mr. Moody, the Sunday School Superintendent?"

"Weell, you know how it is, Mac. He has eleven kids; he needs a gallon a week. I'll just take ma hundred pound o' sugar and be on ma way."

"What's in that sack you brought, that's ajumpin' up and down?"

"Oh, I almost forgot, tha'sa iggle. I tol' ya they wuz up ther."

"Jack, don't you mean some kinda big ol' hawk or somethin'?"

Jack shook his head and said again, "Tha'sa iggle. Caught him in a trap. Moody won't buy him so I'll give him to ya. I ain't about to turn him aloose. He dang near tor' the back of ma hand off."

Jack Hatchett loaded the sugar, stepped up on one of the wheel spokes, pulled himself up, and settled on the bench. He gave a little twitch to the reins as he made a kissing sound and said, "Come up there!" The mules and wagon pulled away with the grinding, crushing sound of metal rims on chert and the clink of metal and slap of leather harness.

At the doorway, Mr. Mac and Emmett looked back from the disappearing wagon to the tow sack jumping and flopping about on the floor. The sack was torn to a dangerous degree. One hole showed enormous feet with huge talons tied with a light cord. As the sack rolled over, an eye peered through holes and parts of the beak showed through.

"Lordie, Mr. Mac, what 're we gonna do with tha ...that monster? You ain't gonna turn it aloose in here are ya?"

Mr. Mac located some of his mill workers and they built a heavy wire cage with a door at one end and mounted it on short legs.

"Now, how we gonna get that beast in the cage, Mr. Mac?"

"Emmett, you get in the cage and pull him in; then we'll get you out."

"Lordie, Mr. Mac, he'd eat me fa sure. I'd sooner go back to the sawmill."

Mr. Mac and Emmett jerked that beast out of the sack, cut the string and threw him into the cage in a cloud of dust, feathers and strong words. They closed the door, but had difficulty holding it. Fingers made a good target for beak and talons. After the door was wired shut, they stepped back. Before them stood a full-grown American bald eagle. He walked the length of the cage threatening everybody who came close with those terrible talons and beak. He did not walk horizontally like a chicken, but upright. He did not hop. He strutted with an arrogant unblinking gaze. He was king of the air, being held by earth bound beings.

"What we gonna feed that thing, Mr. Mac?"

Twelve-year-old Gaston came out from his hiding place behind the counter. "Gaston, your Momma has an old crippled hen; run home and ferch it,"

After the eagle got over his initial anger, he ate the hen. When Fanny discovered the truth, suppers were silent for a week. She said absolutely none of her chickens were to feed that devil. Gaston and his friends caught rats and fed them to the eagle. Crowds of people came from all over the county to see Mac's eagle while the bird stalked back and forth like the caged monarch he was. Over the next two months, Mr. Mac and the eagle tolerated each other, but barely. The eagle glared at his keeper and followed his every motion as he moved about the store. After a time, the bird no longer tried to attack the hand that fed him when the cage was opened. Mr. Mac couldn't pet him like a dog. Monarchs are not to be petted, not even caged monarchs; they are to be served. Sentiment between the two was not affection, but cautious respect.

One day, Mr. Mac came in and stood by the cage. He and the arrogant eagle stared at each other a long while. "Folks, this is a wild thing; he doesn't belong in a cage. He should be free. He should be in his home up in the mountains."

They took the cage out back of the store and opened the door. The two men helping Mr. Mac ran for cover. Gaston watched from a respectable distance. The eagle wouldn't leave. Mr. Mac took a stick and poked him out. He walked stiff legged, stood on the edge of the ditch, glared at all around him and very slowly began flapping those huge wings: swish – swish--swish. After several minutes of this exercise, he flew, but only a few feet across the ditch behind the store. There was more flapping, slowly, slowly and then a little faster while he stretched his neck.

Then he flew again a little farther and landed on Ira Pearson's picket fence, where he walked up and down flapping and stretching for a half hour or so. Finally, the flapping became faster and faster and he rose in the air. He made a majestic sweeping circle, flew in the direction of the lake and disappeared.

Early the next morning, Gaston was sleeping in the second floor of the family home near the lake when he was awakened by a terrible commotion. Dozens of birds of all kinds were chirping, screeching and flying in circles around that eagle in the top of a tree overlooking the lake. By the time Gaston got out of the house, the eagle was gone. He was walking through the yard as three breathless men ran up the hill.

"Quick, where's Mr. Mac? We seen his iggle. We know whur he is!"

"I'm afraid you missed him. He left on the six o'clock train for Chattanooga on business. Where's the eagle?"

The three looked at each other in amazement. "The last time we seen him, he was flappin' them big ol' wings flyin' real fast and low like he knowed whur he was agoin', right over them railroad tracks northeast toward Chatt'nooga."

Written in 1994 from history given to me by my father *Gaston Grady McGinnis*

Afterward

Jack Hatchet had increasing trouble evading the revenue agents in those changing times. For a while he found an ideal location for his still in a cave with a convenient spring. Finally somebody wondered why smoke was coming from a cave. Eventually he resorted to setting fire to the woods when he was cooking off a batch of mash. One more fire wasn't noticed. Ol' Jack Hatchet was last heard from in the early forties. He didn't fit in this changing world and faded away.

Jack Hatchet had two sons. In the late thirties, they were described as raw big-footed country boys. They wore tattered overalls, which had lost the metal buttons on the bib. Through the holes where the buttons had been they placed a man's cufflink to hook to the strap.

In this day of progress, a dam built on Doumas Creek made a lake that blocked their usual route to town. These two refused to change their routine. On Saturday, they walked as they always had along the trail from their house on the mountain. At the bank of the new lake, they took off their shoes and swam fully clothed the half mile to the other side. By the time they walked to town, their clothes were dry and they had their weekly bath. At the end of the day, they retraced their steps, swam back and picked up their shoes and went home.

They also, could not adapt to a changing world.

* * *

In 1926 Dr. Clayton traveled from Springville to Odenville and delivered a baby for the Courtney family. The baby weighed 10 1/2 pounds and came breech. Even today this would be a difficult delivery. In those days a section was out of the question; either the baby was delivered or mother and child died. In their gratitude for the delivery, the parents named the child Gerald Clayton Courtney. Some years later this baby grew into manhood, married and named his first child Gerald Clayton Courtney Jr. This child grew, married and named his first child Gerald Clayton Courtney, III. The child's mother is our daughter, Donna.

We live in a small world.

Peddlers
3

If we need groceries or new clothes or a tool today, we jump in our car and drive to the store to see an overwhelming selection. We may even sit at home and order by phone or E-mail, put it on plastic, and wait for delivery.

There was a day when shopping was not so easy. Farmers were isolated by distance and transportation and their days filled with hours of work. Roads were poor, cars not dependable and mules slow. Every farm home had two Sears Roebuck catalogs: a new one in the house and last year's in the privy. Both served a great need, but the one in the house was not enough for weekly or monthly needs. A trip to town took away a full day of work. The trip wasn't just for shopping, it was a social event that couldn't be rushed. Sometimes needs were other than Saturday. If people couldn't go to the store, the store came to them. In days gone by, numbers of men and occasionally women went from door to door selling things: the Fuller brush man, the Watkins man, the Hoover vacuum cleaner man and a host of others selling a limited number of items. Some had goods everybody wanted; others sold things people didn't know they needed, like encyclopedias or lightning rods. These salesmen worked appropriate areas. A farmer without electricity doesn't need a vacuum cleaner, but his wife would buy vanilla extract from the Watkins man. Some farmers reversed the process and came to town on a regular route selling produce to city people. These traveling salesmen, whether they came from the city or the country, were called peddlers. Those selling to stores were usually called drummers. Some covered large areas, even whole states.

Today with our locked doors and burglar alarms, we look with suspicion on a smiling stranger coming up the walk carrying a satchel. In older days, these men weren't feared, but welcomed as a source of news, gossip or just a break in the monotony of the day. Besides, they might have something the lady of the house just couldn't live without.

The Calendar Clock peddlers sold clocks, which TV says today, were never sold in stores, probably because most people didn't know how to set up a clock and start it. Fashion Calendar Clocks were made from 1875 to 1889 by The Southern Calendar Clock Company in St. Louis and almost all were sold in the rural southeast. The double-faced clock indicates not only the hour and minute, but also the month and day of the month. This mantel or shelf clock was a marvel to people of the South in the drab years after the Big War. They were passed on to children and grandchildren in the twentieth century.

A team of four or five peddlers would locate in a small town or city in a hotel or boarding house, that even small towns had, and cover the surrounding area by horse and buggy. The captain scouted the best roads and prospects and directed the others each day. The captain was said to have driven a buggy drawn by a snow white horse and the peddlers drove black horses. They carried ten or twelve clocks and sold to small town people and farmers for amounts depending on the time of the day. The price was $40 to $45 in the early morning. If the peddler had lunch with the prospect, the price went down. If he ate supper and spent the night, the price could be as low as $32.50. After a sale, with great ceremony the peddler placed the clock on the mantel, wound it, started the pendulum and recorded the exact time. The document inside the door of the clock in our family room says the clock was first started at 1AM, September 1, 1875.

These peddlers sold single items. There was still a great need for food, clothing, and tools. Small towns usually developed around a railroad. The little town of Steel in St. Clair County was typical. Nobody used the real name, but called the town "Steels. These little communities had small general stores, which sold anything that could be shipped by rail. My grandfather, L. L. Owen had a successful store in Steel. Old ledgers show entries for groceries, clothing, hardware, medicines, mule shoes, people shoes, and a host of other items. Farmers in isolated areas still had to lose a day's work to go for supplies. A hard working farmer might make a trip to town once a month.

In the late nineteenth century and early twentieth century there was a great need to make goods more available. When there is a need, someone will fill that need. Bill Trotter equipped a covered wagon and traveled the back roads of St. Clair County selling anything he could haul. He loaded his wagon from my grandfather's store each day and traveled a regular route like the mail carrier. He stopped at a home, tied the team and let down the sides of the wagon to show the stock. His store was then open for business. If the farmer's wife had no money, he took chickens or eggs or other produce in trade. On both sides of the little wagon, shelves were filled with piece goods, notions for sewing, tobacco, snuff, candy, gum, flour, sugar, coffee or just anything that would sell. My mother remembered this peddler as a kindly old gentleman with long gray hair and beard. He had lost his right arm in the Big War. He and three unmarried daughters ran this little business. He also bought scrap iron. As a child, my uncle Jake made a few cents selling scrap metal to ol' Bill Trotter.

Space in the rolling store wagon was limited, so selection was limited. This caused social disaster on at least one occasion. There was a good stock of different sizes of dresses, but all the same fabric pattern. Five ladies showed up for a social event with exactly the same dress. Bill Trotter did not go to the event or he might have had his other arm broken.

Bill Trotter and others served little communities in buggies and wagons for years. As roads were improved and automobiles more dependable in the early thirties, a few entrepreneurs began taking truck bodies to a plant in Georgia to have a custom body built. Others bought an old school bus and converted it. Each day, these vehicles were loaded from a warehouse with anything that would sell and driven on a regular route. They were called rolling stores. The same uncle who sold scrap iron to Bill Trotter sold groceries to eight rolling stores out of the little town of Boaz. They traveled the back roads bringing goods from the outside world to isolated people in the most densely populated rural area in the country. Farmer's wives and children knew the approximate arrival time and looked for the store that appeared in a cloud of dust. If nothing were needed, they waved and the store moved on. Most of the time somebody left their drab surroundings, climbed the steps and entered a portable store displaying what seemed an enormous array of goods to those who had little. In the vehicle were concentrated smells of coffee, vanilla, spices, tobacco, leather, candy, hardware, and clothing. If the sights didn't make the family become customers, the smells did. Every space in the store was filled with something. There was always a supply of coffee, tea, sugar, flour, and salt. There were a few ready-made clothes, but a good supply of cloth and notions. The driver carried a few plow points and nuts and bolts and nails. A tank of coal oil was kept away from the good food smells. An egg crate was at the back of the store, and tied to the back on the outside was a chicken crate for the birds that volunteered to take the trip to town in exchange for a new dress. Children could always trade two or three eggs for candy or gum. To those isolated people, the rolling store was evidence of an outside world.

Sometimes, the rolling store was flagged down crossing a stream in a dark bottom. The driver tried not to look, but if he did, he saw the brother or the cousin in the shadows with the gun. They always bought sugar, in large amounts and for cash. A farmer might buy an extra ten pounds of sugar. The exact amount depended on the size of their churn. They also bought three cakes of yeast and a can of Blue Ribbon Malt. This was still called a "set-up" in 1951 when I worked in a small town grocery store.

The driver completed his rounds, bringing the city to the country, spreading gossip or news, and bringing a little of the country back to town. When the store bounced its way back, the produce had to be unloaded and the store stocked again for the next day.

Paved roads are everywhere today. Cars are faster and stores larger, even in small towns. Most people don't work long hours in isolation. Most of the peddlers and all of the rolling stores are gone forever. But just suppose instead of a trip to Wal-Mart, you looked out to see a man with a satchel and smile coming up your walk with all sorts of things you didn't know you needed? Or suppose you saw a store on wheels with a whole world of wonderful things? Or, better still, if you looked out to see a wagon pulled by a pair of black horses, wouldn't you be tempted to buy every clock he had?

I saw some of this. My mother, father, and uncle gave me parts of this story,

Life In The Thirties

Cotton

4

In the twenty-first century, few farmers grow cotton in northeast Alabama. In the fall, scattered fields wait for the huge harvester. Most farmers have no picker. Rains come, leaves fall and cotton hangs in long strips waiting weeks for the mechanical picker. But there is faded evidence of cotton's glory days. Broken terrace rows lie hidden in woodlands, some climbing the foot of mountains and hills. Once, every usable acre was cleared and planted.

Before the mechanical picker, families and neighbors picked the cotton. On Sand Mountain in 1940, School officials knew country people kept children out of school to pick in the fall. The children came back a month behind the others. The school tried starting a month early and closed for picking so all students would have equal opportunity. After the month break, teachers and students felt they were beginning all over again with little recall of the first month.

The next year, school began at the usual time. When the cotton was ready, schools closed at noon and children had the afternoon to pick. It was still the cash crop. It was beginning to fade, but few knew it.

In 1942, our home for a year was Albertville. On most days of the picking month, after lunch I walked a mile or so to a farm to work. Farmers were anxious to have their fields picked clean in the dry fall weather. I was handed a sack and told where to pick. I collected my pay in late afternoon. Fifty to seventy five cents was serious money to a thirteen-year-old in 1942. When the fields were clean and the gins working, we went to school full time.

Years before that day, Alabama was called "The Cotton State." The crop was truly King. I was almost five in 1933 when we lived with my grandparents on the little farm at 602 West Mill Street in Boaz. In the back yard, the wash shed, well and garage were close to the house, then fruit trees, grapevines and last of all a privy almost hidden by tangled muscadine vines. The lot to the south surrounded a weathered barn of stalls, sheds, corncrib, feed room, hall and loft. A chicken house was in the corner across the fence from the privy. The garden was south of the barn and the pasture was a strip along the branch. Fields lay west of the house, south of the garden and beyond the pasture. Every foot not in yard or pasture was planted in cotton. Even when the price fell to a nickel a pound in the depression, farmers still planted it. It was plowed and planted by mule power and weeded by hoe power.

The cotton grew and in the fall the bolls burst. Weather was hot and clear with white fluffy clouds in the sky like cotton on the stalks. This was picking weather. A crew picked half the fields and was to finish the next day. I watched people in their work. Even in these drab days, they talked, laughed and sang. Somebody always brought them water and seemed to appreciate their simple honest work. To a five-year-old, picking cotton looked like a fun job. I asked my mother if I could pick. Either I was persuasive or she wanted to teach me a lesson, because that night she made me a little cotton sack of the same closely woven material like the big sacks. Big people had sacks with a single strap for the shoulder and were long enough to drag the ground. The object was to pick all the cotton the picker could drag before making the long trip to the weighing station. My sack was scaled to size.

Cotton can't be picked until the sun burns away the dew, so I impatiently ate breakfast the next morning. My mother went with me to the field. Leaves were drying and some had fallen from the stalks. Bolls had burst and cotton pouted out; some hung down. Plants were decorated with soft white clouds floating and drifting in the breeze. Two teenage boys and Dealie Trammell were picking. Dealie lived in the little house at the foot of the hill. She was a widow and worked at every chance. She was not a young woman, but could pick three hundred pounds a day. She was pleasant and smiling, happy in spite of circumstances. She never went outside without her bonnet and long sleeves. Like Momma, she didn't want to get swarthy and look cheap and trashy. My mother talked with her as I began to pick. Dealie was to make sure I wore the red straw hat Mother had put on me as I left the house.

Dealie stopped in the row opposite me, "Honey, don't you get too hot now. Keep that hat down a little more over your face. Don't hurt yourself on them bolls now; the corners is real sharp."

What looked like fun was hot hard work. The bolls had a hard, dry shell with sharp points. I learned to snatch the cotton from the boll and dodge those painful spears. The sun was hot and the little sack filled slowly.

I did have the advantage of being closer to the cotton. I picked my row slower than others, but Dealie always came back to check on me and to remind me, "Pick it clean now."

Down by the branch, stalks were so high I had to reach up to pick. The willow tree hanging over the stream at the bridge made the mossy bank so cool I had to stop and watch minnows in the clear water. The stalks were so thick I didn't think anybody would see, but Dealie finished her row and saw me.

"You not pickin' much cotton in the shade, honey!"

So I began again. The sun was so hot, even the little lizards were in the shade. In this shimmering heat, bees and other insects made buzzing sounds as they passed. July flies made the grating, grinding sound from the distance. The scraping of the sacks pulled along the ground blended with the faint rustling as the cotton was pulled from the dry boll. These were the only sounds, other than our voices. We filled the bags and dragged them to the hall of the barn for the weigh-in. Papa hung the old scales from a joist in the hall of the barn. He moved a weight along notches in the long balance arm to measure the weight of the sack on the other end. In spite of the hard hot work, everybody laughed and joked about the heat or putting rocks in their sack or the depression, and I was a small part of this time.

We emptied our bags in one of the cotton baskets of woven oak strips. The two boys dumped them in a wagon. A pair of mules pulled the full load to the gin. I picked all day, or at least until my mother came to collect her little field hand. My tally was thirty-two pounds. Papa smiled a little when he put the money in my hand. Mother snapped it up when I walked home. She put away these coins to save as the first money I ever earned. Little field hands are tired after such a day. My number three tub of sun-warmed water almost put me to sleep. I went to bed very early after supper.

I never pass a cotton field when bolls are open in the bright sun with white fluffs hanging down, without thinking about that day so long ago and the mother who sewed the little sack and the grandfather who weighed the cotton.

I wonder what happened to my 32 cents.

Wash-pots
5

There are hundreds, even thousands, in antique shops, Halloween decorations, yards, or patios. Some rust away in junkyards. People see them as a thing of the past, now nothing more than an ugly sturdy decoration. The time is coming when people will not know, or will not care what wash-pots were and what they did.

A wash-pot is a short, fat, round cast-iron container about two feet across and eighteen inches tall sitting on three short legs. The bulging convex sides end at the top in a lip that curves outward. Loop handles are on either side of the top. Two men can carry it; one can tip it over. The design changed little over the years because it was perfect for its purpose. It held a lot of water, or whatever was put in it, and absorbed heat from its entire surface. The pot must have its legs set on three rocks, or better still three bricks, partially set in the ground. This keeps the pot from sinking and makes space for a fire under the pot. Flames wrap the rounded bottom and sides and are turned away by the flaring lip. The outside of a pot in use is black with carbon from a thousand fires. Spots flake off in areas so the surface is pitted and rough. Carbon covered cast-iron does not rust. With some uses, the interior of the pot has a clean cast-iron appearance. If the pot is used for cooking, the inside is covered with a smooth layer of carbon like its cousin, the cast-iron frying pan.

The first wash-pot I remember was when I was five in 1934 and we lived in Boaz with my mother's parents. One late fall day, Momma and my Mother rushed through breakfast, put a jacket and hat on me and sent me to the barn where Papa was working.

Nights were below freezing, days were a little warmer; skies were clear and blue with no wind. The moon was full, certainly not waning. The signs were right. This was hog-killing time.

Papa and two other men were working at the hog pen by the barn. Papa stood in front of the pen so I couldn't see. There was a loud bang and a big grunt. I looked around Papa, and saw the pig lying on the ground. I couldn't play with that pig like a dog or cat, but he was sort of like my friend. Any scrap of food we had left and whey from the churn went into the slop bucket on the back porch. At the feed room in the barn, we added shorts to the bucket and dumped it in his trough. The pig was our garbage disposal. I could watch him eat and scratch his ears. Papa said pigs were here for us to use, and he was fulfilling his purpose in life. I was not allowed to see the more gruesome part of butchering. After the pig was killed, bled, and gutted he was hung on the side of the barn by tying the hind legs to a singletree. This is part of the rigging of a horse or mule for plowing or pulling a wagon. It's a wooden cylinder, thicker in the middle than the ends. A metal ring is attached to the middle and smaller rigs on each end. The pig's legs were tied to the small rings and a rope tied to the center ring and hoisted up on the side of the barn. Men could work on the hanging pig without bending over.

I didn't see the wash-pot until Papa warned me not to get too close. A fire was going, and water was beginning to boil. I thought Papa had bought a new pot. It never occurred to me that men could take it from its place in the back yard. Long before I got up, they had moved the pot, filled it and built a fire.

We had a mismatched collection of every knife we owned: some long, some short, some old, and others very old. A new knife in the depression would have been an extravagance. Men poured boiling water over the pig and everybody scraped, even me. We scraped and washed and scraped over and over until the pig was slick. Every hair was gone except on the tips of the ears. The bubbling black pot furnished water for the scalding and washing of the pig and our tools.

After the pig was butchered, parts were taken in different directions. Papa packed hams, one shoulder, most of the loin, side meat, and white meat in salt and sugar in the box in the loft of the barn. One of the men took lean trimmings and one shoulder to a friend who would grind them in a sausage mill. The other man took the head and other scraps to a butcher shop to be made into souse meat or head cheese. Papa took the rest of the loin to the house and put it in the icebox.

Papa gathered fat scraps, brought them to the kitchen, and cut them into strips. Momma turned on all the kerosene burners of the stove. She fried the strips in cast iron skillets and pots, black from years of use. In spite of the temperature, every window was open. The kitchen was still filed with smoke. She poured liquid from the pans into old churns--pure lard. The wrinkled strips left were cracklings. For the next few days our dinner menu was fresh loin--a country pig has no pork chops--sometimes with homemade sauerkraut and cracklin' cornbread.

The next day the old pot was back in its usual place, waiting for the next job.

The pot's next job was soap making. Papa dumped old lard and bacon grease in the faithful wash-pot. As the fire melted the grease, Papa added the proper amount of water and the proper amount of Red Devil lye--too little and we had greasy soap, too much lye and our clothes dissolved.

I always asked Momma to tell about making soap in the old days when there was no store-bought lye. She told how they put boards across the bottom of a barrel, then layers of brush and packed the barrel with hardwood ashes. Hot water poured through ashes over and over made lye, which drained to a barrel below. I later learned this was potassium and not sodium lye like Red Devil and made a milder soap.

After the mix in the pot cooked, Papa poured it in an old churn and stored it in the basement. It set up to a not quite solid and not quite liquid jell.

And the faithful wash pot waited for the next job.

Hog killing and soap making were once a year, but weather permitting, washday was once a week. We went to church and rested on Sunday so we washed Monday. Three #3 galvanized washtubs sat on a stand a few feet from the well under the shed in the back yard. One tub had a washboard. We filled the wash-pot with water and Papa built a fire. We filled three tubs with many, many buckets from the well. Momma scrubbed dirty clothes on the board in the fist tub and took them to the boiling pot. After a time, Papa dipped out the clothes with an old broomstick bleached white by hundreds of baths in lye soap. Momma rinsed the clothes, and rinsing had to be good or somebody lost skin. This kind of washing was a test of fabric; if the cloth survived lye soap, it was good quality. Momma wrung out the wash by hand and hung it on lines in the yard. The wash was clean--probably surgically clean. Sometimes, small rewashing occurred. In mulberry season, Momma found her sheets with purple streaks from berries reprocessed by the birds. What she threw is called a conniption fit.

Other pots were used for cooking batches of something like Brunswick stew for parties or picnics. Nothing cooks like well cured cast-iron, whether a wash-pot or a skillet. Both last a lifetime or more than one lifetime; many are handed down.

There are still wash-pots out there. They sit on patios or in yards with holes drilled in their bottom, forever impotent to fulfill their function the molder intended. If you look carefully, there are no rocks under the feet and the pot sinks in the dirt with shame. Nobody knows how to care for them. Some are painted; some suffer the indignity of holding limp petunias. There is no fire under the pot.

These pots were a vital faithful tool of the farm family. In their present state, don't look at them with pity; look at them as you would an old man or woman in a nursing home, out of the mainstream of life with the end near. Don't see them for what they are, but what they have been, what they have done. What has been has been and cannot be erased by whatever is now. If we could see old wash-pots and old people this way, we might learn something more of human values.

Old Woman at the Well

6

Early in the 20th century, people in cities or towns turned a handle and the glass or the tub filled. Water in the country was not taken for granted. Those on a farm carried water from a stream, spring, or well. Some wells were drilled, but most were hand-dug with pick and shovel. Hot water might come from a tank in the stove or a kettle on top. In 1934, if we had water of any kind at my grandparents' house in Boaz, we drew it from the well, hauled it up the back steps and put the bucket on a shelf on the porch just outside the kitchen door. For a bath, we heated water on the stove and poured it in an enameled basin. Our water was good, but one summer we couldn't fill a bucket without scooping up mud. The walls of the well had crumbled away and filled the bottom.

A man knocked at our door at mid-morning. Papa and my uncles were away. Mother was never an outside person, so I went to the shed with my grandmother and the man who had come to clean out the well. For a deep well, he would have needed a pulley and rope hoist and men to haul him out. After he finished with our shallow well, he could pull himself up the 14 or 15 feet. He took off his shirt, shoes, and socks and left on his ragged blue pants. He attached a rope to a rafter of the shed and lowered himself through the aboveground concrete tube into the darkness of the well. He was a muscular man in his twenties. His shoulders barely slid through the circle of concrete. From the bottom, he began to send up our water bucket filled with mud. It hung by a chain that passed through a squeaking pulley just above the opening of the well and then to a horizontal peeled log with an iron crank on the near end. We cranked the log to wind the chain and draw the bucket. I could bring up buckets of water if they weren't full, but I couldn't crank up mud. Momma Owen had to help me or do it herself. After we emptied each one, Momma called to the man to make sure he was all right.

After several buckets, she called down again; there was hesitation and then came a voice from darkness, weaker than before, "I just opened a gas pocket. I ... I'm gonna have to come out."

Momma pushed me away and stared in the well. There was nothing she could do, but say words of encouragement--the words got louder and more frantic. The rope swayed back and forth. We heard the man grunting, struggling to breathe as he tried to pull up. Finally, his arms then his head appeared at the opening as he strained to pull. His shoulders were out when he gave a gasp and passed out.

As he slumped against the shelf of the well, Momma grabbed him. This dumpy little old lady barely five feet tall reached around his chest and pulled the unconscious man out of the well. She held him up until he became awake enough to sit on the shelf and pull his legs out. He sat gasping on the concrete ledge at the top of the well, his shoulders and arms shivering. When he recovered enough, he put on his shirt, picked up his shoes and said the well was cleaned out as much as it was going to be for that day.

As he left on shaky legs, I said, "Momma, you had trouble pulling up buckets of mud. How could you pull that man out of the well?" She leaned against the concrete, mud smeared on her arms and face, taking quick short breaths.

Momma finally looked up, "Sometimes–not always--but sometimes when there is great need, God gives great strength."

She was unsteady, but made it up the steps to the back porch. She didn't tell Mother why she was lying down in the middle of the day.

The next morning, I drew up a bucket of clear water.

Testament
7

In late winter 1936, conversation was strange because of the place. Walls and ceilings were dark tongue-and-groove with matching wainscoting and chair rail. Floors were painted pine. A single drop with a bare bulb hung from the center of the 12-foot ceiling. The room was filled with Victorian dark mahogany furniture with round velvet cushions at the back of wicker-back settee and chairs, made for style, not comfort, and an out-of-tune piano. We rarely used the parlor except for company.

I knew the story, but Papa told me again, "God has something for you to do."

"Why, Papa? "

He told of being called to a neighbor's phone one night in 1932. His only daughter had called to say his only grandson was having emergency surgery and was not expected to live. He had done the only thing he knew to do. He gathered friends and went to their little church and prayed.

Papa said it again, "God has something for you to do, or you wouldn't have lived to see this day."

"But what must I do?"

"I don't know."

"But how will I know? Will I see visions or hear words from the sky, like the preacher said?"

"I don't know--you might--I never did."

"But what must I do?"

"Just live the best life you can by the rules we have to live by, believe, trust, and wait on God."

I heard the words, but was still troubled. It would be so simple if somebody would tell me something to do.

Spring turned to summer and people in the little town of Boaz came out of hibernation. The man from the hollow at the foot of the hill tipped his hat as he walked the road past our house and said to my mother, "Yes ma'am, hit's warmin' up rite nice. Purdy soon, be warm enough to take a bath agin." Summer had come to Boaz.

In the depression, social events were few in this town. People were more worried about eating and keeping warm in winter. The county was so dry that the Watkins man had trouble selling vanilla extract. Most social life centered around churches. The community was divided by denominations: Baptists, Methodists, and a few Presbyterians. Other than morning and evening service, we had Sunday school, Missionary Society, men's groups, and children's groups--with little crossover from one congregation to another.

Bible School was an exception. I was welcome in the Baptist Church, although everybody knew my family was Methodist. Children went for the social aspect, lemonade and cookies. They also got a subtle dose of Christian principles. Some teachers understood that children learn more from what they see than what they hear. They used something they could hold in their hand to illustrate truths.

Once, we were asked to bring nails of all kinds. The teacher lined them up in order. There were shiny new nails, those with a speck of rust, then more and more and finally one crooked, shriveled and covered with scales of rust. She said rust on nails was like sin in our life, slowly eating away. She bent the last rusty nail and it snapped. The sound seemed to echo in the room.

Toward midsummer, each church began preparations for revival. No matter how good a congregation was, they needed reviving once a year.

A week before the Methodist revival, Momma put on her best hat, reserved for holidays and funerals, and went to visit wayward sinners on the rolls and not attending, or those unchurched. These were considered fair game. She came home late in the afternoon, walking unusually fast. She was huffing and puffing; if she had been a man, she would have been sweating.

She slammed the door as she came in and between gasps said, "I should not have done that, but I did."

When she caught her breath, we finally got the full story. She had visited a wayward sinner, who had not been seen in church since Easter two years ago. The lady had given assorted excuses: nothing to wear, too busy, kids, sickness, and other lame reasons.

Finally as Momma got to the door to leave, the lady said, "Well, Della, you know this is July. I would come, but that church is so hot."

As Momma went out the door, she looked back and said, "There *are* hotter places." Momma left for the kitchen saying, "Lord help me! I shouldn't have done it, but I did."

Julia Street Memorial Methodist Church was a typical small-town church. Two central aisles divided rows of plain wood pews with no cushions. The sidewalls had tall stained-glass windows. With mid-day sun, the sanctuary was filled with splashes of red, yellow and orange. On Sunday night, the same colors glowed to the outside. The platform at the front had a center pulpit. Tall awkward looking chairs sat in front of the choir loft for an assortment of preachers. A scoreboard to the left of the preachers told of contributions and attendance. A piano was on one side and a choir loft above and behind the platform. A balcony at the back opened to several small Sunday school classrooms. Children's Sunday school was in the basement.

Revival began in the hottest week of the year. Services were at night, but even then, with the lights on, the heat was intense. The lady Momma insulted came the first night only. She probably figured Hell couldn't be much hotter.

I was forced to sit with the women on the right, second row from the front. Nobody ever sat on the front row. Mother sat to my left and my Grandmother to her left. I sat at the end by one of the windows. Everybody fanned with pasteboard fans with a loop or paddle-shaped wood handle, a funeral home advertisement on one side, and a religious picture on the other--that is, everybody but me. The windows along the sides were raised for ventilation. An assortment of bugs flew toward the lights through the open window with no screen. Mother had just stopped me from swatting at flying bugs; I was using the fan handle to push along an exceptionally evil-looking, black flying hard-shelled beetle with sharp legs and big pinchers. I was encouraging it to move along the back of the pew in front of us and all of a sudden it did move. It flew up Mother's dress.

When a woman is attentive to a sermon and all of a sudden a big ugly black bug is up her dress, a scream is the first thought. She managed to strangle the scream and make a high-pitched choking sound. She tried to grab it, but it had those sticky legs and pinchers. I couldn't grab it because it was up a lady's dress. After she heard a whispered shout, Momma figured out what happened, and leaned over, because the bug was on the far side. Those two women writhed about like wrestlers trying to get the bug without touching it. The poor bug was climbing higher on her leg trying to get away. Finally, they mashed it between two fan handles while Mother stuck an elbow in my ribs to stop me from giggling. By that time, there were so many strange sounds and so much thrashing about in the pew, the preacher thought the two women were getting happy and had come to the wrong church.

Methodists won't do that, don't you know. I got a bug lecture later and was never again allowed to sit next to the window.

Brother Rice, the evangelist, did not shout and scream like some, but spoke calmly and clearly of vital matters. I even listened--that is, after the bug episode. That week, I learned that truth spoken softly is stronger than shouted words. The preachers were to visit Momma and Papa toward the middle of the week. This was a special event; we ate fried chicken in the dining room and it wasn't even Sunday. But it is a well-known fact that country preachers only eat fried chicken.

After supper, I talked with Mother in private. She said, "Oh, my, we must talk to the ministers."

She took me to the minister and the evangelist and spoke with them. The minister said, "He's too young, Ruth."

Brother Rice said, "Just a minute," and began to question me in great detail, with simple pointed questions: "Do you know you have done wrong things, and will continue to do wrong things? How can you account for your sins? Do you understand Jesus died for you and could accept responsibility for your sins?"

After a long series of questions, for a seven-year-old--or as I said, seven and-a -half--Brother Rice asked the local pastor, "Aren't we called to come as little children? How can you keep him out? Why would you turn him away?"

In those days, small Methodist churches were fundamental and conservative. The revival routine was different from others. After each sermon, the pastor did not have a plaintive altar call while the choir sang all fourteen verses of *Just As I Am*. Those so moved were to come for an altar call at the end of the last service of the revival on Sunday. They were not said to be saved, but converted.

At the last service, my family positioned

themselves near a center aisle. As the sermon progressed, people tried to guess how many would go down the aisle. Last year, five made the trip. The Baptists had had more than that last month. There was hope that the Methodists would outdo the Baptists.

After the altar call, when the last note of the song faded, Brother Rice looked down to see one very small boy standing alone.

He looked down the aisle and around the congregation, now in total silence and began speaking slowly. "We have had a revival for a whole week in this heat. Many of you worked hard for it. Some have been here every night. Now we come to the end and we have one little boy to show for all that work. Some would say all our efforts were in vain. But I say, who here can say what this little boy will do? Who knows the lives he will touch? For only one soul, even a little one, I would do it all again next week. The revival *was* a success."

Then, came the questions and the answers and the baptism. This church didn't sprinkle. There was only one to baptize, so I got the whole pitcher. It drenched my head, ran down my shirt and pants, and into my shoes. The Holy Spirit was poured out over me. I was filled with it. If a Baptist deacon had seen it, this might have qualified as an immersion.

After the service, I had to shake hands with adults who crowded around to welcome me. I was embarrassed, but Papa, Momma, and Mother had trouble hiding happiness.

Almost three quarters of a century has passed since August 25, 1936 when I stood in the center aisle of that little church in a baptismal puddle. I have never seen a vision, never heard sounds of cymbals and trumpets from above, never seen a blinding light from on high, never heard a voice from somebody I couldn't see telling me to search for the Holy Grail or do some wondrous work. Has God forgotten, or did a message come unseen? Has my life been wasted?

Or did God speak in the voice of my grandfather so long ago when he said, "Live the best life you can by the rules we have to live by, believe, trust, and wait on God?"

122·664 C
ALA. FRONT 37

The Tacky Party

8

In the winter of 1937 and the following spring, while the nation still wallowed in depression, we lived in Andalusia, a little town in Southern Alabama. The three of us lived in an apartment on one side of a house of faded elegance. The space was small, but convenient to town and across the street from school. The plainness was fitting to the times.

This was a difficult year. My father lost his grocery store to the depression six years earlier. He was a stranger to me because he had worked out of the state while Mother and I stayed in Boaz. After he worked a few weeks at a new Alabama job, he had surgery for a ruptured appendix. He was hospitalized for fifteen days, with nine days of special duty nurses. This left him with a hospital bill of $87.60 and a surgeon's bill of $100.00 and prevented him from working for weeks. When he did go back he made $40 a week. After a month, he lost that job and had to take another for $32.50 a week.

I had a series of winter illnesses. With no medicines stronger than Vicks salve, my mother was overprotective. When I was sick, days were spent in treatment with bed rest, proper diet according to Mother, and such remedies we had. In the long recovery time, there were endless hours of nothingness. The rule was strict; I could not even sniff and go back to school. Mother had enough college work to get a teacher's certificate and had been an English and Expression teacher. She made sure I had schoolbooks and studied everything required for the third grade. After classes, a healthy boy of nine fills his hours with play, and sometimes things as important as looking at clouds or seeing Indians behind trees. When my schoolwork was finished, there seemed to be endless hours.

We had a tiny Emerson radio. The plain face had two knobs, a dial and a central speaker covered with drab tan fabric in keeping with those plain days. I knew all the local stations by day and the clear channels by night. I knew how to avoid *Stella Dallas, Young Widow Brown, John's Other Wife,* and other mushy programs. But there were *Tom Mix, Jack Armstrong* and at night *Sherlock Holmes, The Lone Ranger,* and dramatizations of good literature, though I didn't know it at the time.

But there were still endless hours. Mother encouraged reading of books. I read *Treasure Island, Just So Stories, Robinson Crusoe,* and an old copy of *King of the Golden River* until it was almost worn out. Books and radio offered an escape from illness, boredom, and loss of school time. They became my virtual reality. I became so absorbed into these stories that with little effort I could become Gluck and deal with evil brothers; I could see the Indians behind the tree and feel the wind as it filled the sails of the ship. There were sailors, pirates, Indians, and cowboys in my room. There were ships and desert islands and airplanes. I didn't have hallucinations. The shadows faded when Mother came in.

At last, I was well enough to go to school. I said, "Why bother? There is only one more week of school."

My mother went with me to explain the long absence. The teacher said about all students would do in the next week was take the standardized test. She wouldn't give me the test because I might fail and couldn't be promoted.

On Monday, I went to school and acted like any other student. On Tuesday the teacher brought in the standardized tests. As she passed by my desk, she hesitated and then put one down.

I looked up as if to ask a question and she said, "Yes." I took the test, but didn't tell Mother.

The end of the school year was to be celebrated on Friday with a tacky party. I didn't want to go because I had missed so much school, but Mother insisted and went with me as some other parents did. There were dozens--and it seemed hundreds--of kids with all the released energy at the end of school. There were the usual games, much running, more shouting and giggling. There was food of a simple sort: ham, bread, pickles and mountains of potato salad that must have been brought in a washtub.

Finally came the judging. Even then, some didn't know how to be tacky and wore ordinary clothes. Some kids dressed in clown suits and painted their faces. They were funny, but not tacky. Some had hobo outfits. They looked like the depression, but weren't tacky. Kids had Halloween masks. They might scare people, but they weren't tacky.

I wore my dad's shoes with the toes turned up and laces long enough to drag. My pants were loose with the cuffs rolled up. The end of the belt hung down almost two feet. The baggy white shirt had garters holding up long sleeves. My tie had the small end six inches lower than the wide part. To top it off, I had on a pork-pie hat; my hair was slicked down and parted in the middle; I had a little painted mustache. I was so tacky I won first prize.

On the Monday the teacher sent for my mother. Mother expected the worst when she went to the office.

My teacher said, "I know I said I would not, but on impulse I gave your son the test. He placed fourth grade, ninth month, a year ahead of his class. You are a better teacher than I am, and I wanted you to know it."

And so this tacky child passed to the forth grade.

Brown Eggs and Vicks Salve

9

I was a sickly child, or so my family said. I had been at death's door a time or two and had desperation surgery once, but never thought I was different from any other kid. My illness did make my mother determined to raise her problem child through supreme effort and will. She didn't work after she married. She devoted herself to a problem child until my sister arrived when I was twelve.

In the 1930's, the first true antibiotic was years in the future. We did have sulfa drugs, but they were not very effective and some had side effects. If a child were sick, a visit to the doctor might produce a diagnosis, but there were few effective drugs. Families managed illness with home remedies or something from the drug store. Most parents read books and magazine articles on disease, health, and nutrition. In the depression years, few had the money for doctor visits. Drug stores had an assortment of vile-tasting cough syrups and tonics guaranteed to make a puny child strong.

Mother had specific and fixed ideas about health. She did take me to the doctor on occasions, usually for a second opinion, but she managed most illnesses.

She treated injuries at home; some would have been sutured today. She cleaned simple wounds and put in a few drops of Pinezone. This was a purified form of turpentine, but much more modern. Later, she used even more modern mercurochrome or merthiolate. Simple wounds had to be treated because people did die from infected cuts and certainly from furuncles, carbuncles and erysipelas, especially during Dog Days. Sprains and strains were treated by elevation, soaks and primarily time. I never had an X-ray for an injury. The body in its wisdom heals itself if possible; otherwise, none of us would survive.

In my childhood, few medicines actually worked. Laxatives did, and all too well at 3 A.M. This effectiveness is probably why so many mothers used them for so many things, like being 'bilious.' I tried not to look bilious, but from time to time I had to take some vile mix. Epsom salts, castor oil, calomel, cascara, and milk of magnesia were possibilities. Adults sometimes took the ultimate, bought one at the time from the drug store: a CRC capsule.

This situation did change once. When I was nine, we had a black and white cat named Butch. The whole family liked Butch, and we were distressed when he became sick. Mother thought he had been poisoned like other animals in the neighborhood. She thought he needed "a good working out" to get rid of the poison so she gave a dose of my laxative to the cat. It is difficult to calculate a dose of people medicine for a cat. Butch died. What a way to go. He went out like a jet!

Mother felt terrible, but she had the best of intentions when she gave the potion. After the services were over and the marble tombstone placed, I admit I did exploit Butch's death.

Whenever I was about to be given a dose of some vile mix, I would open my eyes wide, and with a little quaver in my voice say, "Is that the same stuff you gave Butch?"

It worked for a year, but Mother read about a much more modern natural laxative called senna leaf tea. There is something impressive about the ceremony of preparing a potion like tea. It was so effective I couldn't drink any kind of tea for years. It may have worked; I have not been bilious for seventy years.

Mother's concepts about true illness were to avoid contact with the sick, stay in good general condition, and if illness did strike, treat it with what was available, but primarily with bed rest. All treatments began with a good working out. The rule was simple: rest the body and let it heal. But clean it out first. I was afraid to sniff or sneeze for fear I would have to stay out of school and take a purge. It is hard to find fault with her concepts; I did survive.

Respiratory illnesses were probably no more common than today, but more frightening because they could progress to pneumonia and death. Mother prescribed bed rest with lots of liquids as the primary treatment. She applied a thick layer of Vicks salve to my chest and covered it with layers of cotton cloth pinned to my pajamas. Vicks could also be put up the nose or the victim could breathe vapors from a heated paper bag with salve in it. Mother bought the giant economy size of Vicks. With a protective mother in charge, the patient could have a bath with a bath cloth--except for the chest where the cloth was stuck. I couldn't have a real shampoo; I might get a chill from damp hair. I got dry shampoos. There were preparations at the drug store, but Mother used oatmeal. All this did was take out oil and make me smell like a cookie. Treatment of any illness meant days of boredom and loss of school time, even weeks at a time. Mother was determined that I would have an education. She taught me from the schoolbooks and encouraged reading of books advanced for my years. Through boredom, I developed a love for the written word.

Of all the factors concerning health, Mother thought diet was the most important. There was an expert who once said, "You are what you eat." So it's simple; eat right and be healthy.

There are foods one may eat and foods one may not eat. There must be a good breakfast; it must include an egg or preferably eggs. My Dad ate two every morning. The eggs must be brown. Those weak-looking white eggs were not served at our house. Potent brown eggs were offered fried, scrambled, boiled, coddled, and poached. I hate eggs now, and I hated them then with a passion--white, brown or speckled.

When I was twelve, in hope of a source of fresh eggs, Mother allowed me to borrow a hen and setting of eggs from Momma Owen. I also took three duck eggs. We were close by in our one-year stay. This confused hen rode the few miles from Boaz to Albertville in my lap in the back seat of the family car. The hen cooperated and hatched the chicks and three ducklings. The ducks were a problem from the first. I built a small cement pool and filled it with water. The little ducks didn't just drink; they jumped in to swim as they were born to do. The hen, considering herself to be the mother, ran around squawking and having a duck fit. As soon as the chickens were large enough, the hen went back to the farm before she needed tranquilizers. We didn't have those back then anyway. The family discussed destiny of the chickens. Mother wanted to keep them for eggs, but Daddy said that chickens raised on the ground were much better to eat than those in a pen. My opinion was obvious. The final decision was, if I could do the job, we would eat the chickens. I tried to wring a neck like I had seen Momma do, but I only stretched it a little. The sore-neck chicken ran off and told the other chickens and I had a hard time catching another one. I found I could do the job with a hatchet if I held the head on a board with my foot and closed my eyes as the blade fell.

Desperate measures are needed to avoid eggs. Eventually, we ate all the chickens and left the three ducks. But mother continued to buy eggs and serve them every day.

One day I was sitting and picking at a cold hard-boiled egg, trying to leave parts under the toast or plate, when I happened to look down and see the hole in the floor. Prior tenants had used this hole to drain their icebox. We were more modern. We had a small Crosley refrigerator that even made two trays of ice. The hole was there and unused. Just at that moment, the ducks walked through the access door under the house, and the big green-headed drake turned his head sideways and looked up through the hole at my feet.

I had a flash of insight. *That hole is boiled-egg size. I wonder ...* The ducks were quacking wildly when Mother came in the kitchen and complimented me on cleaning the plate. In the next weeks, breakfast progressed to two boiled eggs. The ducks loved it. Mother did wonder why the ducks came and quacked at the same time everyday.

One day, disaster struck. I sat at the breakfast table and discovered the hole plugged because of cool weather. Over the next few days, Mother would say, "You were eating so well for a while."

If she had understood duck, she would have known. They complained violently every morning. While dawdling over a cold boiled egg one day, I happened to notice the space between the top of the kitchen cabinet and ceiling. When nobody is looking, a boiled egg, or even two, can be tossed into that space. Any kid who throws rocks can do it. I had no more problems with breakfast for a while.

After weeks, maybe months, I came home one day to find the atmosphere in the house so cold there were almost icicles. When Mother called me by all three names, I knew I was in trouble. I was ordered to sit in a chair in the kitchen.

Mother towered over me and said, "You know that Louise was coming today to help me, and I told her that we had to find out what smelled so bad in this kitchen. We tore this place apart for over two hours and had about given up. What–do–you–think–we--found?" When mothers say one word at the time you are in deep trouble and it's about to get worse.

I said weakly, "An old dirty diaper?"

"You know better than that. We got almost a bushel basket of dried and rotten eggs off the top of that cabinet."

I had no idea what my punishment would be. I had to endure a lecture on and on for days and was worse than a quick job with a switch. Mother finally said she would give up on eggs and hope I would survive. It was days before the icicles melted, but I never ate undisguised eggs again. I did survive, but maybe there was something to that egg business after all. I never did grow to six feet like my uncles.

The ducks went back to the farm. People always wondered why they had a habit of turning their heads sideways and looking up through knotholes and quacking like crazy.

SIR WALTER RALEIGH
PHONE
866
413 WEST
WALNUT ST.

Last Weekend in Boaz

10

At the low point of the depression in the winter of 1932, my father lost his grocery business. We drove the Blue Front Store delivery truck 500 miles back to Alabama through snow, detours, one blown tire and a wreck. Two parents, a three year old, a rider to Birmingham, and a dog endured hours of dismal cold.

In the dark days that followed, Mother and I lived on the farm with her parents while my father went back to the job he promised to never do again. As a private investigator, he had to change cities every few months. We tried to live where Daddy worked in St. Louis. We stayed one night. The encephalitis epidemic drove us back to Alabama. Later, we did live where he worked for three months. Before I started to school, we left Brooklyn for Alabama. Mother knew I would have a language problem.

When my dad finally got a job in Alabama and the three of us could live together, he was transferred every year, sometimes more. In the depression, people were too glad to have a job to question a transfer. We moved from town to town, never unpacking half the boxes and losing things with every move. My thirty Big-Little books, my ten-year collection of Life magazines and other childhood treasures were left, lost, or given away. Mother never saw the house in the new town until the moving van unloaded. When Daddy picked poorly, we moved again in the same town. Mother wouldn't accept a kitchen when she could see dirt of the crawlspace through cracks in the wood floor.

I felt no attachment for any town we lived in. I made few close friends in school and never remembered all the students' names. I knew we would leave soon. After we moved away when I was almost nine, I spent part of each summer at Boaz. I knew every inch of the house, barn, and farm. The clock struck the same harsh sounds on the hour. The basement was damp and smelled of lard, lye soap, onions, and potatoes. The house was always there, stable and unchanging. If I left my hooks and line on a shelf in the corncrib or a corner of the loft, they were there when I came back. The tree I planted in the front yard was green and growing. I missed my parents, but the farm was more home to me than any town we moved to.

I heard my grandmother making kitchen noises when she called me. As I dressed, I remembered this was the last weekend of my summer visit.

As soon as I walked in the kitchen, Momma sent me to draw water from the well. "And don't let the bucket get in the mud like you did yesterday!"

I said, "Yes, Ma'am," and carried the bucket from the screened-in porch down the high back steps. The well was under a shed a few feet from the concrete landing at the foot of the steps where we had eaten watermelon the day before. Ducks were picking at the rinds.

A concrete slab covered the well site with a three-foot tube in the middle. The square shelf on top was waist high for adults, chest high for me. The wood lid was held at one corner by a loose rusty bolt. To the right, an iron crank stuck out of the end of a peeled log mounted between two boards. A chain wound around the log and then through a pulley above to the bucket waiting on the cover. I pushed the cover aside, moved away from the crank and let it spin. The bucket dropped like a stone and hit the water with an echoing splash. I let it go as deep as I dared. The bucket came up full and dripping with clear water. No crawfish like yesterday.

As I carried the bucket up the steps, my grandfather came in from the garden. He had long since milked, and my grandmother had strained the milk through a white cloth and put it in the icebox. Papa was a tall, imposing man with snow-white hair and mustache, serious and strict, but with a dry wit. I respected him, but was a little in awe of him.

Momma was a contrast. She was a step-grandmother, but I doubt if that mattered to either of us. She was a short, squatty woman, who wore small wire-framed dime-store glasses, round like her face. She had black hair pulled back and tied in a bun. The wrinkled face didn't match her black hair. She had a small wart on the end of her nose, sometimes growing, sometimes quiet. When the wart got too long, she tied a silk thread around it; she told me it must be silk. The wart fell off in a few days, only to come back after a few months. In contrast to Papa, she did and said funny things without meaning to. It was never "Pass the salt," but "I thank you for the salt." She never said a lot of something, but "a right smart" of whatever. She might say, "What has that dog rolled in? He smells like pure dee kearn!" When I was in college I figured out the word was 'carrion.' Whenever I was about to do something she didn't like, she would call the roll beginning with her brother Roy, then her two sons, and by the time she got to my name, I had done what she was about to tell me not to do.

She mixed a handful of this and that and a pinch of the other and patted out cathead size biscuits with her hands. She didn't own measuring cups or spoons and had no recipes. She cooked with real eggs, butter and lard. Sometimes there was side-meat or sausage for breakfast, but not this late in the year. There would be no pork until the pig was killed in the fall. I ate two biscuits with butter and sorghum syrup, drank milk and was off to check on things.

My grandparents had a two-story white house on the corner of a small farm. Fields were planted in cotton. The house had an address of 602 West Mill

Street, but was the first farm home in the country. Sidewalk and paved road ended a few feet from the farm. The road in front was rutted and deep in dust. A cloud followed every car that passed. Wind from the north pushed the cloud to the house. Trees by the road, chairs on the porch, shrubs, and grass in the yard were gray-white.

On Saturday, traffic was heavy because this road led from the farming area to Boaz. Travelers had been passing for hours when I got out. Some drove cars, more drove pickups with passengers in straight chairs in back. Others came in two-mule wagons and there was an occasional surrey or buggy. Almost everybody waved. This was a happy day; there was no work and they were headed to town. Traffic slowed at midday and began again in the afternoon and into the night in the opposite direction. Late travelers on foot or in wagons were sometimes loud.

I left this dusty place and went through the barn lot to the pasture to check on the branch. It was too small a stream to have a name. The water was so clear I had to hide behind a gum tree to fish. There were bream, frogs, lizards, salamanders, crawfish, turtles, water moccasins, "muss-rats," red-horse and silverside minnows. I knew every turn, every major rock, where the muskrat lived, and deep holes where the fish were.

I wanted to try one last time to get that big water moccasin. There must be a weary guardian angel watching little boys or I would have been bitten by poisonous snakes or broken my neck when I fell out of the barn loft. I didn't get the snake! I checked on the cow and chickens and fed coal to the pig. They eat it like candy; I never knew why.

After doing these important things, I went back to the yard. Momma was working in the shed with her back turned. My Uncle Jake had given me Zebra firecrackers on the 4th of July. I had a few left. Since I was ten years old, which is old enough to carry matches, I lit a firecracker well back from Momma. I knew exactly what would happen. **Kapow!** She threw her hands up and hollered, "Whooeeee!" I had never heard anybody else say that.

"Yes, Momma, I didn't see you so close there."

I ran to the ice truck as it pulled up in the yard. I knew Uncle Jake would let me look in the back. He threw back the canvas cover and plowed a shallow line across a big block with an ice pick. He drove the pick in and split off a small piece. Then he split off an even smaller block. He picked up the blocks with tongs, carried them to the back porch and put both in the icebox. This was our regular every other day dime block and an extra nickel piece. I knew what that was for.

Dinner was early on Saturday. The main meal of the day was at noon. We had fresh vegetables, cornbread, no meat, milk for me and tea for adults. Whatever was left was covered with a white cloth and left on the table or put in the icebox or pie safe for supper. Papa ate a few bites and left for town. I gobbled my food because I was going to town, too. I wore nothing but short pants around the farm, certainly no shoes. For town, I had to wear a shirt, but I didn't tuck it in. I had to comb my hair with water so I looked like a fresh-licked calf. But I got away without shoes. I crossed the yard, kicking up dust from clumps of weeds, frightening a thrush from her search for worms, and began the half-mile trip to town. The sidewalk was smooth enough for children to skate on. Adults walked this way even if they had a car. To burn gas for a trip to town would have been an extravagance. These were hard times. I didn't know they were; they were the only times I had known. I stopped at the bottom of the hill to look at the branch that ran through our pasture. The fish were smaller here. I walked up the hill past little stores and the street where the mule barn was, and then to the main street with bigger stores.

Most of them had a plate glass window. The merchants cringed as farmers leaned back and propped the bottom of their high top shoes against the fresh cleaned glass. Scratches along the bottom of the glass showed marks of other Saturdays. Some stores had an awning or marquee to partly shade their window and the lookers.

The sidewalk was wider in town. Boaz was crowded on warm Saturdays. Women walked the sidewalk only as they went from store to store. Most were in stores, looking, sorting and fondling fabrics, sometimes buying. If they talked or gossiped, they did in a store and not on the street.

Men gathered in clusters at the corners and along the sidewalk. Some dressed like Papa: dress shirt, no tie, and dark trousers, which had no crease since they left the store, held up with galluses. Those at the corner stood in full sun. Fresh scrubbed faces of younger farmers glowed with redness from sun and wind. Older faces were wrinkled and leather-like from a lifetime in weather. Farmers wore their newest overalls and a dress shirt with the collar buttoned and no tie. A gold or silver colored chain hung across the bib of their "overhauls." The left end of the chain was pulled through a buttonhole. The right dropped into the pocket of the bib. The bulge in the bib was a pocket watch, usually an Innersole dollar-watch. They cost a few dollars, but were called dollar-watches. A few with an Elgin or Hamilton checked the time more often. Most wore high top shoes that reached just above the ankle. Hooks held laces at the top. All wore hats in various states and ages. Some wore a sweat-stained work hat with drooping brim. Others wore a dark Sunday hat.

When we greet each other today, one says, "How are you?" and the other says, "Fine" or "Good," even if he isn't.

In depression days, one farmer asked the other, "How are ya?" The answer was "Fair" or "Fair to middlin'" if he wanted to use the whole cotton grade. Some said, "Tolerable well." Others said, "About like common."

Men stood on the sidewalk, talked, told stories, laughed, chewed tobacco and spit. After they spit, they made a downward swipe with index and thumb to take away the evidence. They talked politics, depression, and above all, crops.

Farmers might say things like, "I'm atellin' you, Luke, if'n hit don't rain soon, I'm might near rurnt!"

Then Luke says, "I know what ya mean, and sumpin' else, this here daylight savin' time has might near burnt my corn up. I shure do wish we'd go back to th' Lord's time".

A third says, "If the price of 'guanner' don't quit goin' up, I'm agona have to give up farmin." Farmers are rarely a happy lot, even in a good year.

A small man with weathered face and twinkle in his eye said, "An' do whut? Ya don't know nothin' else. They ain't no public work jobs nohow. Whatarya gonna do, take up bootleggin'?" They all laughed.

The offended farmer took out a square of Schnapps, unwrapped it and took off the small red metal tobacco tag and clipped it to the top of his overalls. If he collected enough he could get a premium. He cut a plug for himself and offered the square around. Two shook their head. The third took out a square of Day's Work and cut a plug. "Didge new neighbor help ya when ya cows got loose cross the branch?"

"Naw, he never holp me; he's a republican! An' you know whut the Bible says about them 'publicans!" They laugh again.

"Ya'all got eny worms in ya corn this year?"

"Weel, I tel' ya' Willie Joe, hit'll vaary. Some places the corn is fair an' others the worms has eat the tossels off. I won't get narie rosnear in them places."

A stranger might think the farmer a hopeless pessimist. No man plants a lifeless seed in spring with hope and faith looking for the miracle of rebirth could be a pessimist. But he knows--*you do not know what misfortune may occur on the earth.* (Ecclesiastes 11:2) Disease, insects, storms, floods and drought were specters haunting the farmer. Just as there were no antibiotics for people, there were no effective insecticides and herbicides for plants. The farmer openly expected the worst and secretly hoped for the best. If disaster came, he expected it; if good crops came, he enjoyed the blessings. He was prepared either way.

Voices were much the same corner to corner. These people did backbreaking work in the heat of summer and tried to survive the cold of winter with nothing more than a fireplace. Some would die without seeing a single drop-cord light bulb in their house. Phones were almost unheard of in the country. Some had a battery-operated radio to bring in the outside world. The battery was about half the size of a car battery, almost as big as the radio itself. Saturdays were important to these hard-working men.

As I passed the little stores and groups of men, Saturday smells were everywhere: chewing tobacco, sweat, Rose Hair Oil, Blue Waltz perfume, coal oil --kerosene in this day--and food mixed together.

On the sidewalk in the front of little grocery stores crates held chickens fresh from the farm. They waited for an invitation to Sunday dinner. The housewife selected the victim, pointed her finger and said, "How about that Dominecker there; she looks rite peart." The clerk snatched the squawking chicken in a cloud of dust and feathers, took the bird back of the store, killed it, dressed it and wrapped the parts in brown butcher paper.

As a barefoot walker, I had problems. The sidewalk was hot to bare feet. I tried to walk in the shade, but I couldn't step on a crack; there are rules about that. I had special problems at the corners. When clusters of men are standing around chewing tobacco, there are splat marks everywhere and some even left the whole used chaw on the sidewalk. I was very careful. I turned to the right past the dry goods store, passed by the dime store and the drug store and on to the Rialto on South Main Street. I figured that was the only movie house in the world with that name. Since my visit was ending, I had spent most of the money my mother had given me. I didn't need much. Admission on Saturday afternoon was half price.

For one nickel I entered a world of magic; there were no problems, no depression, no homework and it was cool. The first movie was a detective story with not too much mushy stuff. Next came the previews, Movietone news, a cartoon and then, *Flash Gordon on Mars*. Last week he was in terrible trouble from the evil emperor Ming. He got out of that problem today and as it ended, he got into another problem with some of those flying people. I would probably never find out how it ended. Next came the cowboy show: Hopalong Cassidy with his white hat, fancy clothes and two guns. The bad guy wore black.

When I got out of the movie, I was like a mole; I couldn't see and it was so hot. I stopped at the drugstore to look at the funny books. Mother said that they were trash, so I couldn't actually buy one. If I had an extra dime, sometimes I bought a Big-Little book.

Those were allowed. Now began the trip home. It seemed much longer. I stopped again at the branch at the bottom of the hill. The little fish darting here and there looked like those rocket ships in the Flash Gordon movie.

I had been gone for hours and was almost in trouble, but I was in time to help hem up a chicken. Momma took the chicken by the neck and whirled it round and round the right number of times: she held the chicken with the left hand and pulled the head with the right and pop, off came the head. And the chicken did run around with its head off. When it fell over, I brought it to her. She picked the chicken, cleaned it, singed the pinfeathers with a burning newspaper, cut it up and put it in the icebox.

For supper, I ate cornbread with sweet milk poured over it. Momma ate hers with buttermilk. Papa ate his with clabbered milk while I gagged just watching. I talked Papa into a checker game. We played on a board made from the side of a packing crate. He had drawn squares with ink and colored them black and red. The men were bottle caps kept in a kitchen matchbox. We didn't buy soft drinks; the caps were throw-aways at stores. Papa would help me, but wouldn't let me win like Momma did. We couldn't sit on the porch because of the dust. I listened to the radio, but about dark when we turned on the lights, everybody else in town did too and the power went off. Papa said the generator in town had blown and it might be hours before power came back on. At this hour, I was sure the heat and noise of the traffic would keep me awake, but sleep comes easy to busy little boys.

Sunday morning things began later and slower than the rest of the week. The cow had to be milked. Cooking and milking were the only work Papa would allow. Sometimes we walked the three quarters of a mile to church, but today a friend came to take us in a car. After Sunday school, because of some prior indiscretion, I was required to sit with Momma and other ladies on the right side of the church in the second row from the front. Most of the older men sat together in the center section.

Service began with testimony time. I could not believe it; Papa stood and talked. He had caught me saying "Heck" or "Darn" one day and among other things he told me I might as well have called on the Devil himself. I would have never thought he ever did anything wrong, but there he was, saying he had. Maybe there was hope for me. Women didn't give testimony. I wondered if they didn't sin or just didn't admit it. Now, the singing began. I looked down the pew to my left. Momma and her friends reminded me of a row of birds on a telephone wire opening their mouths and stretching their necks to get their voices out of joint. I didn't know anybody could sing that high! But birds don't wear hats and glasses. Each hat was like a dish or pot; most were dark with some sort of flower or a pin. The preacher said we should all sing, even if we couldn't sing well, because it sounded good to God. He must be tone deaf.

Now, the sermon began. We had cardboard fans with vine loops or flat wooden handles. There was a picture on one side and a funeral home advertisement on the other. After the singing, these were in constant motion by women. 5 Men gave testimony, admitted sin, but didn't fan. I wished the preacher wouldn't preach on hell in summer. When the service and the socializing were over, our ride took us home.

We found Mother and Daddy at the house. They were to take me back to Dothan on Monday. I gave my mother a hug and a peck on the cheek and allowed her to hug and kiss me. I really was glad to see them, but I didn't want anybody to think that I liked mushy stuff.

Now the questioning began, "Well, nothin' much."

Momma reminded me, "Oh, yeah, I did go to the city pool until they closed it because of polio, and uh... I did go with Papa in the Model T to the farm and to take the corn to the mill. I did some painting and lots of other work." I didn't mention spilling the paint on the Sunday coat. We got it out anyway. "And I caught some fish and we ate 'em."

This was true, Papa helped me dress the little fish and we ate them for breakfast. He said that they were good. I thought they were the best I had ever eaten.

"Uh, no ma'am, I didn't do much reading except *National Geographic*." I was hoping that the little light on my forehead wouldn't come on that said, "He is not telling the truth." I had read the *Geographic*. These were copies back to 1928 and I liked stories and pictures of strange lands. I had also been into the library upstairs and into books of wars and battles and history and adventure stories for adults. I was not sure I was allowed to read these. There were even medical books. Papa was not a doctor, but he treated animals and children. He had books for references. There was an anatomy book that showed a drawing of a naked woman. Even though it had been established from age three I was to be a doctor, I was pretty sure this was a wicked picture I was not supposed to see. I had gone into my uncle Ray's room when I was sure he was away and read some of his dime novels. Momma said that they were trash. I *knew* I was not supposed to read these. This exchange is a tug of war between parent and child. The parent wants to know all; the child wants to be noncommittal, not being sure what is acceptable.

Besides, it is always easier to say "Uh ... nothin' much."

Preparation of dinner ended the conversation. Uncle Jake had already started our job on the back porch. He broke the nickel piece of ice with a hammer and packed it in a wooden bucket with rusted iron fittings. In the center a metal container of this ancient freezer waited for the ice cream mix. We poured salt over the ice. Momma poured the whole milk, eggs, sugar and vanilla mix in the galvanized container in the middle of ice-salt mix, and closed the lid. I cranked the freezer until it was too hard for me to turn. Jake finished the job, and the cream was so hard we couldn't get the dasher out. I missed getting to lick it before dinner. We covered the freezer with a retired black overcoat kept on the back porch for that purpose.

We didn't eat much meat, but on Sunday there must be fried chicken, and only on Sunday, except for company. It was free-range, but we didn't know the name then. Meals for family were around the kitchen table. The dining room was for company. The chicken was battered and fried in lard. A chicken has a limited number of parts, so with this many people at the table each had an assigned piece. I was privileged to have the pulley-bone, cut before the breast sections were separated. I always got somebody to pull it apart with me. It broke unevenly and the lucky person got the biggest piece of bone and his wish. I was always concerned that Momma killed, dressed, and cooked the chicken and her piece was the back, which doesn't have much meat. My uncle Ray was a somber person. I thought he never smiled because his piece was the gizzard.

We had to hear Papa's story again of visiting his girlfriend's house for dinner. He was on his best behavior and tried to pick a piece of chicken he could eat with a knife and fork. He couldn't tell one piece from the other because of thick batter and got a foot. Because he was company, he was passed the chicken again. He picked the other foot. Whatever piece we had, there were always biscuits and gravy and vegetables, but I never learned to eat my peas with a knife like Papa did, though I tried.

No matter how much people ate, there was room for vanilla ice cream. It was so cold and good I always ate it too fast and gave myself one of those terrible headaches. If any were left, we covered the freezer with the retired overcoat and left it for supper.

People began to move to other parts of the house slowly, bragging about how much they had eaten. We ate eggs, butter, milk with cream, pork and lard in ignorant bliss. We didn't know about cholesterol.

Papa always took a nap on the daybed after dinner. After he got up, I went with him on his Sunday afternoon walk. He didn't work on Sunday; he walked and looked. Sometimes, we had serious discussions. On some of these walks, I asked him what he was looking for. He said, "The signs." I thought he meant weather signs. I later wondered if he had meant something more than weather.

I got back in time to help take food to a family at the foot of the hill beyond the farm. I couldn't understand this. I knew my Dad had lost his store and Papa had lost one farm to the depression, but Momma said we had more than the family, so we should share. We took what we had: milk, eggs and butter.

We just made it home before the rain came. It washed the dusty trees and house. It was not a blowing storm, so we cleaned the chairs, sat on the porch and enjoyed the coolness. When the scent of dust is washed away, nothing smells as clean and fresh as air after a summer rain.

When the rain stopped, the frogs began to sing. I knew what came next. Momma said, "Them frogs are acallin' for more rain." And somebody said "They're gonna get it, too."

A small boy does not say much. He listens. On summer evenings on the porch and nights around the fireplace in winter, I heard stories of the past, philosophy and morals using words and manner of speech from the past. Simple wisdom lasting a lifetime is unknowingly absorbed in this way.

We watched birds pulling worms under the oaks and people walking and riding along the road. After dark, the barn cats and the same old chicken came to hunt for flying bugs under the street light at the corner of the yard. The cats jumped and the chicken ran and flew to catch circling beetles and moths. We never knew why the chicken decided not to go to roost with the others. She may have known her performance kept her out of the frying pan.

Bedtime was early because we had to leave the next day for Dothan. The rain began again and the house was cool enough for me to sleep upstairs. I had already done things in preparation for leaving. I had put up my hooks, line and onion sack net I used to seine minnows and had put corn in Momma's flowerpots. I snickered a little because I knew we would get a letter from Momma in a week or so saying the strangest thing had happened: corn had come up in all her flower pots! I lay on the cool straw mattress. The streetlight flickered as the wind and the rain moved oak limbs and made changing shadows on the wall.

I listened to rain beating on the roof. *That sounds like those flying things on Mars, maybe. ....* With sounds of rain on the roof a few feet away on a cool summer night, sleep is irresistible.

There is little physical evidence that this time and place ever was. The largest oaks were lost to the paved road. No dust settles on the porch. Cars speed by and few people look. None wave. The sidewalk is broken, and crumbled. Weeds grow through holes. The enameled streetlight at the corner is gone. Much of the year, the branch is dead and dry as the dusty road of the past. It runs part of winter and after heavy rain in summer. The cotton fields are gone. The barn, the well, and outbuildings are gone. A cousin owns the house; it is remodeled, has a new color, is well cared for, but hardly recognizable as the house I knew from top to bottom so long ago. Before the back porch was torn down–where we kept the ice-box and the water-bucket–where I cranked the ice-cream freezer--I went back to see the railing where I had carefully recorded the length of each fish I caught by cutting a notch at the head and tail. A strange thing happened over the years. The sun and rain had shrunk that rail. The notches were so much closer than I remembered.

In my heart, the little stream so important to me is not *really* dead; it runs clear and free. Minnows swim in the pool beneath the willow. The sidewalk is smooth and straight. Rockers sit on the dusty porch looking at gentle summer rain. I feel the velvet darkness with splashes of light from the corner. I hear soft voices with strange words and manner of speech. I smell cool night air that comes with rain. These Forever Summer scenes live in the little boy part of old men's minds that always remains.

I have the medical book with the wicked picture. I have the world's best checkerboard and the dipper everybody drank from, but physical things were not the important parts of these visits. This was a time of learning and growth as much as if it had been a classroom. I was shaped and formed by these days. I learned of family love and security. I learned self-confidence and formed my love of the fantastic world we live in.

There is in the child an inquisitive nature, a spirit of anticipation, hope for the future, wonder and amazement at the world around him, and a sense of what next. These qualities fade as problems of the world mount. But as long as the zeal and ardor of youth can be remembered, though years pass and the body ages, in our hearts we are never truly old.

Depression Changes To War

One Sunday Afternoon
11

Sunday was a break in the daily routine. There was none of the rushing around to get out of the house to school or work. We slept late and read a little of the Sunday paper after breakfast. After church, we had the usual fried chicken noontime Sunday dinner. The house was quiet except for an occasional outburst from a small sister I was supposed to watch and keep out of trouble, but that was impossible. We never listened to the radio on Sundays; there was nothing on but screaming preachers and bad quartets. After dinner, we four drove our 1940 Chevrolet the few miles from Albertville to Boaz to visit Momma and Papa Owen. The car was typical of the stripped-down cars of the depression with no accessories except a Southwind heater.

The day was warm and clear for December--a late Indian summer day. Sunday drives meant more then. Without televisions and computers, families were forced to talk to each other and look at the world around them. The drive was unhurried as the day. Part of the joy of a Sunday drive is seeing what others are doing along the road. On the east side there was a huge pile of sorghum cane where the mule went round and round pulling the pole to turn the rollers to crush juice from the cane for the cooker. Daddy said with all the development along the road, the old mill might have to move. The highway brought us to the center of Boaz and we turned right on West Mill Street. There was little traffic, a few other Sunday drivers enjoying the day of rest. We pulled up in the yard of my grandparents' house and Momma came running out of the house and across the yard toward us. We thought the house must be on fire. Nobody had seen her run since the milk cow butted her. She was at the car before we could get out.

"Have ya heard--we done locked horns with the Japs?"

We hurried to the house and sat around the little radio and listened for an hour, until we realized they were saying the same thing over and over because nobody knew the whole story. The Japanese had attacked Pearl Harbor. We didn't know the damage was worse than we could imagine. I didn't know what war meant.

Our ride back to Albertville was somber and silent. The same houses, same stores, same mill, same sights were there. Nobody looked. We heard the same story over and over on our radio.

The next day the President spoke, and for the first time we began to understand a little of what war meant. In the next months, lives of everybody in the nation were turned upside down. Recruiting stations had long lines of volunteers. The draft was instituted. We began meat rationing, gas rationing and shoe rationing. Tires were unattainable. When men joined the army, they sold their tires and put the car on blocks "for the duration." The War Production Board, the Draft Board and other boards appeared to control our lives. Anything with metal or rubber was unobtainable. Manufacturing plants sprang up everywhere, even in Alabama. News was grim. We lost parts and then all of the Philippines and other lands in the Pacific. "We regret to inform you" telegrams began arriving. No community was free from death. There was a nationwide fear that the Japs would invade California. A submarine had surfaced and shelled the coast. Japanese-Americans were interned in California because of a fear that some were loyal to the land of their birth and were spies. Americans were rapidly learning to hate Japs and these were Japs. Their businesses and farms were mobbed. It was difficult to tell good from bad, so all were rounded up. They were isolated for their own protection. We were a peaceful nation with a small army in the late depression. After December 7, 1941, we created the largest manufacturing system the world has ever seen and trained a huge army. A sleeping giant had been awakened. If the Japanese had formally declared war and not made the sneak attack, the outcome might have been different. In their desire to dominate the world, they underestimated The United States. They united us like no time before or since. If they could have foretold the future, events might have been different after that Sunday afternoon.

The Last Cornstalk
12

Papa Owen was a healthy man for his sixty-eight years, but he had a respiratory illness that didn't improve with treatment by Dr. Horsley, the one and only doctor in Boaz. With care in The Holy Name of Jesus Hospital 25 miles away in Gadsden, he improved and was allowed to go home, only to get worse and begin a slow decline. The family discussed more hospital care, but Dr. Horsley said little could be done anywhere. There were no antibiotics in the summer of 1942. Treatment of pneumonia was supportive with a Calvinist attitude.

I was a teenager, but as his only grandson, was allowed, even encouraged, to see and be with him. My mother, who was so much like her father, carefully coached me, explaining that death is a part of life.

Papa lay in the double bed in the back bedroom, the bed I slept in until I was nine and in later years when I visited in the summers. Dark stained wainscoting ran from the painted floor to the chair rail. The walls above were covered with faded wallpaper with a snag here and there showing cheesecloth underneath. Three pictures hung by wires from the picture molding near the top of the twelve-foot ceiling. A dresser, wardrobe, and sewing machine were arranged along the sides of the room. The bed was under a window, against the wall opposite the fireplace. An oval multicolored crocheted rug covered the floor in the center of the room, just out of range of sparks from the fire in winter. A collection of straight chairs and rockers gathered about the fireplace across from the bed. A kitchen clock with carved wooden bonnet and sides sat on the mantel, loudly ticking.

Each time it struck, there was one less hour. The clock belonged to Papa's father and had been running over half a century. Papa always cared for it with such ceremony. I wondered when it had been wound. At the end of a center twisted yellow and black drop cord, the brass socket held a black double socket. On one side, light from a bare bulb was harsh and glaring, throwing shadows beyond the bed on this overcast day. The other side of the socket held a cord that angled across to a small radio on the bedside table. It was respectfully silent.

Uncle Jake, Papa's youngest son, sat by the bed. He stayed in the daytime and Uncle Ray stayed at night. I sat at the far side of the room, felt helpless, and said nothing. I wound the clock, sat staring at the cold fireplace and listened for sounds from the bed. I thought of words I should have said. The ticking of the clock seemed louder. I dreaded the strike at the hour.

Papa was six feet tall with snow-white hair and mustache. He was not thin, but trim for his years with hollowness to his cheeks that gave a distinguished presence. He was a strong man, well read, and respected, an authority figure in the family. What I was seeing was a man frail and weak in his striped nightshirt, so much smaller and without his usual intellect. He was picking at covers and hallucinating at times. Jake talked with him and laughed with him at times. There was little we could do except be there.

A man in his final hours may cry out, hallucinate and babble senseless words, even without drugs. Sometimes-- not always--but sometimes, there is a lucid time filled with strange words, profound wisdom, even poetry, as if a window of Heaven opened for an instant. Then, the moment is gone.

Papa had just said something about a pinch of sugar that made no sense at all, when he suddenly sat up. He seemed to regain his statue.

His eyes a little brighter, he said in a low clear voice, "I feel like a cornstalk."

Jake laughed and said, "What, Papa?"

I turned to watch. Papa looked straight in Jake's eyes. "Have you never seen a cornfield in winter when plow and stalk cutter missed just one cornstalk and left it standing all alone in the center of the field? My Momma and Papa are gone; Wiley and my other brothers and sisters are dead and gone. I am the only one left. *I am* the last cornstalk."

Then the window closed. It was almost sundown when I left.

That night Papa died. He just slipped away. It seemed so little was done for him, but there was little to offer.

Two days later, men brought him from the funeral home and put him in the parlor where we rarely went. I ran to see as soon as they left. I took a quick look and fled as people crowded through the front door. I sat in a rocker in the empty back bedroom and stared at the fireplace. The shaggy mustache and the white hair loosely "roached up" were gone. The hair, eyebrows, and mustache were trimmed like a twenty year old. His hair was slicked back. The shirt and coat were so smooth they could have been painted on. The body in the casket was artificial. It was a stranger. I didn't know him.

I hope he knew the words I never said. I know the words he left unsaid–I read it in his eyes. I looked up. The clock still ticked.

Strangers ran his funeral. They didn't know even the last cornstalk falls to life's storms.

More than half a century later, I miss him at times: when I think of a true Southern gentleman, if I would like to talk to a father figure about some weighty problem, or when I see his old clock in our bedroom; now it ticks for me.

In my mind's eye I see that cornfield in the weak light of the setting sun of late winter. The cornstalks are cut and plowed, save one. It stands, but leans, and twisted leaves shudder in the cold wind. There is snow in the middles and against terrace rows.

But I now know what Papa must have known. As surely as day follows night, spring follows winter and then summer. I see that same cornfield in the golden light of summer sunrise with voices of birds, sounds of bees and the smell of fresh turned earth. Row on row stalks of corn sway in the summer breeze. One stalk is greener and a little taller than all the rest.

Courthouse Steps
13

The year 1943 was not just a time more than a half century ago; it was a different world, different life, and different dimension--never understood by those born since. It's hard to describe to one who was not a witness. To begin with, this was before color--back when the world was black and white. Look at old photographs: black and white, and old movies: black and white. There were some like *Snow White* and *Gone With The Wind,* but they were apparitions. In real life there was no color. Men's suits were drab; houses were drab; army uniforms were olive drab. The navy wore blue-black or white. Even Lucky Strike cigarettes' green had gone to war. A stifling grayness hung over the nation at war, dominating everything. Morals and standards were either black or white. The war was clearly right; marriage, honesty and piety were right. Hoarding and dealing in the black market were clearly wrong. Situational ethics had not yet been invented.

Life in the little town of Roanoke was slow and isolated--even worse in wartime--more black and white than other places. The town was connected to the outside world by a railroad, a Greyhound bus that traveled poor roads, and a primitive phone system. Movietone news did come to the Marion Theater, but the subject was always war. It dominated everything. Cars had A, B, or C stickers on the windshield, lower right side, to show the amount of gas the owner was entitled to. There were stamps for gas, stamps for canned goods, stamps for shoes, red points for meats, and give up on tires. Anything metal was hard to come by.

A constant answer was, "There's a war on, ya know" or "That went for the war effort."

Crews of kids collected scrap metal and paper. We bailed paper like hay and shipped it out by rail.

The oppressive weight and grayness of war was everywhere. There was a little unwanted color here and there. Mothers who had lost a son in the war were encouraged to place a gold star in their window.

In this sleepy little town, I was attending my tenth school in nine years. I was acquainted with the problems of the eternal new boy, but didn't accept them gracefully. A stranger, especially one a little shy, doesn't fit well in established groups.

I had two local castoffs as friends. We were fifteen--an awkward stage--just finishing rapid growth with enough hormones to confuse--not still children, but certainly not adults. Sledge was older, larger, a little stooped with small almost recessed eyes and small mouth, which never showed teeth. His words were a little thick, and he spoke even slower than I do. He had lost a grade in school, but was ostracized because his parents were never married. His name was Sledge. We called him Sledgehead. Charlie Barber was small and blond with delicate, almost bird like, features and hands. He was ostracized because he was a little different. He had no interest in social events, but was skilled in building things around the house. He was as agile as Sledgehead was awkward. We would have given him a nickname, but what could be done with a name like Charlie? I was painfully thin with brown hair, which had a red cast in summer. I was Ginnis, Ginnie or Ginnie Pig. We were free spirits, each in his own way. We were driven together by this black and white world.

How would we entertain ourselves in this summer of '43? We did not worship before the great TV god and were forced to read books, which of course, were black and white, and publications such as *Saturday Evening Post, Reader's Digest* and *Life*. The pictures generated by radio and books could be brighter and clearer than TV. Radio was a link to the outside world, but everything we heard was war. H. V. Kaltenborn, Gabriel Heater, Lowell Thomas and Walter Wenchell brought us war news, sometimes a little distorted. These were nighttime occupations; the three of us searched for daytime diversions. Summer days were long in little towns.

Toward late evening, we could hear the lonesome, mournful sound of the train a long way off. The sound of a steam whistle is not at all like a diesel whistle. The three of us went to the station to see the Seaboard and Coastal train pull in. Newspapers and strange packages were unloaded. All sorts of people got off. We could only imagine the far off places they had been and strange things they had done. Then the train pulled off in a cloud of steam and gray smoke and was gone. Dumps of sand, gravel, and stones were along the track. As the train faded in the distance, we loaded up on smooth rocks of proper size at one of the dumps. Nobody ever told us we couldn't, so we helped ourselves. My mother never understood the holes in my pockets.

In his entire life, Sledgehead had never been out of the city of Roanoke. One day the three of us rode our bikes down the path beside the railroad track seven miles to Dickert, a crossroad with a few stores. It had a name. *Now*, Sledgehead could say he had been somewhere.

We built our own transportation system. The route from my house to Charlie's house through ordinary means was about two miles. The three of us cut a trail through Red Bug Hollow and a swamp along a branch and connected the two houses in three-fourths of a mile. Sledgehead lived a mile away, but he was there almost every day to help. We built a bridge frame of saplings across the branch and floored it with old barrel staves from the syrup mill. We floored the drainage ditch from the pipe under the railroad spur.

We used scrap metal and pipes to build stoves in the clay bank and stabilized the pipes with wires. We had cookouts, camp-outs and used slingshots on snakes, birds and suspicious bushes. There could have been an Indian or a Jap in there.

We might have made a little noise, but we were well away from houses. One day we arrived at our camp to find Mr. Myhand and his black employee chopping our stoves with an ax and saying unkind things about "those boys." We couldn't believe it. It wasn't even his property. It wasn't ours either, but we were there first. This meant war, but how? We blocked the drainpipe under the spur, but it might be months before it rained enough to flood his pigpen.

Mr. Myhand's coal-yard was fifty yards from my back yard across a field of broom sage beyond the elevated railroad spur that blocked the view of all the buildings except for the roof. He had a house, a barn-like storehouse, and smaller sheds. All had a corrugated metal roof. I established the range and discovered from the edge of the broom sage, I could use my sling--not slingshot, but sling--and throw a big smooth rock across that field and railroad track, and drop it on a metal roof. Bam, bam, scrape. scrape, thunk over and over again. We figured everybody was in the house during supper and sounds were good for the digestion.

Within minutes Myhand and his hired hand were out beating the bushes with a big stick saying, "It's those boys again! I know they're here somewhere." He never climbed the railroad track and looked our way and never heard us laughing.

In 1943 we were not held captive by spectator sports, but movies were a diversion, even if they were second-run. One afternoon on the way home from the movies, we discovered an abandoned church a block away and parallel to the main street. It was locked, but there was no "Don't come in" sign. Sledgehead thought it would be a sacrilege that we should try. He didn't say the word. He had trouble with that many syllables, but he expressed the opinion. The small Victorian building had weathered gray, almost black, walls with dirty amber windows. In the graveyard to one side, weeds almost hid overturned pots and tombstones tilted at odd angles. Around it, a rusty wrought iron fence had sections leaning almost to the ground. The walk to the door was broken and weeds grew from cracks. A twisted oak hung over the church. It was spooky, even in daytime.

We finally convinced Sledgehead this was no longer an active church. Besides we weren't going to do any damage. We opened an access door in the ceiling of the entranceway and climbed in the space above and then across into the building and down through another access door. As big as he was, Sledgehead had to go second. Charlie went first to help him through, and I stayed outside to make sure he went. True to our promise, we didn't damage anything, but explored in the dim yellow light from the windows. Sledge walked stiffly, hugging himself as if something were about to snatch his shirt away. He knew what would happen, but still hollered and threw up his hands when one of us jumped out from behind a door. Before we left, we found the old pump organ.

I don't remember what excuse we gave our parents, but we borrowed a flashlight and went back to the old church one night and were inside before the late movie turned out. We raised one window a few inches so we could see and hear a group of people coming down the dark sidewalk toward the church. At the corners, a streetlight with flat enamel reflector cast a dim light. In the middle of the block, the church and graveyard were lit by moonlight throwing strange shadows through trees, bathing the church and crooked tombstones. At this hour, there were no cars and no motor noises. It was truly quiet as a tomb in this black and white world. We heard people laughing and talking as they walked under the light at the corner.

There was no sidewalk across the street from the church. To go home, they had to pass the church and graveyard or walk a half-mile around. As they came closer, the walkers and talkers became softer and softer. Even whispering stopped. They were trying to tiptoe past the graveyard filled with strange shapes and shadows.

They hesitated, almost stopped and stared across the iron fence. One walker pointed. Did they see a flicker of motion at a window? They couldn't have seen the dirty string coming out of the window, but they did see the white cloth it jerked up from behind a tombstone. I pumped like crazy and played a mournful scale on that old organ. Charlie rattled a chain. Sledge was supposed to moan, but he was in a stupor and drawn up in a knot. We goosed him in the ribs, and he screamed instead. We head shouts and shrieks and feet hitting the sidewalk. One guy went through a hedge. Another ran over a garbage can. As soon as we recovered from our laughing fit, we left for home to polish our halo in case we heard the story the next day.

After I fed the ungrateful chickens the next morning and did a few jobs for mother, I listened to the radio as I finished reading the new *Saturday Evening Post*. Every few minutes there was a war bulletin. Most were not good. After lunch there was a knock at the door.

I heard the door open and the hesitant question. "Is…is Ginnie here?" By now, Mother knew my official name. I walked with Sledgehead down the trail through the hollow to our "camp."

After Sledge located Charlie, we sat on our bridge across the branch. "Anybody hear anything about last night?"

"Not a word. Maybe those folks are afraid spooks will get 'em if they talk about it."

Sledge squinted, making his eyes look even smaller. "I wanta do sonethin'; Momma's lookin' for me to weed the garden. I'm not goin' home 'til dark. What ken we do?"

"We could cook out."

"We did that Tuesday; besides I don't have anything to cook. We could ride bikes down the railroad tracks."

"We did that last week. Besides my bike is broke."

"We could visit Mr. Myhand."

"Naw, him and his man are lookin' too close. We better wait a while. Movie doesn't change 'till Monday. What do you want to do, Sledge?"

"I-o-know, what do ya'all want to do?"

"War's on and everything is dead in this town. Nothing is goin' on anywhere and there is nothin' to do. I reckon we'll just have to go downtown and pee on the courthouse steps."

"What! You cain't do that. Somebody would see you."

"Sure they would, Sledge. How else would they know we had made our mark?"

"You cain't do thaat!"

"Yes we can. Dogs do it all the time."

"That's different. I won't do it."

We said nothing as we listened to the familiar sounds of birds and insects and looked at their flights around us. "Do ya'all recken them snake-doctors really hang around snakes? They're just everwhere down there toward the branch."

"Sure, Sledge, that means there's a snake under ever rock. Remember how many snakes there were in the wash-hole we swam in down the railroad track. There were snake doctors everywhere there."

A five-foot black snake slithered down the bank by a post under the bridge. We watched in silence. Now, Sledge knew the truth about snake doctors. As the snake glided toward a bush, we saw snake doctors with transparent wings and iridescent bodies resting on a limb of that bush.

"See, there's three of 'em an' not only that, I saw a cat bird fly to that bush, an' you know they're always 'round snakes. An' there's some snake spit on a weed next to that bush. I betcha there's a whole mess of moxicans under that bush. Do ya recken that was one of them hoop snakes? My gran'pa says they grab their tail and turn theirselfs into hoops and roll down the hill and chase ya. When they catch ya, they stick in ya leg."

"Even if that's true, he'd have to be on a hill above us to get us."

"Oh, I guess so. Anyways, he didn't look like one of them corchwhips. Grandpa says them will chase ya and whup ya somp'en terr'ble."

"That's a black racer."

"We better be quiet; if he hears us, he'll chase us. That's why they call 'em racers."

"Sledge, do you see ears on that snake? He's not going to hear us and not going to see us unless he grows an eye on the top of his head."

The tip of the snake disappeared under the bush, and the flying visitors left for other snakey areas. After the display just for our benefit, Charlie said. "Okay, if ya don't want the courthouse, how 'bout the post office steps."

"That's worse. I'll go home and pull weeds."

"Then you're chicken, Sledgehead." Subtle humor was wasted on Sledge, but Charlie and I loved it. After we talked and argued for a while, we noticed the shadows were longer and the day about gone, so we split up and agreed to meet the next day and try to decide what to do. Two of us said we might have to go downtown and pee on the courthouse steps. We never did, but whenever boredom and the doldrums set in, we threatened to do it. We never told Sledge that the courthouse was in Wedowee. Roanoke did have a post office and with steps.

We did go to social events, but rarely. The school had a picnic with lots of food, games and contests. I was thin and didn't have much to move around. I won the sack race. My prize was a piece of lemon pie. As I picked up the pie at the table, Clarence came over. My dislike for him was not because he was fat and not because his family was rich; it was because he was the most obnoxious guy in school. He picked on everybody and could be downright cruel at times. He proceeded to jeer at me and hit my hand and elbow to try to make me drop the pie. I still didn't understand that new boys never win anything--not even a piece of pie. He said something once too often and hit my arm once too often. The lemon meringue pie made an enormous splat.

There was a little color in my life in the form of lemon yellow on a howling face when all the world was black and white. I might not have to go to the courthouse steps after all, I had made my mark.

My First Visit To Anniston

14

After the big picnic, life settled into deeper summer doldrums. At fifteen, we were beginning to function more independently away from direct control of parents. I did have to mow the lawn, take care of the chickens and do simple repairs. Once these jobs were done, I was off and gone on bike trips, cookouts, or down the trail and through the swamp, always with a big sling shot, a little one and a pocketful of rocks. I left the sling at home for Mr. Myhand. My poor mother would go down the trail to the edge of the swamp to call me for a meal.

I didn't have a watch and sometimes was hours late. I was forced to hang my head and listen, "Well, young man what do you have to say for yourself?"

"I'm sorry. I just got to talking with Charlie and Sledgehead and forgot the time."

She probably thought I needed a change of scenery, so arrangements were made. Or did she hear about our threat to the courthouse steps? Daddy saved enough gas stamps to make a rare trip to Birmingham. I was to be left for several days at one of his sisters with one set of cousins and then go across town to another sister's house with other children of my age.

The Winter family lived in East Lake, near the airport. The country mouse was visiting the city mouse, so we did city things. I was impressed with the ride downtown. Streetcars make strange noises, different from bus sounds. The car made faint noises when stopped. As the car pulled away the motor hummed, making a whirring grinding sound as it gained speed. The wheels rolled over the joints in the rails with a clicking sound. The cars jerked and lurched as we turned corners. The conductor pulled the cords to make clanging sounds at intersections. For a few cents we could ride downtown or across the county. At the edge of the airport we saw industries involved in the war effort. There were big warning signs everywhere:

UNCLE SAM WANTS YOU!
LOOSE LIPS SINK SHIPS!
THE ENEMY IS LISTENING!

One said, BE ALERT. Somebody had written under the sign "That's just what this country needs, a buncha lerts."

When we did get downtown, I found a trip to the Alabama Theater was like visiting a palace to a country mouse; there was a spot of color in this black and white world.

I spent more time at the Edwards' house in Homewood. My uncle and aunt had two girls near my age. There were no gas stamps for another drive in the car, so I began making plans for my bus trip. I wrote one of my "I am fine. How are you?" letters to my mother and told her I would come either Tuesday or Wednesday. The city was too much for the country mouse, so on Tuesday morning I took my satchel of dirty clothes, and went to the Greyhound Bus Station. I checked and rechecked the schedule and connections. I had enough foresight to come early and was number three in line to load. With gas rationing, buses and trains were crowded. A ticket meant you could go if you could get on the bus. Every seat was filled, and every inch of the aisle had standing passengers, with two on steps at the door. The bus pulled away, leaving as many as were on the bus. The old bus groaned and lurched as it made turns out of the city to Highway 78.

Stops and turns made standees sway. There was no room to fall in the aisle. Some fell across people in the seats. Even in a window seat, I feared for my life. If the fat guy fell, he would squash us all. Highway 78 was a narrow curving, patched asphalt road and the only route to Anniston and Atlanta. Traffic was thin, but troublesome. Military convoys and an ancient truck sometimes ground along ahead of the bus, even slower than the wartime speed limit of 35 miles per hour. Any town with a name or a crossroads store could put up a bus stop sign and get service. Sooner or later, a Greyhound or Trailways bus would come by. We stopped at every pig trail. Sometimes people flagged down the bus in the middle of nowhere. Passengers getting off were always toward the back, so people in the aisle would have to get off the bus and then get back on. One soldier, tired of this game, muscled himself up and lay down in the overhead luggage rack. There was an open luggage rack over the seats. Bags fit into this rack or were left at home. We picked up a few passengers, but put off more and slowly the aisle cleared. People were pleasant. They gossiped and talked war, children, recipes, crops and destinations. We delayed several times at bus stops to deliver a package or message or get a Coke. Even when we were rolling down the highway, it seemed we were crawling. I could see my neighbor's watch so I knew we were late, but there was a 90 minute wait in Anniston for the connecting bus, so there should be plenty of time.

As the man in the next seat said, "That bus will probably be as late as ours."

In Anniston, we pulled in a drab station on Gurnee Avenue, two hours late. As soon as the bus stopped rolling, I was out like a shot. The station was empty except for two people at the lunch counter. The last bus of the day had left on time. My mother had given me a little money. I had spent most of it. I had 35 cents after I bought my ticket in Birmingham. I used a nickel for a collect call. My mother would know what to do. I called the number and instead of a mother who had all the answers, I got a trouble operator who talked as if she were holding her nose. Wires were down somewhere in Randolph County.

"When will they be fixed?"

"Too late today--maybe tomorrow; they's a war on, ya know."

So, I was left with a satchel of dirty clothes and 35 cents in a strange town with no hope for a bus until morning. Through the smeared glass, I could see the sun going down. The soldier who had climbed in the luggage rack saw something was wrong and stopped to talk. He even bought me a lemonade at the lunch counter. After he heard the story, he wished me luck and left. A skinny kid with a satchel of dirty clothes is not popular.

We are a product of our experiences. My children never understood why I insist they carry emergency funds when they make a trip. I always gave them a bill to put away. They spent it, but I tried. As they walked out the door, I always gave them a quarter for the phone.

I had functioned on my own in the past without my parents telling me what to do. I even broke an ankle miles away and managed to get home on my bike, but there was always the possibility of getting home. I was in a strange city and knew nobody.

Or did I?

I used a dime to check my bag, looked up an address in the phone book, asked directions at the lunch counter and went several blocks to the Brown Service Insurance Company office. I went to the counter at the front.

"Ma'am, could I please see a list of your agents and superintendents?"

"Well, ah ... I suppose so."

I looked down the list quickly, because the clock on the wall showed five o'clock coming quickly. "Ma'am, this Mr. Boozer--was he in Dothan three years ago?"

"I don't know, I haven't worked here that long."

"Is he the one they call Bunion Boozer?"

"Well... I think they do."

"Could I have his number and maybe use your phone?"

This was not permitted, but by now she was dying to find out what this kid was up to. I called and talked to Mrs. Boozer. I almost called her Mrs. Bunion! I explained who I was and the problems I had. Mr. Boozer and my father had worked together in Dothan. He had been transferred in one direction and my Dad in another. She had never laid eyes on me, but knew who I was. She patiently explained how and where to catch the bus for Oxford and was waiting at the bus stop. An angel couldn't have looked better. We walked to her house and tried to call my mother again without success. Mr. Boozer came home after a bit and found a surprise visitor.

Breakfast had been a long time before. A bath and a hot meal did wonders for my morale. I slept in a spare bedroom on the second floor. Mrs. Boozer woke me early the next day. At 6:10, I used my wrinkled ticket and left on the bus headed for Roanoke. The trip was slow, but not like the day before. I got off the bus, took my satchel and walked the mile and a half to the little house on South Government Street by Red Bug Hollow. I opened the front door before eight o'clock.

My mother jumped up and said, "Goodness, you're here early. What time did you leave?"

"Mother, you just wouldn't believe it!"

My Most Unforgettable Teacher
15

Education should be a life-long experience. Twelve years of public school and college years are structured and intense, but learning should never end. In the years of school, working and beyond, we come in contact with those who teach and mold our lives. At first, we may have only one teacher. As time passes, we are taught by increasing numbers. We are exposed to hundreds--even thousands--of men and women who impart knowledge, shape lives and exert influences lasting a lifetime.

Of all the teachers I have known, who was the most unforgettable? If I close my eyes, who can I still see and hear? I eliminate those of recent years for whom I have no true perspective. I eliminate my first teacher; my mother is not to be considered with others. Wives are also in a special category. After marriage, husbands and wives begin a lifetime learning experience. I have learned both with my wife and from my wife. If men listen, they learn caring, devotion, love, and family relationships. Who then, of the hundreds of teachers is the most unforgettable?

In a weeklong medical meeting, I may hear ten, sometimes twenty-five people. In the years since medical school I have been exposed to thousands of speakers and teachers. Most were just-look-what-I-have-done people, which is one way to teach. Few have a vast body of knowledge and truly want to impart this to their hearers. There are exceptions. Laslo Tabar knew more about mammography and breast disease than anyone I have ever known and had a missionary zeal for teaching. Even with his Swedish accent, he wasn't my most unforgettable teacher. Big John Slaughter was my Chief when I learned the art, science, and practice of surgery at Lloyd Noland Hospital. He guided me through my first operation. More than surgical technique, he taught there is one standard of care for all patients. He taught pursuit of excellence. He shaped my concept of surgery more than any other, but he is not the most unforgettable.

Hugh Trout, Jr. taught me the only operation I never changed. When I questioned his technique of appendectomy, he said his father and Dr. Jones had founded Jefferson Hospital in 1907 and one operation had been done the same way all those years. There had never been a blown stump. I never had a blown stump and saw no reason to change. Dr. Trout is not my most unforgettable.

We had dozens of major teachers and hundreds of lesser teachers in medical school. Dr. Tensley Harrison and Dr. Champ Lyons, were world-renowned and had written books, but they don't fit requirements. I remember others faintly.

J. Henry Walker taught biology. Septema Smith taught parasitology. But they are not the most unforgettable. Dr. Toffel, taught more than chemistry. He taught how to think and reason, how to use words, but avoid domination by words. I remember reading *Tyranny of Words* for extra credit for an average of 105 that quarter, but even with his '34 Ford called the *Brown Beetle*, Dr. Toffel is not the most unforgettable. Dr. Russell taught about life in his English literature class, but he doesn't fit.

I remember the high school teacher who gave me a love for chemistry and let an eager boy run the lab. I remember the teacher who showed me that geometry is more logic than mathematics, but I don't remember their names.

Others left their mark. In 1944, when we moved from the little country school in Roanoke to Gadsden High. I learned to say sophomore and not Senior I.

Even if I had known the teachers, I wouldn't have had a choice in most classes; there was one Biology teacher and one Latin teacher. They were good teachers, but nameless now.

And then there was algebra. Even the name strikes fear in the hearts of naive students. It was taught the first hour after lunch, guaranteeing indigestion. There was one algebra teacher. Ms. Whorton was not just short, she was pathologically short. She had a round, puffy face, small nose and mouth, an expression as if her lunch had been dill pickles. On bad days, she looked like she had eaten a green persimmon. She squinted through round wire-rim glasses, too big for her face. She had short arms and tiny swollen hands. One was wrapped around a long piece of chalk that looked even bigger as she waved it about. She could write only near the bottom of the blackboard. If you stood up to see, you were glared at for making short jokes; if you didn't try, you were not paying attention.

On her better days, Ms. Whorton was sullen. On others her wrath was severe. Discipline was assured in her class. A grayness from her room seemed to flow from her blackboard to the hall and wrap students as they came in the door. Except for her small voice, always sharp and biting, there was gloom and silence in the class. She was too small to be an ogre and didn't have the nose for a troll. To us she was an evil gnome, and we were under her spell as she waved her white stick. She must have known algebra, but few did well in her class. I had a low passing grade when I missed the final exam due to legitimate illness.

I went to Ms. Whorton to see about a make-up test. She gave a curt answer, "No, you cannot have another test. I'm not going to waste my time and energy giving a make-up exam. You can take an F for the semester. You'll never finish high school anyway."

I knew better than to argue with an angry gnome, so I left. I didn't bother my mother with many school problems, but I couldn't handle this one. She was in the principal's office when he arrived the next day. I took the test surrounded by sullen, sarcastic remarks and was given a D- for the semester. I passed, but there was Algebra II the next year and something else gnawed at me. Could the gnome be right? Was there something wrong with my brain? Should I change my plans for medicine?

I registered for summer school and took Algebra ll taught by a pleasant human. I was making A's when another disaster struck. Chicken pox is bad enough, but my case was so bad the county health officer was sent to see if it could be smallpox. It wasn't, but he told us I couldn't go to school until the last scab fell off. To complicate matters, an ironclad rule limited absences to two weeks in summer school. The last day came and I still had two scabs. I did the only thing any red-blooded American boy would do; I put band-aids on the scabs and went. The two weeks with chicken pox cost me my A, but a B in algebra is still a good grade. There was nothing wrong with my brain, and I had avoided Ms. Whorton.

I would never have had her as a teacher anyway because my father was transferred and I entered Huntsville High School in the fall. As I registered, I began to take stock of where I was. The algebra in summer school was an extra credit. I took Latin as an extra class in Roanoke and Gadsden. I was one credit short of senior level, but they wouldn't put me in the class. After my junior year, I took the last of my sixteen credits in summer school and left for the University of Alabama in the fall. When I graduated from college, I sent one of my five invitations to Ms. Whorton with a little note. When I finished Medical School, the bitterness had faded and I didn't send one.

Ms. Whorton, I have long since forgiven you and asked God to forgive me. You must have had tremendous physical and psychological pain that made your classroom a dungeon for you and your students. If you were a cretin and not a genetic dwarf, what a difference a little medication might have made in our lives and yours. I never saw you have a happy moment. My forgiveness is not through my own wisdom. When Joseph was thrown in the pit and sold into slavery, he suffered hardship and misfortune, and yet was molded, strengthened and became a great leader in Egypt. Years later, he faced his brothers and forgave them, saying though they meant their actions for evil, God meant them for good.

How many times have I had to learn that lesson over and over? If a door closes, blocking me from what I thought I wanted, another opens down the hall to something better than I ever dreamed of. I try to remember, but I still complain when that first door closes. Ms. Whorton, it was not your intent, but you propelled me and exhorted me through terror; you were my goad. I fled from you, gained a year and my self-respect. *You* are my most unforgettable teacher.

And technically speaking, you *were* right. I never did graduate from high school.

River
16

We turned off highway 431 to Rainbow Drive that passes within sight of the Coosa River for the first few miles. Traffic was heavy in both directions on this first Saturday in October 1993. The stream of cars and trucks made it hard to make the left turn to the parking lot for the Alabama Princess. My wife Betty and I boarded this 83-foot stern-wheeler and sat on the top deck for the hour and a half trip up the river. The Princess looks like a 19th century steamboat with two stacks, but is not. The boat is moved by two paddle wheels that move together for straight ahead, and separately for turns and are powered by a diesel engine. The stacks are fake. The boat is steel, not wood. As we left the dock, there was a constant chunk, chunk, chunk of the paddles. We passed under the 1920 highway bridge with its tall, sweeping classic arches, and the old railroad bridge that once rotated to let ships pass, and the 1950 highway bridge with functional square uninteresting shape. Little houses, trailers, fishing shacks, and piers were thick on the west bank for miles. To the east were the rubber plant and farther on, large homes and a golf course. As we turned to go back down the river in mid-afternoon, boat traffic began to increase. Large powerboats passed our slow moving paddle wheeler. Near the dock, thirty to forty boats gathered for a fishing contest. Bright glitter finish Ranger fiberglass boats with huge Mercury motors were in the water and on trailers on the bank. Hundreds of people watched as the boats were pulled out of the water for the fish weigh-in. Traffic was even heavier when we drove way from the lot. The policeman had to move a traffic cone to let us out.

A hundred years ago in a different world and different life, I saw that river. We moved from Roanoke in 1944 when I was fifteen. We had lived in Gadsden when I was in the sixth grade, but there was not one familiar face in Gadsden High. As always, I was the new kid.

Outside of school, I entertained myself as well as I could. Besides listening to the radio and reading books, I rode my Schwinn all over the city. With gas rationing there was little traffic, so I was reasonably safe even on main roads. In wartime days, high school students didn't have cars, not even seniors. When I rode on Rainbow Drive, only an occasional car passed. I was without wheels for a while after a disaster. I pulled out a tube to fix a flat and tore the tube in half. There were no replacements in wartime. I took six hot patches and stuck the ends together. The deformed tube thumped, but lasted the war and years later for my sister.

I met two boys in school I probably thought to be Gadsden versions of Charlie and Sledgehead. I did have to let my mother know where I was going on my bike and have permission to spend the afternoon with these newfound friends.

"Oh, yes, Mother. They are good boys. I met them in school."

"And you will be in their house or yard?"

"Uh ... uh... sort of out back of the house, but not far."

"Well, see that you get back on time."

A lot of the trip was downhill, especially the stretch toward the river at Brown's Landing. It was back of the boys' houses--about a mile back. Mother didn't ask how far and she didn't ask about the river. Both boys were waiting.

Ben was taller than I was and just as skinny. His expression was glum and gloomy. His outlook was sometimes similar to his face. Pete, thin and short, was sometimes called Pee Wee, but hated the name. He smiled a lot, talked a lot, usually about trivial things. They were cousins, but didn't look related.

"This is Rudolph. He's part Feist."

That dog might have been ten percent Feist, but ninety percent was some strange hound shepherd mix, with a little beagle thrown in. His thick body and short legs did not resemble any known breed. His coat was mostly white with strangely located splotches of black, brown and a little rust. He looked like he had been put together by a committee and was the ugliest dog I had ever seen. But he was a happy dog and wagged his tail and smiled a lot, like Pete.

"We wuz gonna go fishin', but I don't reckon we will now."

"Why not?"

"Come on. I'll show you."

We walked the smooth path to the river. There was not another living soul on the river or the bank. The murky water looked as if it were not moving until a leaf floated by or a ripple from a fish bothered the surface.

Trees hung over the water. Snake doctors flashed iridescent blue as they flitted back and forth on transparent wings, sometimes resting on tall weeds on the bank, always facing water. Crickets chirped and July flies made their grating, buzzing noise from the trees on the hill. Except for these sounds and the catbird in the bush, the river was peaceful and quiet. The shade made the bank cool and dark with spots of sunlight.

"See, lookie there."

I saw a riverboat of the day: thick wood, curved sides, square end, front and back. A chain passed through a drilled hole in the smaller front end and was wrapped around a tree and padlocked to itself.

"That's ol' man Johnson's boat. We wuz gonna use it like we been doin', but the ol' stingy thang has taken to lockin' it up just 'cause we sort of borrowed it a time or two. We hid it in the bushes up a ways, but he found it. He's been raisin' cane to ever'body about that ol' boat. We're just going to have to go up river and find us another one."

"They got some mean dogs, or we would go today." Pete said with his only frown of the day. Ben continued to complain about the boat. He wouldn't consider fishing from the bank. Then we talked about other things. We talked about students and even a little about school and teachers. Ben and Pete had just recently relieved a garden of a watermelon. They told how sweet it was. They told about hunting in the wintertime, work in a garage and life on the river.

"Come on, we best get up some wood." We built a fire in a clearing near the riverbank and then pulled away branches hiding supplies. In some fashion Ben had secured a loaf of bread. Pete had an iron skillet, blackened from a thousand fires. He had also taken from his mother's pantry a blue quart fruit jar with zinc lid filled with cooked sausage patties packed below a thick layer of lard. Pete pulled the rubber ring. The dog suddenly woke up. He knew that spewing sound. All of those sausage patties and the lard went into the hot skillet. As the grease sizzled and popped, the sausages began to turn an even brown, making red flecks of pepper shine. By his time, Rudolph was as close to the pan as heat would allow. He could not contain the water in his mouth. He licked his chops constantly, ringing one side of his mouth with his tongue and then the other. Finally, the moment arrived. We pulled the pan to the side of the fire and speared the sausages with a stick and folded bread over them.

If I live another hundred years, I don't think I will find sausages like those. The setting or the method they were acquired may have had something to do with the flavor. Rudolph was not forgotten. Slices of bread soaked in grease and broken sausages suited him just fine. Three boys and a dog ate the quart of sausages and most of the bread. We lay down, propped against a tree trunk feeling stuffed like ticks we pulled off the dog. "Mebe you shuda got two jars, Pete."

"I can't do that; they may be countin' the jars!"

The shadows were getting long. Even without a watch, I knew it was late. Pete said he had to get the skillet back before suppertime. It was already clean. As soon as it cooled, Rudolph had seen to that. I walked the pedals to pull up the hill from the river toward home.

My mother couldn't understand why I ate so little at supper. After I went to bed that night, I thought about the peaceful river and boys I had met. *I'm afraid those boys may get into real trouble someday. Maybe I will look somewhere else for friends. Still ... those were good sausages and after you look at him a while, that dog really wasn't as ugly as I thought.*

In spite of all this, I never went back. The company was better on the riverboat. Except for that, I liked that river better a hundred years ago.

Preparation for Life

The Last Act
17

Rain fell in great sheets of water. Gusts of wind twisted trees and sent shifting crooked lines down the window. Blue-black clouds covered the late evening sun. Fog wrapped trees like an evil blanket. The glare of lightning made trees, streets, and cars look unreal as in a dream. After each blinding flash, darkness settled like a velvet curtain. In this increasing darkness, rumbles of thunder shook the window and one of the bars. A dim light behind a wire cage lit the cramped room--a cell with bare essentials: bunk bed, toilet, and table with remains of a meal. Most of the food lay untouched. The room filled the request for a cell with a view of the outside world.

A man stared through the single barred window. Stenciled letters were hardly visible on his pale blue shirt. Bursts of light reflected in the room outlying his shaved head. He was still a handsome man, but lines were beginning to creep in around his eyes, making him look a little hard.

Richard Martin rested his hand on a bar and muttered, "What a lousy day for my finest performance. Oh well ... things will look better in the light of day."

"Anything ya need, Mr. Martin?"

Rick turned to see Sam, a six feet eight inch man with a round somber face and a much smaller David who never had much to say. Rick never used their real names and called his guards "Igor and friend."

"It's Sam and Dave, Mr. Martin. Ya sure ya don't want the chaplain?"

"I told you a thousand times, I don't want to see any slobbering chaplain, and I don't want to see you jerks. Go torture somebody else and leave me alone!"

"Okay, Mr. Martin. If ya do need anything, let us know. We just come on and we'll be with you till... well, you know."

Rick Martin sat on the cot, propped a pillow against the graffiti on the wall and thought on his life and plans. This was to be his last day on earth. A smile showed in the glare of lightning. *Just wait till morning. All of those slobs will change their tune when they hear the news. They'll know who is a real star.*

Richard Martin had been a star, but the star faded. Through good looks and dumb blind luck, this high school dropout had become an over night success in Hollywood. He wasn't prepared for success. He pursued excesses of anything money could buy: houses, cars, clothes, boats, women, alcohol, and drugs. After years of success, self-indulgence and arrogance gave him the reputation of being an unpredictable troublesome star. As quickly as his star rose in the east, it set in the west. In this declining state, Rick married an older woman who had been an even greater star in the past. He thought headlines of a marriage would restore interest in his career. There was no affection; he actually hated her. It was a marriage of convenience and ambition, although his wife loved him and abandoned her career to help her husband.

Rick's plans brought frustration and bitterness because he was offered even fewer roles. He was abusive to his friends and wife. He could not stand his wife and told her how strange she was. She liked black: black clothes, black jewelry, and black sheets. She even kept an old black touring car when bright colors were the fashion. With her coloring, black looked good on her, but it was strange. Rick told her she was crazy.

After months of strife, in a final rage Rick physically threw his wife out of the house. "Take your stupid black clothes and your stupid black car and get out of my life! You and your craziness have ruined my career."

Rick Martin's career had failed; he had alienated most of the people in the movie business. His fair weather friends were gone and he had disposed of his wife of convenience. He had two friends left. They could hardly be called good friends, but they were friends of a sort.

Moe had worked for Rick since his early days in the movies. Rick found him in the group of extras on some monster movie set. He didn't know or care what Moe's real name was. Besides, a dummy wouldn't know who Quasimodo was--or Moe for short. He was a strange little man with distorted features and twisted body, not quite a hunchback, but with some sort of progressive disease. Rick never remembered what it was, but complained about the expense to diagnose something that couldn't be treated. Moe had little time left, a year or so at most, but that didn't matter. His ambition was to do anything Rick wanted: drive the car, yard work, house work--anything. He followed Rick like a twisted puppy. To Moe, Rick had everything he did not: sound body, fair face, and clear mind. Moe was happy to serve his personal idol.

After his rage at his wife, Rick sent Moe for groccries. His one other friend and agent, Abe Rothberg, arrived shortly after Moe left. Abe was a heavyset man with long stringy hair, rough features, and rasping voice. Rick and Abe sat in the den discussing the possibility of a part in a play. Over and over, Abe emphasized better acting and better attitude. Abe went over the script in detail. The two of them read the lines. They stood and went around the room reading words from each violent scene. They came to the end of this murder mystery and were shouting angry words and going through motions of the struggle in which Rick was to be killed in the play. At this climactic moment, Moe come in through the kitchen door. To his twisted mind, the only person in the world he cared about was being killed. He dropped the groceries and rushed in the room, snatching a bookend as he went. There was a sound as if a melon had been dropped and Abe fell to the floor. Rick screamed at Moe, cursed and called him foul names.

Moe cried pitifully, "Oh, Mr. Rick, I thought he was killin' you. You know I wouldn't hurt nobody."

Rick kneeled by Abe. He was not breathing and there was no pulse in his neck. Blood oozed from the depressed area on his scalp. Hopes for a comeback were fading. He looked at Moe. *Why not? Abe alive was helping. Maybe dead he could do more.*

"Moe, do you want to make this right? Do you want to do something to help me?"

"You know I do, Mr. Rick, anything."

"Listen carefully. Take the car; have it washed, do anything, but stay away from this house for three or four hours. You were never here since early morning. Tell not a single person about this. Do you understand me?"

"But don't we have to call the police?"

"I told you; do just as I say. You were never here. You saw none of this. I will be gone when you get back, but I will contact you. Do--as--I–say!"

Moe left. Rick took the bookend, carefully protecting fingerprints, and put it in a floor safe not even a persistent policeman could find. He took the other bookend, wiped it clean, put a little blood on it with his own prints and called the police.

The arrest made headlines. The trial made bigger headlines. Rick was again the center of attention. He attempted a melodramatic performance, protesting innocence. Rick had publicly fought with his agent and threatened his life a week before the death. With this knowledge and with prints on the bookend, the outcome was obvious. Rick was abusive and arrogant to the attorneys, judge and jury alike. They felt a sense of relief after they condemned and sentenced him.

His greatest performance, the one that would restore his rightful place in the public eye depended on twisted, totally loyal Moe. At the last minute, or better still an hour to avoid cutting it too close, Moe would arrive at the prison, sobbing and saying he had committed the murder through mistaken identity. The hidden bookend could be retrieved for proof. Rick could see the headlines now of his noble sacrifice to save his faithful servant.

He laughed to think of twisted Moe with canine loyalty willing to do anything. Rick warned him not to be late. He gave him one of his watches and told him to come a little early because of the storm.

"Mr. Martin ... it's time."

Rick jerked his head around to see Igor and friend staring through the bars like mismatched pallbearers. "Time, what do you mean, time? It's no where close; I just ate!"

"Mr. Martin, look at my watch. We got to go. You know the warden is punctual and your lawyer is here. Said you wanted a witness to somethin'."

"I will not go; someone else is coming. We have to wait. We have to wait for the truth to come out--for justice to be done!"

"Mr. Martin, nobody is going out on a night like this. We got to go. If we don't take you, we lose our jobs."

Three men struggled and made slow headway down the dark hall. They went like stair steps--one tall, one ideal height, and one short. A third guard helped strap Richard in the chair. He was screaming now and cursing. The skin of his face was a strange violet color. His features were twisted and distorted and covered with sweat as he shouted, "Someone is coming--coming with the truth. Wait ... wait."

Lights do dim when the switch is thrown.

"Sam, he didn't go out like them characters he played in the movies."

"No, Dave, he didn't. What you s'ppose he meant about somebody coming?"

"They all say things like that. Let's finish up."

There were front-page headlines, though small and below the fold. After all, he had once been a star. His final hour was gracefully not mentioned. On page three there was an article about the irony of death within the prison and death without. Just before Richard Martin was executed, a man was killed in the street in front of the prison--a hit-and-run victim. There were witnesses. As the car sped past, a flash of lightning showed an old black touring car driven by a woman with a black scarf about her head. In the darkness that followed and with swirling fog, nobody could read the tag.

EPILOGUE

This story doesn't seem part of my life, but it is.

In 1946, I was a seventeen-year-old freshman at the University of Alabama. Of the of 10,000 total enrollment, 5,000 were freshmen. The school gave the men's main campus dormitories to women and put most of the men several miles away at Northington Campus--an army hospital just given to the University.

Most of the men were veterans. Some considered this a paid vacation and never studied.

Many nights, poker games kept us awake. We lived a separate existence from the rest of the college. The University hired new instructors and told them to get rid of us. There was no room for that many sophomores on the main campus. Courses can be fortified so few can pass.

Toward the end of the first quarter I counted quality points I hoped to get: an A in chemistry and B in algebra. I hoped to pass German, but with no points. I had five. I needed one more or I would leave with the others. My other subject was English and I was struggling and failing English 101. All grades were from themes. Three grammatical or spelling errors earned an F on any paper. My high-school English teachers were usually substitutes or coaches. I knew little grammar, was a poor speller, and didn't know what a theme was. I passed my first theme at mid-term: a D-. I celebrated.

The final exam was to be a short story and would count half our grade. It was my only hope for my sixth quality point. Our instructor, Mr. O. B. Emerson, loved murder mysteries. I thought I could write a story so intriguing he would not see my errors. We could work at home, so I wrote and rewrote the story, had friends read it, stopped people on the street and asked them to read it. I bribed a friend to type it, turned it in on Friday and spent the weekend wondering if I should start packing.

On Monday, Mr. Emerson made his entrance after we had time to fidget and sweat. He had bad little-man's disease. We had never seen him smile.

He slammed the papers on the desk and said, "Where's McGinnis?" I raised my hand. "I fooled you–you so and so; I read it twice. You made three mistakes!"

After letting us suffer through announcements, he handed papers to a guy on the front row and told him to pass them out. He kept one, walked down the aisle and put it on my desk face down. He stood and tapped the paper with a finger. Eventually, I had to look up.

He said, "You had three mistakes and deserve an F ... but ... I liked your story and I *gave* you an A-."

For the first time, I saw him smile–just a little. Maybe he had a heart after all, at least a small one. He walked back up the aisle, told us good-by and left. We never saw him again. There were sighs and groans around the room. The guy next to me groaned loudest over an F. He thought he had a great story; he copied it from a comic book. His work was either transparent as mine, or our teacher read the same comic book.

I passed English with a C-, a minor miracle. Because of this naively written tale, I made my sixth point to stay in school this difficult first quarter.

This story was and always will be part of my life.

What I learned In My Sophomore Year
18

In the days before computers, registration for classes for 10,000 students took two days of confusion. The first day began with A-named students and worked half way down the alphabet. The next day began with Z and worked backwards. At the next registration in three months, the first day began with Z. As it worked out, those whose name began with M came at the end of the day either way. I made the trip from Northington Campus to the intimidating University of Alabama main campus. The guard at the door of Foster Auditorium checked the name on my student activities card and let me in near the end of the second day. Hundreds of tables filled the auditorium. Each had a sign on a pole listing subjects, hours and location. A person was seated at the table with sign-up sheets for each class. I knew the subjects I wanted, but had to schedule classes so I had time to go from one building to another. Some were on one side of the campus and others on the far side.

The floor was littered and patience short at some tables. It was evident registration was coming to an end. I made several tries, only to find that classes that would fit my schedule were filled. Finally, I got everything, except English Literature. When I found the right table and looked at the sign-up sheets, the one open class had one spot left.

I said, "My gosh, who wants to get up for an 8 o'clock class Tuesday, Thursday and *Saturday*--and it's football season."

The man at the table shrugged and said, "That's it."

I signed.

On the first Tuesday, the bus was late so I was late to class. All students know to avoid the first two rows. I had no choice. I sat in a center front row seat. I looked up at the teacher standing three feet away. How was I to know the guy with rolled up shirtsleeves at the registration table was Dr. Russell? He starred at me, as the room got quiet. He turned and began to write on the blackboard such words as:

Kiln	Five
Nine	Line
Lion	Oil
Ant	Aunt
Fine	White
Warn	Worm
Cool	Roof

He pointed his chalk at me, "Pronounce those words, please."

He heard me speak. He knew I was country and dumb enough to do it. When I said the words, there were snickers. We had great numbers of students from the north because of low tuition.

He pointed to a boy in the back of the room, "Pronounce the same words, please."

He got his mouth out of joint and read the words. In his speech, the letter i had two sounds. His words were quick with sharp corners; some had more syllables than mine. Dr. Russell pointed his chalk at a girl on the second row. "Who is right?"

"The boy in back, of course."

Dr. Russell walked to his desk and sat on the corner. "You are totally wrong. The boy in front pronounced the words the way he heard from his parents, grandparents and people in his hometown. He *is* right. But the boy in the back is right, too ... for the same reason."

He looked around at startled faces. He spoke slowly and clearly.

"There is nothing wrong with sounding like where you are from.
Never try to be something you aren't.
Always be yourself.
Never apologize for who you are."

When I registered at the beginning of the next quarter, I signed up for Dr. Russell's class first.

Governor's Day
19

In the summer of 1948, Governor's Day was announced at the University of Alabama in Tuscaloosa. "Big Jim" Folsom had campaigned with a mop and suds bucket. He lay down on courthouse steps to prove some point. Rumors of scandal and corruption were linked with his administration. He was considered uncouth and an embarrassment to the academic community. He was Governor of The State of Alabama, but there was a lack of enthusiasm for his visit.

The week before the event, the Advanced ROTC Coast Artillery class was held outside the military building under the big oak trees.

Our instructor, a regular army major with a sergeant standing just behind, explained this unusual class, "Boys, as you know, we are to have Governor's Day next week. We will have a formation of the troops. A 19-gun salute will be given to honor the governor. You seven are the entire class of Coast Artillery; it will be your duty to fire the salute. I know you have just started and have not had training with weapons, but there should be no problem."

Several of our class said they thought the old gun we gathered around was for decoration. The major agreed, but said, "This French 75 mm is a trustworthy old gun. Just be here in uniform a half hour before the parade."

"Could we have a trial run today and shoot it a time or two?"

"It would disrupt the campus and besides, there is nothing to it. It's simple to operate. What could go wrong?"

"Major, do you think we could maybe move the gun a little and shoot over the reviewing stand?"

"You mean with a load of confetti?"

"We sort of had in mind a load of rotten eggs and tomatoes."

"Don't be ridiculous, and you boys are to stop referring to him as 'Large James.' He is Governor and is due respect. Remember, he has a lot to do with funding of the university."

On the ill-fated day, the reluctant seven gathered around the old gun on one of the hottest days of the year. The paper mill smell seemed worse in the heat. The governor was late. Somebody forgot to put the troops at parade rest and left them at attention. With the delay and in the heat, several cadets passed out and had to be dragged like sacks of cow feed to the nearest shade. We should have seen the omen of things to come.

The Major made assignments showing the routine of passing the ammunition, loading blank rounds, firing rounds and removing spent cases. Arthur Gates was made gun commander because he was larger than the rest, or maybe because he was the loudest. One cadet had as his only duty the counting of shots. He was to mark down each round as it was fired. The major warned us this was old ammunition and would make heavy smoke.

After initial assignments were made, I was left out. The major said, "Boys, there is one problem with this old cannon; the ejector doesn't work. Each time we fire the piece, someone will have to go around to the muzzle and knock out the empty case."

He handed the ramrod to me. At 127 pounds, I was about the same size as the ramrod, though not as straight.

I looked at the ramrod and the muzzle, "What happens if they shoot before I get back?"

"Ah ... you don't want to think about that. We will try to not let that happen."

The great moment arrived. One passed the shell from the stack; one threw the shell in the chamber; one closed the breech and one pulled the lanyard. There was a flash and a ka-boom! This was the worst noise on campus since the Yankees came through. The wind had totally died. An enormous cloud of black smoke wrapped that old gun and just sat there. The smell of burned gunpowder was everywhere. I ran around and disappeared in the smoke, but couldn't find the muzzle. I was feeling along the barrel, burning my fingers until I found the opening. Then swish--clunk--clang--clang; I could hear the case fall and then hear them reload.

"Don't shoot, don't shoot! I dropped the dumb ramrod and can't find it in all this smoke!"

The second shot was a little delayed, but after that, firing was more orderly. Everything was going well except for the smoke getting worse with each shot.

After a round, I would disappear into that choking smoke, knock out the case and scream, "Don't shoot, don't shoot!" until I got back. By now I looked like a skinny black cloud with eyeballs.

After several shots, I entered the cloud one more time, drove in the ramrod–swish--clunk--cling--clang. As I was feeling my way back, I heard a scream, scuffling noises, curses and a thud. I came out of my cloud to what looked like a war zone. One guy was on the ground out cold and one was sitting on the ground holding a bloody hand. There was blood on the gun and on the ground. The rest of the crew were standing around with their mouths open--dumb struck. Smoke was now covering the rear of the gun. In the poor visibility, one guy had closed the breech on the loader's hand as he was pushing in the round, causing bloody, but not serious cuts. The counter saw blood and passed out.

After a lot of shaking and pleading, the Major got the counter awake enough to mumble," Uh ... seventeen shots."

"Good, I'll help you boys. Two more and we're through." The Sergeant left with the wounded man. They fired the shots, the Major gave a signal and the parade began. By this time the counter had fully recovered, found his paper under his leg and counted his marks.

"Uh, Major, I told you wrong."

"You what!"

" I've found the paper and checked it three times. We gave the governor a fifteen-gun salute. Could we fire a few more?"

"You mean five minutes into the parade?"

So the entire Coast Artillery troop--less one--stood around that old 75 looking at each other and at the ground. This dejected silent group considered their failure.

"Boys, forget it. It never happened."

"What do you mean, Major?"

"The ******can't read; he probably can't count either. Maybe he won't notice."

The Major was right. Large James--excuse me--Governor Folsom, never noticed. Strangely enough, nobody else did either.

The Convention
20

Two of us propped up on our beds in Room 22, Lupton Hall and a visitor sat in one of our two straight chairs listening to my radio. The speeches and the shouting at the Democratic Convention of 1948 seemed strange and disorganized. The chair-sitter got up and said," That's about all of that stuff I can stand. To think, those are people who make laws and tell us what to do."

As he got to the door, crowd noise became louder and the announcer was almost shouting. The Alabama and Mississippi delegates were walking out.

Over the next days, newscasts were filled with interpretations and predictions. I saw pictures in a day-old paper in the lounge downstairs. The split in the Democratic Party had been years in the making. After the Big War, in 1865 the Republican Party had insisted the Union army occupy the South and dictate standards of their choosing. When the army left, the South went back to its old ways as much as possible. Because of bitterness after the occupation, the South became solidly Democratic. It was assumed the South would always vote a straight ticket in any election. The South was taken for granted and almost considered a vassal to the national party. In the Great Depression, the party became more liberal in the eyes of the conservative South. Introduction of the civil rights plank in the Democratic platform at the convention in 1948 was the precipitating factor for the split. It came after more than a half century of change.

A few days later, the three of us listened to the radio describe the big split in the political party. People could see integration was coming. It had happened all over the world and was beginning in the South. President Truman integrated the armed forces by executive order. Instead of waiting for social change to occur, the Southern way of life was to be changed by edict or law. Those who walked out and others were having their own States Rights Democratic Party convention on this July 17th. The name was too long, so people called them Dixiecrats.

I said, "None of us are doing anything. Nobody has tests on Monday. Why don't we go? We'll never get to see another convention."

"You know that place will be packed. We would never get in."

"The bus schedule would put us in too late."

After arguing several minutes, we agreed to try for a while. We stood on the corner in front of the Supe (supply) store and stuck a thumb toward Birmingham. Cars had to stop when the light was red. That gave us a chance to look pitiful to any driver who looked our way. Somebody had just said something about no rides today, when the slickest black limousine I have ever seen stopped at the light and the driver motioned. It took a few seconds to recover. We couldn't believe it. One sat in front and two in back. The uniformed chauffeur gunned the motor and said, "Where you boys goin'?"

"Boutwell Auditorium where they're having that convention. It's late, but we're gonna try to get in."

"Just so happens that I'm gonna go to that very place. This is Governor Wright's car. It's his ride back to Mississippi."

We tried to see somebody we knew so we could wave. We couldn't. We waved at strangers we might meet later. We slowed for traffic around the University, but on the highway our driver knew no speed limits. I have never made such a fast smooth trip from

Tuscaloosa to Birmingham. And it was cool on this summer day. The driver was talkative. We were well prepared for the convention, if we could get in.

The parking lot was full and people were standing around the entrance door. "We'll never get in."

Our driver looked around. "Oh, yes you will. I'll take you out right to the door. Tell them you're on his staff, if you have to."

He let us out a few feet from the door. The two guards looked like they were local and not secret service. People at the entrance couldn't help looking at the limousine. We said our thanks and good-bys to our driver and walked toward the building as if we owned the place.

Steve was taller and a year older than my roommate or me. He walked past the crowd at the door and said to the guards, "We're running late; heavy traffic at the line. Where are the seats left?"

One guard turned to look at the tag of the limousine as it pulled away. "Uh ... all those down front are gone. Might be a few in the back--way high up. Sam will show ya."

We didn't turn our heads, but heard complaints from the crowd at the door. The guard said, "I had to let 'em in. Didn't you see tag on that limo' they came in?"

We probably got the last three seats high up in the back with a direct, but distant view of the platform. We saw events that matched sounds we had heard on the radio. Politicians made speeches about preservation of way of life and changes in the Democratic Party and need to split away. Finally, Strom Thurman was nominated for president. Signs on a stick suddenly appeared. People jumped up and began milling about shouting and waving the signs. After order was restored, Governor Thurman was selected.

Then, Governor Fielding L. Wright was nominated for Vice-president. We didn't have signs, but jumped up and cheered. "This is our guy. He gave us a ride and got us in the front door. He didn't know it, but he did." People around us thought we were crazy.

After the long convention, we had a long walk to the bus station. Another limo' ride was too much to hope for. It was late when we got off the bus and ate a burger at Pugs.

On the way back to the dormitory, I told the others, "Good or bad--right or wrong--I think we've seen a little history today and I don't think we'll *ever* convince anybody we rode to Dixiecrats Convention in the governor's limousine.

My Worst Christmas
21

My rule was simple: stand on the corner in front of the Supe store on the University of Alabama campus and point a thumb toward Birmingham a half hour before the Greyhound bus came through. If I got a ride, money and time were saved. If I got no ride, I rode the bus. This was late December 1949, time for Christmas vacation.

I was a day late. The campus was almost deserted. At registration in the fall, I had counted my credits and discovered I needed one more hour than planned to have enough for graduation in the spring. The only one-hour course I could work in was Choral Union. I have trouble playing the kazoo and I sure can't sing, but I got an A for showing up for all classes. At registration, they didn't tell me we had to give a performance of Christmas music the night after everybody else had left. In Foster auditorium, I sat in my usual spot between the tenors and the baritones since they didn't know what I was. I was proud of our performance. For the first time in all those months, in the silent pause toward the end of The Hallelujah Chorus nobody said **Hal ...** . This ended my singing career. I slept in the empty dorm and tried for the early bus.

A few minutes before the bus, I got a ride with a man driving a brand-new Pontiac. He had a used car salesman's smile and talked incessantly to his captive audience. I didn't want to hear how much money he made, how much his car cost, or his sexual exploits, especially not today. His bragging did make me compare my life with his. He chose work and not college and was making what sounded like big money. I had almost finished four years of college, maybe for nothing. This talkative driver didn't know an experienced student could tune out irritating sounds and voices. I nodded and grunted now and then and he thought I was hanging on his every word.

As we drove toward Birmingham, I remembered coming down this road in 1946 as a naive 17-year-old with sixteen credits and no high school diploma. The University had the largest enrollment in history. I had no choice where I lived and went to class. It was not the campus I expected.

The main building of Northington Campus was a rambling cantonment structure: long single-story units at right angles to a central hallway system. Each unit had a smaller hall with private rooms on each side, ending in a 16-bed bay. The dining room, post office, supply store and living quarters were bound by miles of hallways lit by windows by day and bare bulbs at night. These halls were our thoroughfare to class, dining room, supply store or post office. We could walk miles under one roof. The halls were entertainment for some. They took the big wheels off beds and slid them down the hall, hundreds of feet in a single throw. If a heavy wheel comes sliding down the hall as if shot from a gun, quick reflexes are needed at the right second, to jump up and avoid an ankle injury from this sliding discus.

Classes were in the nurses' quarters. These concrete block buildings were just large enough for a single class. They were across the road at the far end of the complex, 100 yards beyond our hallway system. The walk did warm us before coming in the cold rooms in winter. Summer was a different story. Only the movie house showing third run movies was air-conditioned. Over 4,000 of us lived at Northington Campus, ate there, went to class there and studied there. We were a separate existence, remotely related to the main campus and the rest of the world. Our teachers were new. Some said that they had seen a letter of instruction to the professors saying, "Get rid of some of these people. We cannot take 5,000 sophomores." We thought that our instructors graduated from the Marquis de Sade University.

I remembered my parents driving down and staying with me for housing assignments. I am still surprised they left me. My assignment was Ward C-13, the psychiatric unit. We were at the end of the hall, farther from the classrooms than any other unit. Were they trying to tell me something? Before very long, I did feel as if I were nuts.

I had 15 roommates in an open ward with bars on the windows. Beds were lined up head to the wall, foot to center, with about eight feet between the rows for a walkway. This high security area had interesting furnishings. We could tolerate the wavy metal mirrors in the bathroom--like the fat mirror in the carnival. We could operate the push button faucets at the lavatory, but there were no handles in the shower. After an hour's search, we found a locked cabinet in the hall. We didn't have a key, so we used a tire tool and discovered controls 20 feet from the shower. We had to make nude trips back and forth from the shower to controls in the hall to get the water temperature just right. When we got in and lathered up, some guy coming in the hall twisted a knob. Screaming showers were common.

At the end of the 16-bed bay, the door opened to an unsheltered platform with a ramp leading to the drive. When it was a hospital, patients could be taken from the ambulance up the ramp into the unit.

Our possessions hung from a metal pipe on the wall or lived in a footlocker at the foot of the bed. A folding table by the bed was big enough for a few papers and an alarm clock. Sixteen Big Ben type clocks made unbelievable sounds when the lights went out.

With that many guys in a room, somebody is bound to snore. Some saw wood, groan, babble with fluttering lips and some whistle. We had a guy who did it all and added new sounds when we got accustomed to the old. He left the big wheels on his bed so he was higher than the rest of us. He was afraid of falling out of the narrow bed, so he held to the mattress edge, slept on his back, and got the only full night's sleep in the bay.

One cold January morning after midnight, some of his wide-awake roommates opened the door and eased his bed out of the bay and down the ramp to the drive. About two in the morning, the shivering guy woke and tried to pull up his covers. His hand brushed his hair. It felt stiff and cold. He forced his eyes open, saw stars and full moon, felt his hair again and knew it was frost.

The door banged as he pushed his bed in. He took the corner spot. The guy in the next bed helped him get the wheels off. The next day, he found a mattress for the floor in case he fell out of bed. He never did, but was quieter sleeping on his side.

As students became discouraged and left, rooms were emptied. I got a small room with an even smaller half-bath: Room 15 on Ward B-13. Small means long enough for an army cot and a row of clothes hanging at the foot, and wide enough for me to stand in the middle of the room and raise my arms and touch both walls with my fingertips. By the cot, I had a small table and chair. They had to be folded up for me to move around. One visitor constituted a crowd. The room with commode and sink was even smaller. This was the nurse's station with a window opening into a 16-bed ward. Aluminum paint blocked out light, but nothing blocked noise from poker games beyond paper-thin walls. As small as it was, limited privacy allowed me to study better. I wouldn't have survived the first quarter without it.

I was a minority student. Most were veterans, older and more mature. Most non-vets were good students. I was neither. I had never studied in high school. That's not quite right; I studied what I liked. I liked scientific subjects, literature, history and geometry, which is logic, not really math, and made good grades in these subjects. In mathematics, Latin, and English grammar I studied enough to get by. I just needed a pass, and that's all I got. For the first time in my life, I couldn't make it this way. I didn't know how to study. Pre-med students were forced into special classes taught by special ogres. We were forced to take German because advisors said that all doctors had to study in Germany. I thought we had torn up that place! I did have one advantage over most non-vets. They had grown up and gone to school in one place. Now they were in a strange world filled with strange people. I had always been the new kid.

At the end of my first quarter, many were asked to leave. The bays were quiet. It was a matter of quality points: six or you were out. This was not like high school; the instructors gave lectures and tests and didn't appear to care if we passed or failed. The only student I had known in high school flunked out. I talked with him as he packed to leave. To come to college with high hopes and be asked to leave after one quarter was devastating, and he showed it. There was little I could say because I had just enough points to stay. A friend in some of my classes with an IQ of 147 failed. As friends left, I felt alone and vulnerable. We lost over half of the 5,000 freshmen the first year. Four years later, about 1,500 graduated.

In the second quarter I went on to German II, saying that I would do better. It is hard to build a house on crumbling foundations. I made another D. The third quarter I made an F. For the first time in my life, I failed a subject. I was not then, I am not now a good loser. It was a well-known fact you can't get in medical school if you fail a subject.

I didn't have the self-confidence to work that summer. I read a lot and brooded. In the fall, I went back to school and registered for the German class I failed. I sat in the German III class in the first week, looked around at other students and listened to the professor. In our lives are points of crisis when circumstances become clear, and we are faced with decisions. *What are you doing here?* I dropped the course so it was not charged against me. I would concentrate on the other subjects, teach myself to study, try for A's, accept nothing lower than a B, or quit and dig ditches. I never admitted that a 117-pound guy would dig a skinny ditch. Changes came slowly. I made new habits, not just memorizing facts, but philosophy and psychology of learning and use of words to express ideas and facts. I tried to prove what I knew by learning how to take tests. A little understanding of the instructor was helpful, knowing what he or she expected. Some asked "what am I thinking?" questions. The main campus dorms were given back to the men and I moved into number 22 Lupton Hall for the next three years. I felt like a real college student for the first time. To improve self-esteem, I decided to correct crooked teeth. I made a hitchhiking trip to Birmingham every two weeks to have braces adjusted. I needed a new self-image physically and academically. I made mostly A's with a few B's. Success breeds success, but nobody *ever* gets in medical school after he fails a course. In the spring of my sophomore year, a new German instructor came, and the old ogre left. I registered for German I. The instructor never knew I had already endured three quarters of German. He thought I was a brain. I made straight A's. He rewarded his best students. He invited two of us to The University Club for dinner one night.

Summer school followed to make up for repeating the German. The summer after the junior year, I went for advanced ROTC basic training in Wisconsin for six weeks. ROTC was easy, and the government paid $30.00 a month, more than my boardinghouse bill of $19.50 a month for two meals a day. After summer camp, I worked as a carpenter until school began.

In my senior year, I made application to the Medical College of Alabama in Birmingham. I brought to the registrar a transcript of almost 2.5 average--on a 3 point system. I was a member of the honorary pre-med Alpha Epsilon Delta. I didn't wait for her to find the failing grade. I pointed it out, but also showed her that I repeated all the German. We never knew how many were turned down; 470 were accepted for interviews for 52 admissions. I made the interview, but had a disadvantage. There were no family role models. I was the first on either side of the family to graduate from college. My mother and her father had gone to Jacksonville State Teachers College long enough to get a teacher's certificate, but didn't graduate.

Other questions would be, "Why do you want to be a doctor? Do you know what you are getting into? Do you know what doctors do?" How could I convince these people I knew what I wanted?

I lied about finances. The Admission Board turned down anybody who expected to work, even in the summer. Finances were not supposed to be a problem. There were few scholarships and no loans. Students were considered a bad risk. After it was over, I felt pretty good about the interview, but there was that German grade--a black mark that would never go away. Acceptances and rejections would be sent over the Christmas holidays. I had asked that mine be sent to my school post office box. The answer to four years of work would go to my University box, and I was going in the opposite direction.

The man was still grinning and talking when he let me out at the bus station. I thanked him for the ride, and he never knew I heard little of his stories. I rode the bus to Albertville. I remember little of that Christmas. Mother accused me of being sick. I brightened up a little for fear she would dose me with some of that vile concoction I had as a child. I remember only one present. My parents told my nine-year-old sister she couldn't have a Monopoly set because they never bought me one. I bought her the set. Momma's Christmas spice cake lifted my spirits only a little.

A few days after Christmas, the final blow came. College students, especially pre-medical students, have an elaborate espionage system. I knew veterans were given preference. Word was the admissions committee was picking only one student from each county. A veteran in my county got his letter of acceptance. Disaster had struck.

A BS in biology and chemistry doesn't earn much respect if you can't get in medical school. I would join the Chinese Army. My parents never knew of these plans. I didn't tell my wife for years for fear she wouldn't believe me. She didn't! I turned down a scholarship toward a Ph.D. in psychology, but another offer was being held open for me until word came from medical school. Instead of accepting a commission in the American Army after my ROTC, I would accept a commission as a captain in the Chinese Nationalist Army on Formosa. This was offered to the two top Coast Artillery students for two years at $16,000 a year--more money than I could comprehend at the time.

They furnished uniforms, housing, and a fulltime interpreter. This job seemed to be my only choice since I had little chance at medical school.

My letter was in the box in Tuscaloosa. It would be easy to say drive down and check, but roads were poor, driving slow, and my father needed the car for his job. So I stayed for my December 31st birthday and left the next day, two days before classes began. I don't remember what excuse I gave.

It was a depressing trip. The bus went the old highway from Birmingham to Tuscaloosa and stopped at every pig trail. My whole life hung on a decision already made. I had the grades, but nobody in the history of the world has even gone to medical school after failing a subject. Sometimes, hope is the only thing that sustains us. Mine was fading. There was still a glimmer, or I wouldn't have gotten off that bus and walked across the street to the basement post office under the deserted Supe store.

The letter from the registrar's office was on the top of others in the box; I saw it through the glass. Three times the combination lock wouldn't work. I had used the box three years. I knew the numbers. I put my bag down and tried with both hands. Finally, when the letter was out, I couldn't do a simple thing like open it.

Finally--when a letter begins, "Congratulations," there is little reason to read the rest. Big boys don't cry, but sometimes their eyes get a little moist. After a while, I went to a pay phone and called my mother. She did cry. This had been my worst Christmas, but this was the first day of a happy New Year!

The next year, the medical school Registrar told me the admissions committee treated my old German grades like God treats repented sin. They wiped them away, as if they had never been.

Years later, I found a quote that expresses far better than I can what I learned in bitter experience:

Nothing in the world can take the place of persistence.

Talent will not; nothing is more common than unsuccessful me with talent.

Genius will not; unrewarded genius is almost a proverb.

Education will not; the world is full of educated derelicts.

Persistence and determination alone are omnipotent.

The slogan "Press on" has solved and always will solve the problems of the human race.

Calvin Coolidge.

I never did like rice that much anyway.

The Matchbook
22

In the fall of 1951, I was a poor starving second-year medical student at the Medical College of Alabama in Birmingham. As I look back, I do mean poor. I was one of two non-veterans in my class. Veterans had the GI bill; I had to make it with funds from my father, who made a real sacrifice to send me to college. There was no tuition; my total expense for the first year of college was less than $1,000. Now, medical school had a $700 tuition fee. There were still no loans and few scholarships. Against the advice of the Dean, I worked in the summer, but during the school year work was not allowed or even possible. After my first year of medical school, I couldn't get work in a hospital. They said I wasn't qualified for any job--including orderly. I worked that summer in a grocery store.

Most students lived on tight budgets. Few were accustomed to a high standard of living, so expectations were low. Single students lived in three old apartment houses owned by the University. Ours was 1024 9th Avenue, cornering on 20th Street South. Another was west on 9th and the third on 20th Street. Another student and I lived in a room on the second floor, a few feet from a streetlight, neon sign and bus stop. Buses squeaked to a stop at the corner under our window, opened and closed the doors, released air brakes with a gush, and gunned the motor to pull the 20th Street hill all night long. People getting off the bus talked loud enough for us to hear every word. Windows had to be open on warm days; there was no air conditioning. In the heat of the top floor, few of us could study fully clothed. Noise on a 20th Street hillside was impressive to a country boy. Some said this old building had been a floozy house; we never knew for sure. Rent was low, and I tried to get by on $50.00 a month for food, laundry, supplies and gas. We ate two meals a day--actually only one. Several of us went together at night a short way down Highland to Bogue's. They served a balanced meal for 55 cents. For lunch we ate the cheapest hamburger we could find for15 cents or less.

We didn't wear whites until we went on the wards in the last two years of medical school, so in the first two we wore anything, mostly jeans and tee shirts or sport shirts, or old army uniforms. We worked so hard, nobody noticed what the other wore anyway. We understood the pressure we were under. We knew how many were interviewed for the 52 places in our class. There were hundreds of students out there willing and able to take our place. We lost one the first year--a Phi Beta Kappa. Nobody missed classes. We were afraid to blink during a lecture for fear of missing something. Those conditions didn't seem so bad to us then as they sound today. We had lived through the deprivations of depression and wartime and post-war shortages. We had never known creature comforts we take for granted today. Whether by design or accident, some hardships are part of life and instructional, although we don't like to admit it at the time. *Tribulation brings about perseverance and perseverance proven character, and proven character, hope* (Rom.5-3) .... and our hope was to finish the four years.

I survived my first year in medical school, but struggled in one course. My roommate struggled in another. Both of us got threatening letters from the school in the summer. We must do better or find another line of work--or words to that effect. The two of us talked about our troubles in the first week of our sophomore year and decided our problem was burnout. In the fall semester, we had gone to one ball game. Other than that, we had gone to class or studied, and still had problems. Our conclusions were strange. We couldn't possibly study more, so we would study less. We did study, but we began to take breaks; we played pool in the basement, carpet golf a block away, went to movies and some weekends played poker, just penny ante stuff. A few of the more affluent--those whose wives worked--played the big dime-quarter games. The breaks seemed to help. We could work harder if now and then we had a little relaxation from the study grind.

A few weeks into the fall semester of my second year, I decided I was tired of looking at guys in jeans and dirty tee shirts. I needed female companionship. My problem was where to look. The good-looking girls were married or attached. There were only two girls in my class. My two female cousins lived across the mountain in Homewood, and I checked out their friends and met others in different ways. Finally, my cousins said they had no further suggestions except a girl of dubious reputation. I gave her number to my roommate. These events never resulted in anything beyond a single date. I had to look at myself and admit it might be me; I went to class or studied all day, never read a newspaper, and knew nothing of the social life in town. Some of the girls I went out with worked, made good money, and drove nice cars. I had saved a little money from my grocery store job; I considered it mine to spend. I did have a car of sorts--a '37 Chevrolet with knee action front end I filled with oil every week and it still bounced for five minutes after I hit a bump. It had one accessory--a smooching knob on the steering wheel. It was so hard to steer, I had to use it for a sharp corner. I knew it wasn't an impressive car, but I thought somewhere out there, there must be a girl who would accept me, my old car, scholastic isolation, and low finances.

My Aunt Frances lived all the way across Birmingham and out in the country--way out. There are people in Birmingham who don't know where Chalkville is. In my frustration I went to see her and even had a home-cooked meal. She recognized my circumstances and later called to say as usual, all the desirable girls in the area were married, attached or spoken for. She remembered one whose boyfriend was out of the state. It took several days to contact her. As a favor to Frances, she would go out with me, one time only. A dead end street is better than no street at all. I went. I don't remember what I wore. There wasn't much choice--one of two sport coats, slacks, oxford cloth button-down shirt and knitted tie. I did have a secret weapon. My father insisted on loaning me his tan '51 Oldsmobile coupe for the weekend--a hot car that even smelled new. But it was still a long drive across Birmingham and out to the country for a blind date who was spoken for and even engaged. I did hope my aunt didn't think I was terminally desperate and fixed me up with a real dog.

In the country, a neighbor lives a mile or so away. Frances went with me and introduced me to her young neighbor. She didn't know this girl well and introduced her by the wrong name. Apparently, she was too shy to make a correction. Her family called her by her middle name and Francis called her by her first. When you meet a blind date, you can't do like dogs, cats, or cows and walk round and round and size each other up. It's not like walking through a car lot kicking tires. It's more like getting on an elevator. You look at the passengers one quick time. Then, you must turn and look toward the door. So when you meet your date, you look long enough to recognize her if she got lost in a crowd, but it's bad form to stare--even if you want to. I am the first to admit that a woman's largest sex organ is her brain, but it helps to have good supporting structures. A quick glance told me she was not a dog. She was not a raving Hollywood beauty, but she was pretty--really pretty--and had adequate curves in the right places. She was well dressed. I was to find out that she made her own clothes. She was wearing a top that was not too daring, but showed enough neck and shoulders to prove she had pretty skin. My looking showed only one thing I didn't think was just great. Her lipstick seemed bright and overdone, but that was the style then, so I couldn't complain. I don't remember where we went, I am sure to the movies, probably the Alabama. Conversation was slow in the beginning, since I am basically an introvert. It did progress; for a time I forgot she was attached and spoken for. The only thing I knew anything about was medicine so I found out things about her. She was a working girl; she had to be. She was the last of four girls and their father was disabled and retired. She lived with her parents in the country, so far out they had no phone. She had to make her calls at work. That's why my aunt had trouble contacting her. She worked as a secretary for the district office of Allis-Chalmers in Birmingham. Sometime in the course of the evening she showed me a book of matches with the name of the company on it. She left me with the book of matches in my hand. I couldn't immediately hand it back to her, so I put the book in my pocket and forgot it.

After the movie, we drove back across Birmingham and out in the country. It was late when we stopped at her parents' house. We got out of the car and stood on a terrace in front of the house and talked. Light from the house let us see each other, but wasn't enough to block stars of the clear night sky. At that hour, even crickets had gone to bed. Or was it that I didn't hear them? After our introduction, I had taken a few glances as I got the chance. As we spoke from inches away, it seemed all right to look closer. Is that called gazing? I put my arms around her and suddenly the most natural thing in the world happened. It wasn't planned--at least not by me. It just happened.

That lipstick might not have been too bright after all; it came off, anyway.

There are times in my life so indelibly impressed in my mind I can close my eyes and be there again. I see everything as it was. I live in darkness with distant light. I feel the night air. I have sudden new emotions. I sense the event--a time when I could live forever, or forever go back to.

But the magic passed; she said it was late and time for me to go. So, I drove down the long driveway, back from the country and across Birmingham for the fourth time. I wasn't accustomed to a radio so I didn't turn it on. I left the window down to feel the night air. *She didn't seem attached and spoken for... Maybe... it was the new car.* But my ego spoke up. *She didn't kiss the car! I did tell her I had an old car. Maybe.... that was permanent good-bye.*

It was very late when I got home. I had to park a block away and walk across 20th Street traffic, which still runs in the wee hours. As I walked the creaking wooden stairs, I realized I had been gone a long time. I opened my door at the head of the stair and left it open a little so I could undress in the room by the hall light and not wake my roommate.

I was mumbling to myself about the better ones being taken when I felt something in my coat pocket. I pulled out the matchbook I had forgotten. I stepped to the doorway so I could see better in the hall light. The printing on one side said Allis-Chalmers and the address. I turned it over. The other side had the same name, but it also had a phone number.

I think I have just gotten a signal. Maybe, just maybe, I will call that number next week.

I did. I still have the matchbook ... and the girl.

Little White Ducks
23

Little ducks of white, strutting in the light,
Two by two in a row, where do they run?
Hear their bubbling, happy sound of delight.
See their funny hop and lark in the sun.

Do the ducks of white know where they rush?
Do they see the hawk as it circles high?
Or the hungry fox deep within the bush?
Do they see where other perils lie?

Their funny backward hop will stop one day.
Some will fall to fox, some to hawk.
Some will lose their voice and fade away
Other ducks will come and do the funny walk.

There was a day like no other in the spring of 1952. Fifty medical students had endured basic science courses in the first year and basic surgery, medicine and pathology the second year. Ours was the last small class--the last one that went for quality rather than quantity, or so we saw it. We saw and worked with each other every day. We were a close group. Few were affluent. Most of us did well to afford jeans and sport shirt that seemed to be our uniform. We wondered if we would ever become real doctors as we endured the formaldehyde smell of cadavers in anatomy, bad temper of the rats and biting of the dogs in physiology and thousands of hours of lectures. Toward the last of the sophomore year when we had the basic knowledge of just about everything--so we thought--we were given a history and physical course by Dr. Tensley Harrison, of textbook fame. He gave us a little brochure-sized book that was to be our bible for taking the medical history. Hundreds of questions from what we called our Gray Book were to be asked in an organized fashion and recorded as a hand-written history, six to ten pages long.

The day finally came, now that we knew everything. Each student was to be assigned two patients in Hillman Hospital. We were to do a history and physical that would have nothing to do with the treatment because patients were being treated by real doctors--interns, residents, and staff men--but the event would be a learning experience for us. In those days, to go into the wards, medical students were required to wear white pants and intern jackets. We knew it all; the uniform would make us look like we knew it. People might think we were real doctors.

When the big day arrived, there was much fumbling and complaining. The pants were starched and stiff, but the jacket was something new and different. An intern jacket is a tight-fitting short-sleeved garment worn in place of a shirt. It's a little shorter than coat length with a straight bottom worn outside the pants. The collar fits like a tube around the neck to the chin. A row of cloth or bone buttons extends from the bottom, up the right side, in front of the shoulder and to the collar. Our name was stitched in place just above the left breast pocket, supposedly so the patients could identify us. The two lower pockets were for a notebook and a stethoscope to wear like a badge so that everybody would know we were doctors. A guy with a Superman build looked good in one. If a student had a pot or a big behind, the world knew it all the more. If he had a double chin, the collar made it worse. We struggled to get into those tight starched jackets and placed our notebooks and stethoscopes just so. My roommate, Bluitt, and I agreed the top button on the collar had to be left open. After T-shirts and sport shirts for two years, a tight collar was more than we could take.

We were self-conscious as we left the house half way up the steep hill on South 20th Street. We met others, all heading downhill toward Jefferson Hillman Hospital wearing new starched uniforms for the first time, all walking stiffly and awkwardly. We laughed as we called each other "Doctor." The sound of the word against our name was strange, though it had been longed for. We called each other "Doctor" again to hear the sound. We walked down the narrow sidewalk by twos. On a steep hill, a person walking rapidly takes stiff, jerking steps, sort of a reverse hop and seems to sink lower and lower with each step. We went two by two, talking and laughing all the way. We looked like a row of happy little white ducks.

Sounds stopped when we walked in the hospital. Laughter was replaced by new emotions, including sheer terror. I wondered if patients were as intimidated by us as we were by them. We were given names and locations of two patients and were forbidden to read the chart to search for a diagnosis. I made the mistake of talking to others who had seen their first patient. One of my classmates couldn't remember all of the questions in The Gray Book so he interspersed pages from the question book with blank pages in his notebook. He held the book where the patient couldn't see, read the questions and wrote the answers on the other side.

As they got into this long procedure, his hospital-wise patient said, "Little docta, if you wants to, jus' le' me have pencil and paper and that lil' Gray Book, and I'll answer them questions, and you can go on to the movies or sumpin."

The fledgling doctor was crushed. I was determined that my session go well. I memorized most of the questions and would go back for any I forgot. I put on my best serious doctor face. But I must begin in a professional manner and quickly determine why the patient was in the hospital.

So I asked, "Why did you come to the hospital?"

"Cuz I wuz sick."

I lost it on my first question. This was not working. I finished, but went on to the next patient, determined to do better. I would rephrase the question and ask it in a better way.

To add to my anxiety, I found the true reason for the name on the jacket. It really was for the staff to identify sinners. After some trivial event in the hall, one of the "big dogs" pointed to mine and said, "I will personally see that you never graduate." When I realized later, the only medication dose he asked students was aspirin, I knew he probably wouldn't remember my name any better than the drugs. Just in case, I avoided him for two years.

I couldn't find my second patient. His neighbor in the next bed didn't know where he was. A nurse said, "Oh, he's gone to the cardiac lab--not the regular one--the one in the basement." After a few under-her-breath remarks about new students, she gave me directions.

When I found the place, I had no idea what was going on. A doctor who seemed to be in charge explained the room. Two patients were lying on seven-foot long beds of sand elevated about three feet. Patients in the sandbox had a stylus attached to their head. Each beat of the heart caused the body to move enough to make a tracing on the moving drum at the head. I never saw another ballistocardiogram done. It must not have been helpful in diagnosis. When he was finished with the test, I talked with my patient while he waited for his ride to the unit.

"Sir, what brought you to the hospital?"

He blinked once and said, "The am-bu-lance."

How I finished, I don't know. That day proved to me that no matter what knowledge I have, communication is essential. In the afternoon, I applied for a summer job at Lloyd Noland Hospital as an extern taking histories and physicals so I could get a little experience before school in the fall.

In 1989 at our 35-year class reunion, there were eight of us. Some were dead from accident, some from disease, some by their own hand. None came who had problems--health, financial, legal or marital--as if that would have mattered. We were no longer a close group. Most just didn't bother. I have not been back, though we graduated over a half-century ago. For a brief instant, at those reunions, there was a glimmer of the brightness and enthusiasm of that day so many years ago when we wore the little white suits for the first time.

Somewhere this spring, others will put on whites for the first time and so the cycle begins again.

The New Doctor
24

In one month in the summer of 1954, I graduated from medical school, passed board examinations to practice medicine, married and moved into an apartment with my new wife, and when I caught my breath, began an internship at Lloyd Noland Hospital.

Betty and I had an apartment that would fit in an ordinary family room with space left over. She spent her money on the wedding. I spent part of my grocery store job money on a gold ring wide enough to mask the absence of the engagement ring I couldn't afford and the rest on a honeymoon all the way to Cheaha, 65 miles away. We had only a few pieces of furniture. We ate our first meal seated on the floor around a cardboard box, but it didn't seem to matter. The first Sunday told us why our apartment was so cheap, when stock car races began at the fairgrounds a block away! Traffic began just after daylight.

I had taken a rotating internship. In this program that no longer exists, interns worked one or two-month rotations in specialties to let them decide what field they were interested in. I didn't know what I wanted to do. I thought I would like general practice. I was sure I hated surgery. I was one of twelve interns who worked from 6:30 A.M. until 5 P.M. and every second or third night.

I knew the place from my summers as an extern. The Tennessee Coal and Iron Company had brought Dr. Lloyd Noland back from the Panama Canal Zone in 1913 to control sanitation and treat infectious diseases in employees. He convinced them to build the 5-story 320-bed Employees Hospital at a cost of $750.000. After two years in construction, it opened in 1919. Workers could get full medical care by admission or in the many clinics

When nights were slow, I wandered around the grounds and old building, now named Lloyd Noland. I marveled at the six-foot thick outer walls of the first floor clinics. I never covered the forty acres of the hill, but I did go into the underground first attempt at air conditioning, Air was blown from deep tunnels in the cool earth through vents to every room in the hospital. Return air was recooled and sent back. Patients thought they would smother if windows weren't open. All the cool air was lost. The system was shut down after a month. The two silent fans must have been ten feet tall.

One night each month, interns worked in the Wenonah, Muskoda, Ishkooda or Fairfield Steel Dispensary. We could eat, sleep or read in the deserted office. We might see one or two patients, or none. If you wanted a radio, you brought your own. Television didn't exist except for a few huge floor models with six-inch screens. The hospital packed a field-hand size sack-supper for us and paid $35 per night to supplement the $50 a month salary. If the interns' wives wanted to eat, they worked. My being away from home much of the time made it difficult for a new marriage.

We didn't take this year by choice. State law required a one-year internship to practice medicine. Our salaries were low, but we were fed and given uniforms in the form of white scrub suits. After the grind of four years of college and four of medical school, we felt a sense of relief as if a huge weight had been lifted. Appetites came back, ulcers healed, and sense of humor returned. The pressure to finish school was replaced with eagerness to learn as much and do as much as we could crowd in a year. The goal for interns was to make the year pay through knowledge gained. Medical school filled us with basic knowledge of medicine, and we had seen rare and exotic diseases that gravitate to medical centers. The internship showed us the practical side of medicine: the everyday diseases of private practice.

Eagerness caused trouble for most of us sooner or later. One who was not well liked by others overheard two fellow-interns talking in the dining room, "Did you see the eye grounds on that guy on the sleeping porch on Section G? I have never seen anything like that right eye. The resident and even the staff man had never seen one either."

The gullible intern went up and politely asked if he could check the eye grounds in this man's right eye. He adjusted his shiny new opthalmoscope and looked in the eye and then wiped the 'scope and looked again. Finally, "Whah, whah, whah!" The patient couldn't stand it any longer. Everybody on the porch laughed. The intern was looking in an exceptionally well-made glass eye.

Lack of prior patient contact was a problem for some interns from northern schools. They had book knowledge, but had spent little time on the wards. They had to be taught how to draw blood, pass Levin tubes, insert catheters and other procedures we had been doing for two years. Early in the year, one of the Yankee interns was called to Section D at 3 A.M. The nurse asked him to come and pronounce a patient.

"What do you mean pronounce?"

"Doctor, he expired; it was expected; the family understands."

So this sleepy, confused intern came in the room with the nurse standing by the bed, chart in hand. He stood at the foot of the man's bed, thought for a moment, raised his right hand and said, "I now pronounce you dead," and went back to bed in the call room.

All of us had to learn about the operation of an active private hospital. There was no nice electric machine to plug in and put suction to a Levin tube. We used a three-jug system. The #1 gallon jug hung on a stand, the higher the better. Water drained by rubber tube to an empty#2 jug on the floor to cause a vacuum. A rubber tube from #1 transferred the vacuum to an empty#3 jug. That jug transferred the vacuum by rubber tube to the Levin tube in the patient's nose. If there were no kinks in the tubes, the stomach was kept empty. Nurses and interns were constantly swapping # 1 and 2 and emptying and measuring # 3.

Needles, syringes, and gloves were saved. If a needle bounced back when the nurse gave a shot, it went to the sharpening room. In another room, used gloves were washed, powered, packaged in cloth wrappers and sterilized. There were no disposable exam gloves. Rectal exams were done with a finger cot, which sometimes left rusty knuckles. IV sets were made from rubber tubing with glass fittings, sterilized in fabric. Sometimes, there was a diagnosis on the chart of intravenous fever from a simple IV. We used a prepackaged set for blood transfusions. Nurses in the OR packed and wrapped instruments and fabric drapes.

I wondered why the nurse took so long to give shots. One day I watched. She pulled out an alcohol burner on a little stand. To one side, a small upright rod held a spoon over the burner. The nurse put saline in the spoon and lit the burner. She took a tablet with her fingers and dropped it in the saline. When it dissolved and boiled sufficiently, she drew it up in a glass syringe, fitted the needle, and gave the shot. A depot-penicillin was not liquid at room temperature.

The nurse dropped the ampoules down her bra for a few minutes and it was ready. We called it bosom-cillin. The dose for ordinary penicillin had just been changed from 10,000 to 100,000 units.

I was glad we had antibiotics to give. Civilians had penicillin since 1945 and now we had streptomycin and aureomycin. In medical school, we had heard the lectures from old Docs who lived before these magic drugs. For a time, they tried injections of milk to promote an immune reaction to infection. The patient probably worried more about the sterile abscesses on his behind than whatever he had before. I found an antibiotic text from the '20s with an even older attempt to treat infection: intravenous mercurochrome. The author warmed that the margin between therapeutic dose level and fatal level was very narrow.

My first month was internal medicine, which is the backbone of general practice. I continued a lifelong learning process of communication. No matter how much a doctor knows, he must speak a common language with the patient to get the history and to instruct and inform. Interns did all the histories and physicals. Dictation equipment was available by going to the fourth floor to use one of the two desktop units. Most histories were hand-written. There was an almost perverted interest in bowel habits and stool description.

"What color is your stool?"

"Doctor, it's dark down there in that hole. I can't see the bottom." I had forgotten about privies.

And with another patient, "Your stool is what?"

"Bright blue."

"How long has it been blue?"

"Ever since I painted it last week."

Another part of a medical history, which sounds so simple, is the age. Some elderly people had no idea of their age. I took the advice of a staff man and asked a simple question, "Do you remember the dark day?"

"Oh yassuh, I was a boy ten or 'leven plowin' the noth field 'bout 10 in the mornin'. All of a sudden, it commenced to get dark, chickens started to go to roost, people wuz hollerin', the preacher come and they wuz prayin."

He would go on for an hour if not stopped. If the patient were alive on the day of near total eclipse, he knew where he was, what he was doing and how old he was. From that event, age could be calculated.

About the time I was assigned to colored male medicine on section D, a new resident arrived. It took administration a half hour with a Turkish-English dictionary to discover he was their new resident. He was also assigned to section D, and the house staff was told to teach him English. Our staff man responsible for this section frequently called to say he wouldn't be in that day and for us to take care of things. We had about twenty patients in the hospital and busy outpatient clinics. A green intern and a Turkish doctor who spoke little English were left with this duty. After considering the matter, we decided to reverse the roles to give Jim--the closest English word to his Turkish name--practice in language. He took the history and presented the case to me on rounds. He improved faster than I would have in Turkey, but he had his problems.

On the first day he told me in the past the patient had never had any disease. "Come on Jim, what about VD?'

"Oh no, I ask... see. You have gon-o-rhea?"

"Oh nosuh!"

"Jim, use words he understands. You ever had claps?"

"Uh-huh, two-three times."

"Okay, clap, I remember that."

In exchange for language lessons, Jim tried to teach me chess. Any time I got aggressive with him in this contest, he said, "You push me too hard." He then proceeded to annihilate me. I did tie him a time or two, but never came close to a win. He had been playing since he was big enough to move the pieces. As Jim improved his language skills, his knowledge of medicine began to show.

At the first of the month, he was transferred to section K with Shorty Rike who treated female patients. Jim was riding up the elevator to his new assignment with another resident and a group of women employees. The girls were good naturedly giving Dr. Flynn a hard time about something.

He turned to Jim, "Help me out, Jim. Tell these girls I'm a good guy."

"Oh yess, Dr. Fynn ... fine fellow ... most time business ... sometime bull-shit. "

"No, Jim not here!"

"Oh yess here, there, anywhere!"

The elevator stopped. "Jim, get off this elevator with me--right now."

"Oh no, I must rise more floors." After he was forcibly extracted, Jim walked the last flight of stairs.

On his first day, Dr Rike handed him a chart and said, "I want you to take a very careful history on this lady. She is very prominent in the community."

The first part of the exam went well. In the course of events when Jim came to the past history, he said, "How many time you have clap?"

When the screeching stopped, Jim was sent off the unit for remedial English lessons.

I had to be defensive, "Hey, I said he knew enough English to get by. I don't know where he learned those words."

When Jim went back to Unit K, the staff still thought he was a little off. He ordered a gall bladder series on a 13-year-old girl. They laughed and laughed until the report came back showing stones. The staff on that unit began to know what we had known on Section D, that he was a good doctor bound by a language barrier. With time, the barrier faded.

Most of the patients coming for care in internal medicine had self-limited diseases. Whatever was done, they recovered. A smaller number had an acute illness that needed specific treatment. Pneumonia could cause death, but with antibiotics, patients lived. Diabetics could live with insulin, but great numbers of patients had diseases treated with red pills this week, purple pills next week, then striped pills. The next week they died. Many patients, especially older ones, had problems not helped by medicine of any color. There was no bypass operation or angioplasty. There was no kidney transplant or dialysis. Severe heart disease or kidney failure patients were made comfortable until they died. I didn't find a home in internal medicine.

Early in the year, another intern and I answered a call to the ER. The ER doc said, "Ya'all want to do some suturing?"

"Yeah--yeah! Sure."

"You ever done any?"

"Well ... no. None to speak of."

He sighed and pulled down some towels. "There's a woman here whose boyfriend took a broken beer bottle and made zigzags on her back. Practice sewing these towels and I'll be back in a little bit."

He said our work was fine. I started at the shoulders and the other guy started at the waist. We injected the Novocain and waited 15 minutes for it to work. We couldn't inject the whole area because, as slow as we were it wore off before we needed it. We spent two hours injecting, waiting, threading needles and sewing with 0000 silk. The ER doc approved our job and we dressed her back.

We left the ER feeling like experts--tired experts.

The next rotation was Pediatrics, much like internal medicine for little folks. In some ways it is unique. The day began with ward rounds with Dr. McCullough who practiced long before penicillin and had a wealth of knowledge not found in textbooks or related to exotic tests.

We presented a case to Dr. Mac that had confused the house staff.

He checked the child and backed up to stare at him. He said one word: 'Typhoid."

The resident said, "But there is nothing to even suggest typhoid."

"He looks like typhoid. Even smells like it."

It was typhoid. The patient came from an area of Birmingham called Typhoid Flats. I could smell some diseases and infections; maybe I could learn typhoid. After six cases, I began to see and maybe even smell what Dr. McCullough did. Years later in the private practice of surgery, I was laughed at for my diagnosis when I referred a patient to an internist. The patient did have typhoid.

One day on rounds, we saw a baby who had swallowed an open safety pen. Dr. McCullough hardly looked at him. He told the head nurse, "You know what to do."

Others went for coffee. I went back to the ward to see what the nurse knew to do. She was sitting at the bedside. As any mother knows, a baby will eat anything! The nurse was feeding wisps of cotton. In a day or so the pin arrived in the diaper wrapped in a thick protective layer of cotton.

As the group of doctors made rounds each day, the charge nurse, who spent little of her day with paper work, reported the progress of each little patient in minute detail. Again, there was the preoccupation with stools.

Once she stopped at a little boy's bed and said, "Dr. McCullough, I have never seen anything like it. He had a stool that was blue and yellow and green."

Dr. McCullough went over to the bed and picked up an empty crayon box and said, "Son, where are your colors? "

He gave a toothy grin and proudly announced, "I et ‘em."

Clinics were held in the late morning and afternoon. On the first day, there was a well baby clinic. Babies thought to be healthy were checked and given immunizations. On this hot day, the first patient was a screaming, screeching little baby brought in by a huge, round-faced, smiling, black lady.

She sat and tried to console her child, "Now be sweet for the nice docta."

This little baby would have nothing to do with the nurse in her starched white uniform and funny hat and this pale doctor in a white suit. As mothers are wont to do, she figured that food solves all ills. She offered lunch. This was not a bottle baby. She brought out an enormous bosom to offer the little baby who, by now, was screaming, screeching and whooping. He kept pushing the bosom away and she kept trying to give it to him.

In desperation she finally said, "Chil', hush now. You betta take dis ninnie fo' I gi' it to da docta!"

The nurse tried to get around the corner before she lost her composure, but she didn't make it. A child who has good lungs and turns down a big lunch was pronounced healthy very quickly.

I did not find a home in Pediatrics.

Most of the Urology clinics were filled with patients with urethral strictures left from the days before penicillin to treat gonorrhea. The orderly taught me how to pass the urethral sounds.

I worked on the Eye, Ear, Nose and Throat Service and tried to like it because there was such a demand for their services. As with other departments, there were enjoyable aspects, but I was bored with sore ears, sinus trouble and snotty noses. There were breaks in the boredom, such as the obviously pregnant woman who showed up in the eye clinic.

"They told you in the emergency room to come to the *eye* clinic?"

"Yes sir, I just tol' 'em I hadn't seen anything in four months."

My next rotation was Orthopedics. Each time I was transferred, I was supposed to be an expert in one specialty on the last day of the month and an expert in another on the first of the next month. Sometimes I referred patients to myself. As usual, eagerness prevailed. Putting on a cast looked so easy. I didn't see Dr. Yelton, the Chief of Orthopedics, give me the experimental plaster that sets up in one to two minutes, rather than the usual five to seven. They had to cut me out of the cast.

As he was finishing a cast, Dr. Yelton always said to children, "I guess you just wanted a plain white one; you didn't say."

"You mean I could have had a colored one?" Dr. Yelton walked away laughing.

The episode took the cooperation of several interns and residents an entire month to set up. When the interns changed services on the first clinic day of the month, Dr. Yelton opened the door to the waiting room to see twenty children and teenagers with arm and leg casts bright blue, yellow, green, orange or red, some with polka dots, some with stripes. The owners laughed and giggled because they were in on the joke. Dr. Yelton never mentioned white casts again.

I liked parts of Orthopedics, but I am not physically big enough to do some of the orthopedic procedures.

Obstetrics and Gynecology was a grind: on thirty-six hours and off twelve, and the twelve hours were hardly enough to recover from the thirty-six. I was poor company for my new wife in these twelve hours. Obstetrics was rewarding because patients were usually happy when they left the hospital with the product of their labor. Again communication had to be learned. Patients use slang or what they think is a proper word. If they hear a scientific word they don't understand and can't say, they change it to a word they do know or what they thought they heard.

I had to figure out what was meant by, "My body fell, Doc."

"My nature is bad" or "My husband's nature is bad" or "too good."

"I think I got a cysk on my left oval."

"They told me I had fireball tumors so I had a histomorectomy."

"My virginia itches something fierce ... when my husband uses me."

"You have a sore on your what?"

"My tant, Doc--you know--tant rektum, tant virginia, just ma tant."

Babies seem to come when the moon is full or on rainy nights and not in reasonable, daylight hours. In the wee hours one night, I was complaining about the night deliveries. My patient, about to deliver her eighth, casually said "Docta, they's 'ceived at night, they's bawn at night".

I did not feel at home in Obstetrics and Gynecology.

In late summer, I began rotation in Surgery with some experience. When interns worked at night, we took call for all services except obstetrics. We did surgical histories; we repaired lacerations in the emergency room, and we scrubbed on emergency cases in the operating room, mostly to hold retractors, or what we called idiot sticks.

I dreaded surgery, because I hated it in medical school. On the surgical wards and in the clinics, again a common language had to be learned. All patients, mostly men, have difficulty in describing anything south of the navel. Patients refer to the groin, the grine, the crotch, the crunch, the croutch, or just down yonder. A hernia is a Herman, a hernie or a rupture. Hemorrhoids are 'roids, hemrods, or piles.

One man was desperately trying to describe the area of his rash and itch, "Doc, it's you know where those two, uh ... uh ... it's right on my scrotchum."

Patients even invent terms. A whiny man was telling a pitiful tale of all his illnesses and said, "It was terrible. Dr. Henderson took out half of my colon and left me with a semicolon."

Not only did interns have to learn the language of the patient's illnesses, but they had to instruct them on care. Not everyone understands such things as suppositories. One woman said, "Doc, can't you give me some other kind of medicine. Them 'positories you give me last week tasteses awful."

A man said, "Doc, the tinfoil on them supposiqules just tore my piles up!"

We had to unlearn some things we saw in medical school. After any abdominal surgery, adhesions can form and bring on obstruction or pain, years later. In medical school, several surgeons had the answer. After each case they dumped in the abdominal cavity a liter of sterile amniotic fluid. A baby floats in the uterus nine months and doesn't get adhesions so it should work. It didn't.

Patients with large abscesses were given a general anesthetic for fear of spreading infection by injecting a local. This was a leftover from the days before antibiotics.

Again, there was eagerness to learn and practice skills. Tying a knot doesn't sound like much of an accomplishment, but a right-handed surgeon must do an unnatural and awkward thing and tie with his left hand. The would-be surgeon must learn the two-handed tie, the one-handed tie, the instrument tie and the surgeon's knot. Long operations need hundreds of ties. A surgeon must tie a knot as easily as he walks, without having to think about each step. Tying a knot was a basic skill and a place to start. In the intern quarters there were sutures tied on bedposts, doorknobs, and drawer pulls. Interns practiced running down a knot in the bottom of a penny matchbox to learn how to work in small spaces. They snitched gloves from the OR to practice with gloves on. When actually on the surgical service, interns scrubbed on all scheduled major cases in the third spot. The staff man and resident did the surgery and the intern held retractors, looked, and lived in hope that Big John would ask them to tie a knot or do something. They had to be prepared like the reserves on a bench--just in case. Interns assisted the residents and did simple procedures with supervision. Interns made rounds with staff members and went to the surgical clinic.

The Chief of Surgery was Dr. John Slaughter, a strange name for a surgeon. Big John was tall and imposing, but to interns he looked ten feet tall. He was a superb surgeon trained at the Leahey Clinic, which is sort of like coming down from Mt. Sinai, just behind Moses. He was an authoritative figure, a solemn and stern man. He had a sly sense of humor, which he managed to hide most of the time. Unlike some of the other staff men, though he might eat residents for lunch, he was kind to interns, taking time to explain and teach. I decided I hated surgery in the past because of the abusive attitude on the surgical service. I began to see surgery as different from other specialties. Internists were PP doctors--pills and penicillin and hope the patients got better. Surgeons used medication, but their basic instinct was to physically cut away a problem or make it better. They were fix-it doctors. With his hands, a surgeon can physically remove the tumor, the offending organ or correct a defect. Men cannot force healing. Only God heals, but the surgeon can remove the tumor or repair damage and bring tissues together so that the body, in its infinite wisdom, can heal itself. Some patients didn't survive, but most did. If a patient had a surgical problem, it could be fixed today, not next week, next month or never. It was confusing to begin to like what I thought I hated.

The Third One
25

Even at this hour, I couldn't get an elevator. I grumbled and complained to the walls as I stomped up the empty stairwell toward the operating room. *This is the third one tonight. Big John did the first, let the resident do the second, and I'm the lowly intern who has to hold those stupid idiot sticks for the third time. The first two were like rolling off a log; they could've done them through a buttonhole. There is nothing to it. I could do one as good as they can. They're holding me back.*

I was still complaining when I put on my cap and mask and began to scrub. I leaned to look in the OR window and saw Big John and the resident gowned, gloved, hands wrapped in a towel, the patient prepped and draped; I was late. I scrubbed faster, finished, went in the room, and dried my hands without speaking. I didn't look up; I knew they were staring. After the nurse put on my gown and gloves, I pressed my hands together and walked toward my dreary spot at the lower end of the far side of the table.

Dr. John Slaughter said, "No, stay on this side." He went around the table, dropped his towel, picked up the knife and handed it to me.

All of a sudden, it was hard to breathe in that OR; it must have been the heat. I made the few steps, leaned against the table, and looked down. There lay a human being I talked with an hour ago; now I was about to invade his body. I took a deep breath, made a show of measuring the 1/3 - 2/3 line between umbilicus and crest of the ileum, and made the skin incision. *But there are other layers. What did they do next in all those operations that looked so easy?* Illustrations from a dozen books flooded my mind. That night, I made a startling discovery: anything looks easy if the person doing the job has done it a thousand times and is good at his work. I also found one side of the OR table to be at least 10 degrees hotter than the other. There was no air conditioning. In summer, we did surgery from 6A.M. until 10 and after 3. One or even two people might faint as they worked under lights wearing thick cloth gowns. There were always two circulating nurses. One did nothing but wipe brows. Some doctors wore sweatbands. In spite of all efforts, eventually somebody sweated in the incision. God must honor honest sweat because no serious infection happened. Even at three in the morning, I was sweating; the nurse couldn't wipe where the trickles were. A surgeon can lose a pound an hour doing a hard case in a warm room. I was probably losing two. The first two were like rolling off a log, but after I made my McBurney incision, cut the fascia, spread the muscles and got in the abdomen, there were adhesions everywhere. The appendix was hidden far away--somewhere. This was not a doodlebug appendix; I could not stir with a finger and see it jump up.

Big John said, "You obviously need more room. Do a Weir extension."

"A what?"

"A Weir extension."

I wouldn't do anything to jeopardize the patient, but if I admitted the truth, that I had no idea what a Weir extension was, I would lose my case. I did know one of Dr. Slaughter's habits. The extension couldn't be at either end or laterally toward bone, so I moved the knife in a safe area along the fascia medially. Big John said, "Uh-huh." I made the incision right there. Fascia over the muscle separated and exposure opened like magic. I could see the appendix and take it out with Dr. Slaughter leading me from across the table.

When we finished and everybody was headed for dry clothes, I must have looked like somebody poured a bucket of water over me. As I began to recover, I realized a lowly intern had done a major surgical case in the heat of a summer night. I was feeling a little better about myself.

Big John said, "Before you leave, I want to talk to you." We left the lounge for the privacy of the linen room and stood around the seven-foot square table almost filling the room where the nurses folded surgical cloth drapes. Dr. Slaughter leaned against the table and said, "I am glad this happened just this way to show you two things. First, an appendix can be one of the easiest operations in the world, but at times it can be one of the hardest. Second, just when you think you are a sharp doctor and good surgeon, something comes along to take the wind out of your sails and knock you down. When you operate, be ready for anything you find. There will be surprises in surgery ... and in life. You must deal with the unexpected."

What could I say but, "Yes Sir, thank you?" But I thought, *am I that transparent?*

When I finished changing into dry clothes, Big John had left to find a bed for an hour or so. The patient had been sent to his room, the nurses had turned off the lights and left. The OR and the halls were dim, quiet, and empty. A flickering light floated down the hall as a nurse made rounds. Others spoke in low voices in a circle of light at the nursing station. Sounds of heavy breathing or snores came through open doors. But for these signs of life, this big hospital was silent, dark and asleep.

Do you suppose he spotted me because he has been there himself?

The telephone operator blinked fully awake, or at least more awake, "At this hour you want whut?"

"The library key."

I opened the door to the library at 5A.M. I sat in a chair and stared at the row of books. *I don't remember my desperation surgery when I was three. I don't remember saying I was going to be a doctor so I could have a light like the one he used to look in my ear. I do remember Mother reminding me and pushing me, years later. I remember my folks struggling through the depression. I remember my struggles in high school, going to college with little money, and then failing a course. I remember almost failing the first year of med school and the three hard years that followed. I know I came from a family of farmers and tradesmen, but the President of the University himself handed me my degree. No matter where I came from, what struggles I had, or where I finished in my class, after he handed me that sheepskin, people began to call me Doctor. It seems like I have worked my whole life for this night.*

I pulled down a book. Somewhere, there was something about a Weir extension, and I would know all about it before we made rounds with Dr. Slaughter. My life had been changed. I now knew I was a fix-it person and felt at home in surgery.

Besides, I couldn't sleep anyway.

Duty Delayed
26

When I was accepted for medical school in 1950, I declined the offer of a two-year job as captain in the Chinese Nationalist Army and accepted a commission as a second lieutenant in the Coast Artillery Corps, a branch no longer in existence. After advanced ROTC, I had to take some commission. I took it in inactive reserve because I didn't have time for meetings and training of active reserve. The law required two years of military service. At three-month intervals, I was drafted. I had written letters to the Draft Board 50 miles away to tell them I was trying to finish my education. They ignored my request and sent a "greetings" letter. I had to write new appeals and beg deferment. There was the matter of a war in Korea--far different than the war with Japan. Few had the burning desire to fight in a strange land for stranger causes. Friends told me a transfer to Korea made them think they were being sent to the end of the earth and would never come back. Some never did. Even after the war, some resigned commissions and left the army to avoid a transfer to this far-away land. If my duty was to donate two years of my life, why couldn't I wait until I had my education? We were told there was no such thing as leaving medical school and beginning again after two years.

I survived medical school and had the same problems in internship. I finally convinced the draft board that internship was part of my education and a legal requirement to practice medicine.

In my internship year, I learned I liked surgery and needed more training. This was a calculated risk because now I was subject to the regular draft *and* doctor draft. For some reason, the Draft Board left me alone for a year, so I began to think about a residency. Bluitt, my roommate in medical school, also wanted surgery. We talked about choice of programs. The University of Alabama had a huge flow of surgery. The Draft Board could jerk me up any day. We could see more surgery in a shorter time. But could we endure the stress and abuse and were they already full? I made an appointment for us to talk with the Chief of Surgery.

He was kind, pleasant, and flattering. He said he knew our work from medical school and had much rather have us than some unknown. I asked if we could be assured of acceptance if we agreed to come. If so, we could stop looking for another residency.

He said, "Oh, yes. The Board makes the final decision, but they always do what I tell them."

We talked as we drove back to Lloyd Noland Hospital. We didn't ask about pay. It wasn't enough to make any difference. We had heard the University interns made $6.00 a month. Not long after our commitment, Dr. Slaughter asked us to stay at Lloyd Noland. I told him we thought we could see more cases in a shorter time in a University setting. We made a commitment because residencies were filling rapidly. He said he would like to have us, but understood.

In January, people began getting acceptance letters. When one of the interns got his notice from the University, I called the Chief of Surgery. He had the same name, but didn't sound like the man we had talked with. He was abrupt and curt.

He said, "No, you weren't accepted! The board didn't choose you."

I hung up before I said something I would regret. I discovered he agreed to accept anybody who asked and picked those who agreed to stay five or six years. We had asked for four to make us Board eligible. He was so persuasive I didn't see the scales under his white coat. In June, we would have no place to go. I went to Dr. Slaughter. He was as astounded as we were.

He said, "I would keep you here, but it wouldn't be fair. We are full. Two more would dilute the work. Give me 24 hours and see me in my office."

He located a residency at Baroness Erlanger in Chattanooga and one at Jefferson Hospital in Roanoke, Virginia. I had never heard of either. I took the one he recommended in Virginia. It's a good thing Betty said she'd go anywhere I went. We went in faith she could find work. We couldn't live on my salary of $100 a month. We stored what little furniture we had and moved to Roanoke to begin my surgical residency.

Jefferson was an added-to dwelling converted to a hospital in 1907 by Hugh Trout, Sr. and Dr. Jones, who still operated in his late seventies. The hospital of 151 beds drew patients from western Virginia. The nursing units for the patients were old, but functional. The hospital had its own nursing school, internship and residency program. Jefferson was primarily a surgical hospital run by Dr. Trout, Jr., Dr. Jones, and partners, but other doctors admitted patients.

Dr. Trout, Sr. had part of his training in Germany, and designed the main operating room as a copy of a German surgical amphitheater. The octagonal room was covered by a glass dome, giving intense light for surgery. Below the top dome was a gallery of chairs for observers. In front of the chairs, a circle of gaslights with reflectors focused on the operative area. Another glass dome separated the gallery and gaslights from the operating room. If the light was not right, the patient--not the light--had to be moved. In this more modern era, we had lights on a stand. The dark gaslights and empty chairs were symbols of the past.

In the first year, I was the only intern or resident who spoke American English as a primary language. We had Turkish, Mexicans, British, and two former Hitler-Youth members.

Betty and I lived on the first floor of an old house next door to the hospital. The single male residents lived upstairs. We were eight feet from the Emergency Room. In our bedroom, we could hear loud conversation, shouts, an occasional scream and the tics. Tic tic .... tic tic tic; when I heard that sequence in a department store years later, it still gave me a start. There were no loudspeakers, only tic-boxes throughout the hospital, including the wall of the ER next to our bedroom.

I had the same problem with my service obligation. I was always at the top of the list. Draft board locations could not be changed, so my life was in the hands of those who knew me as a far away unfamiliar name. It was easier to draft a stranger than the son of a friend down the street. I did considerable soul-searching over the problem. I was willing to fulfill my duty--my legal requirement of two years, but I had rather save a life with a scalpel than take one with a bullet. It seemed logical to me that I would be of more value to the service as a trained surgeon. There was so much I didn't know, so much I needed to see, but I needed time. I managed to hold off the draft board and began my first year of residency.

The eagerness of internship stayed with me. I wanted to learn and see cases like I would see in private practice, and I wanted to see them as quickly as I could because I never knew how long I could stay. As junior man, I was given the worst jobs by the chief resident, José Maria Tores del Toro. The senior residents admired fast surgeons--the cutters and slashers. The chief resident admired one of the younger partners, Dr. Albertson, most of all because he began the case with a single slash severing all layers of the abdominal wall down to the peritoneum. When Pepé--I assume this is a slang term for José--got his first chance at surgery, he made a big slash, too. His went through all layers and into the liver.

I had to assist the plastic surgeon because he was slow. I assisted Dr. Jones because he was old. I ran the neurosurgery ward of twenty-five beds and scrubbed on the surgery, because it was drudgery. I liked the plastic surgery, and the surgeon helped me with some of my cases. Neurosurgery was another matter. Sometimes I held a brain retractor for four hours and watched the patient die the next day.

Some cases were interesting, even for a general surgeon. Once as we finished elevating a depressed skull fracture with local anesthesia, "Toughie" Weaver, the neurosurgeon, tried to get some sign that the operation had worked. He shouted in the patient's ear, but couldn't get him to move a hand as a signal.

He finally said, "Com'on cough, Sam, cough! "

"Cough, Dr. Weaver?"

"If he coughs, it raises his intracranial pressure and helps elevate the brain which has been compressed. Besides if he coughs, we know he heard us and the coma is not so deep."

"Listen to me Sam, cough-cough!"

After pleading with Sam the third time there was only silence. Then the patient took a deep breath and in a very soft voice said the words, "Cough-cough!"

"Great, Sam, if you can't do the deed, you said the word. You heard us."

Sam was not through, "Cough-cough ..., **cough!"** As his voice fully recovered, he continued to fulfill the only request he understood, over and over, louder and louder.

Dr. Weaver left me to do the dressing. After we finished and they rolled the patient down the hall, I could hear the nurses saying, "Sir, what is it? Do you need to cough?"

I could hear Sam's reply, "Cough-**cough -cough!"**

When I made rounds in the neuro-unit that night, I heard the same serenade. Other patients in this open ward complained. The nurses wanted to sedate him.

"No way; he's doing what he was told. Give him cough syrup and sedate the others."

After a day and a half he quit "coughing" and left the hospital when his confusion cleared. Other neuro' cases were not so happy. I was not attracted to this part of surgery.

Another job the senior residents didn't like was the emergency room. Strange cases appeared and took time that could have been spent upstairs with big surgery. Senior residents did the glory work in the OR and the ER was covered by such low-lifes as first year residents and interns.

Once, an anxious man about 40 arrived in the ER wearing a raincoat on a clear day. He registered, saying he had problems and wouldn't be specific.

When the female German intern came in, he wailed," I want a man doctor."

When the most junior male resident came in, the patient brought out his problem from under the raincoat. He had placed his penis through a steel building nut that was strangling the base. He had an enormous erection of the blue steel type that did not and could not go away. The veins were occluded by the nut. The ER ring cutters lost their teeth without denting the nut. One of the nurses suggested they send for Dr. Butler; he was just out of urology training and should have all the answers. So, the gathering crowd stood looking at each other, the patient and his problem.

The orderly suggested, "Ain't that nut threaded? Can't we grease it, get a wrench and screw it off?"

Finally the door opened. "Mornin', Dr. Butler. Fellow here's got an extra nut."

Dr. Butler had seen nothing like this in training. We sent for the hospital maintenance man. After one look with eyes bugged out he said, "Good gollie... I ain't never seen nothin' like that."

"That's not the question. Can you cut the nut off?" The patient was paler and more anxious by the minute.

He tried with a rotary tool, but the disk broke on the first try. "Doc, that's a tempered nut like you use on structural steel. They ain't nothing what'll cut it 'cept meby an acetylene torch." Our patient lost all color and began moaning. "On second thought, we might could call them folks over at Norfolk and Western Railroad repair shop and see can they help us."

As word filtered through the hospital, more lookers arrived. As men came in, they gasped in admiration at this huge phallus. Men fear that their symbol and instrument of passion will wilt, but after the lookers considered the matter, they realized a greater fear was it would never wilt. They sighed in sympathy.

The door opened and in stepped the man from the rail yards in his work-clothes. He was a large thick-shouldered man in striped coveralls with grease spots. His round smudged face held a stump of a cigar. Half of one of the teeth clamping the cigar was gold, which sparkled in the glare of the ER lights. His thick hands were covered with rust and oil. The short bill striped hat was much too small for his head. The crowd parted so he could see the patient in their midst with the projecting troubled column.

"Gee-man-nette, I never seen nothin' like that!"

His pale blue eyes widened, and he almost lost the cigar. The head nurse managed to get him to part with it before crossing the room.

" I know, but can you cut it off ... the nut that is?"

"His nut. Which one?"

"The metal nut, there at the base. If we don't do it soon, gangrene will set up." The patient moaned again.

The mechanic leaned forward carefully keeping his feet far away as if he were looking at a snake. He scratched his head and adjusted his cap, making it look even smaller.

"Don't rightly know. I just work on locomotives. Never done no work so close to people's ... ah ... you know ... parts. Might cut it with ma high-speed carborundum wheel, but it gets hot enough to boil water when I turn her up. And I just don't thank I could look at that ... ah ... thang and work on it." The patient moaned louder.

When the actual event began, the room was almost full. The patient was in a semi-sitting position with the engorged monument of passion projecting as a focal point. The patient was beyond caring about an audience. The locomotive mechanic with stained hands, wearing greasy coveralls, and hat too small still on his head, held the rotary tool with carborundum wheel almost at arm's length while he turned his head. He couldn't stand to look at the patient's ... ah ... predicament. As the whining wheel touched the nut, two people held the affected member away from the nut as much as possible An orderly with shaking hands poured water on the wheel and nut as the grinding heated up. Dr. Butler and a resident tried to hold and direct the mechanic's arms as he operated the rotary tool. Since the locomotive mechanic was not looking, at times the wheel drifted to touch a knuckle or the engorged member with a resulting cry of pain or curse.

As the first wheel broke, the mechanic announced, "Now ya'all, I only got two more wheels. Ain't no more this side of Richmond." The patient's moans were more like sobs.

Our mechanic with the greasy striped coveralls severed the nut as the second wheel broke. Everybody cheered except the mechanic, "Ya'all are gettin' ahead of yaself. This ain't no ordinary nut. It's tempered steel. We can't spread it. We got to cut the other side."

So the mechanic with the greasy overalls and the hat too small for his head told the doctors, nurses and orderlies what to do, and they did it. The crew moved to the other side. Dr. Butler convinced the mechanic with only one wheel left he had to look. The improved technique worked. At last, the second side was cut and the nut fell away. The obstructive engorgement faded and the wounded monument went down like a petunia in noonday sun. Tenseness was replaced by discoloration, abrasions, and swelling where the nut had been. Dr. Butler sat and was writing admission orders. He was trying to think of a diagnosis.

The patient effected an amazing recovery and said, "Oh no, I have to go home. My wife doesn't know where I am or what I am doing." He signed out of the hospital against advice, but agreed to take antibiotics.

The patient was well dressed, smiling and completely recovered when Dr. Butler saw him two weeks later.

Dr. Butler said, "I've just got to ask you a question. What did you tell your wife? How did you explain the ... ah ... injury?"

"Oh, no problem. I told her I got it caught in a car door."

She never asked why he had it out when he closed the door.

These were days for learning. The way to remove a tempered steel nut from a vital part was interesting, but not the important lesson. I learned no matter how many patients you have seen and how much experience you have had, the very minute you think you have seen it all, some guy comes in with his penis in a building nut or some equally bizarre thing happens. Learning is an unending process. Nobody ever knows it all. I also learned to take help from wherever it's offered, including that from a reluctant mechanic in greasy striped coveralls, stained hands, one gold tooth and a hat too small for his head.

There were other duties of a junior resident I did not expect. On occasion, Dr. Trout operated at what was called the colored hospital. At that time, black patients had their own hospital staffed mainly by black doctors (Burrell Memorial.) The sparkling new hospital and equipment was a contrast to our ancient building. When major surgery was needed, surgeons from Jefferson were called.

One day as we finished a light OR schedule, Dr. Trout said, "Come, go with me to do a mastectomy."

"I thought Pepé was scheduled to help."

"He is. You're going to give the anesthetic. Our anesthetists are off or tied up with cases here and can't go.

"But I don't know anything about anesthesia."

"What's to know? Grab a syringe of pentothal. Give her a little of that, some nitrous oxide, and oxygen. Everything will be fine."

I got the pentothal and an emergency consult from one of the anesthetists.

After we arrived at the hospital, I went to talk to our patient. I tried to look like I knew what I was doing. The patient was a dignified lady of 75 with a dusting of white in her hair. I sat at her bedside and explained the surgery to her.

She said, "Oh yes, I knows what that is. I hep' do one on my aunt-tee when I was a lil' girl. Two doctas, they come, took her out under th' apple tree in a front yard where it was shady. One docta, he po' somethin' on a tea strainer on her face till she go sleep. Then he run around and hep' the otha docta take her bres' off. When she start hollerin', he go back and po' mo' stuff on a tea strainer 'til she hush. Then he hep th' otha docta agin. Must'ave done a good job. She live a long time."

"What on earth did you do?"

"Oh, I wave th' bresh to keep flies off."

So what did I gain in this one more day of learning? I didn't learn much about anesthesia. But what I gave was better than aunt-tee's. My patient didn't holler. I learned I could do procedures I didn't know I could do. But more important, I learned to appreciate living in a modern world. I learned to value efforts of those who have gone before and worked in primitive conditions. What we learn comes from work and experience of others.

I managed to stay the year, trying to learn as much as I could before the draft swept me away. There was so much to see in this busy hospital. They kept me in spite of my twisted sense of humor. I tried my best to get three doctors to go in practice together so I could see the sign: Drs. Grossclose, Clapsaddle and Dingledine. They also saw nothing unusual about the color of doctor's cars. The internist's cars were white, the obstetrician's was blue, the surgeon's was red, the urologist's was yellow and--it had to be--the proctologist's car was brown.

There was no resident ahead of me so, in spite of my strange view of life, I became chief resident my second year rather than my third, never knowing from day to day if I would be drafted into the Artillery or the Medical Corps. We still had two drafts.

I was given six beds. I could operate on whatever I could put in those beds. Ambulatory surgery was years away, but the rule was as same as the rest of the hospital "Get 'em in and get 'em out." A patient had his appendectomy one day, got a laxative the next, and as soon as he had a bowel movement went home. Staff doctors referred charity and destitute people and those from the tuberculosis sanitarium. They helped me with bad cases. Some of my patients from the hills of western Virginia referred themselves. These were descendants of English and Irish immigrants who had settled the mountains and valleys of western Virginia and never left. Surgery was the last resort for these isolated people. I never saw a single patient from this area with an unruptured appendix. I saw some from the mountains for a workup, advised surgery for a gallbladder or some other problem and they packed up and went home. I never saw them again.

One of my first patients from the TB Sanitarium had severe ileus after abdominal surgery. He was not obstructed, but his bowel wouldn't function or respond to usual medications. Dr. Trout said, "Give him a turpentine enema."

He was always in a hurry; he left before I could ask how to give it. The head nurse didn't know. She found a 1930-nursing manual. There was a listing of enemas: milk and molasses, soapsuds, ox-bile, beef tea, nutritive (eggs milk and sugar.) If we added a little flour we might expect a cake in the bedpan. The last one was turpentine enema: six drops mixed with glycerin. After the strange enema, two orderlies couldn't change bedpans fast enough. The patient got well, but I never ordered another turpentine enema.

I was expected to see time-consuming problems the staff doctors didn't want to bother with. I had a cracker-box office and examined my patients in the ER. I did my minor surgery there. I didn't do like Dr Jones. He kept radium sticks in his safe and taped a small piece to any mole a patient wanted off. He took the radium off in a day or two. The mole did fall off later. I can only wonder about long-term effects.

Among those dumped on me was a collection of patients with varicose or stasis leg ulcers unhealed for years--sores several centimeters across the side of a calf. Most had been treated by the series of residents before me. Some had their veins stripped. Others couldn't have surgery because the infection wouldn't clear enough to allow it. I went into surgery so I could physically do something for patients, yet nothing worked for these people. In my tiny office, I read everything I could find on the problem. A single article described a strange treatment.

As chief resident, I made the schedule for surgical assistants in the OR. I scheduled myself for an elective Cesarean section by Billy Hurt. After he delivered and resuscitated the baby, I said, "Dr. Hurt?"

"Yes?"

"Can I have the placenta?"

"What?"

"I mean if it's clean and she has no disease. I want it sterile. Okay?" AIDS hadn't been invented and hepatitis wasn't common. I was worried about syphilis and tuberculosis.

He gave permission for me to have something that was to be thrown out anyway. I set up a sterile table and dissected the placenta. I threw away the cord and membranes. I kept the succulent red cotyledons, which had been implanted in the uterine wall. They looked like a rug of packed rosebuds. Under sterile technique, I cut them into one and two centimeter cubes, half-circles, and triangles. I put all these cubes into Petri dishes, covered them with a solution of penicillin and streptomycin and put the dishes in the refrigerator. I warned everybody not to bother my placenta parts. I didn't tell the nurses I had never done this before.

Over the next days, I called in all those patients with unhealed ulcers for a graft. I cleaned their ulcer and covered it with cubes of placenta, making an exact fit like a mosaic. I covered the cubes with Poro-wax--a wax coated mesh. I sewed the edges down to fix the cubes in place and dressed the leg.

When the cubes were stable in a few days, I took the mesh off. The surface of the cubes turned black, but around the edges I could see placenta growing into the ulcer. It did not just cover; it had healed to the patient and sealed the ulcer. Over the next few weeks, the surface crust of the mosaic crumbled away; the graft became smaller and then disappeared. The ulcer of many years healed with a smooth flat scar. One rejected the first graft, but the base improved and the next one took. There are hormones in the placenta that have never been identified. This technique depended on these hormones.

My friends tried to discourage my enthusiasm for my strange treatment and the one journal article. "Sooner or later somebody is gonna find out what kind of graft you're doing. That's experimental surgery. It's not legal. You're gonna get in bad trouble."

Fortunately, I had heard about the VD twins: syPHILis and GaNORREa.

One day, the dreaded question came, "Doc, just what kinda graft did you put on me? It's worked good, but what was it?"

"Well the exact name was ... ah ... it was ... it was a placenTEAL graft."

"Uh ... okay, I just wondered."

That was the last of the bad ulcers. I never did another. Some day, someone would ask where the placenTEAL graft came from.

As chief resident, I was expected to scrub on the difficult cases. This procedure was fine with me because I needed to know how to do the unusual, as well as the common. I wasn't happy about doing a lot of thoracic surgery because I never planned to do any. I didn't think I could be comfortable doing a chest case just occasionally. I wanted to see operations I would be likely to do in private practice. Chest cases were less then than now, because anesthesia was not as advanced and mortality was greater.

One day in my chief resident year, I scrubbed on a case with Ted Albertson, who was a few years out of training. He was the idol of the Mexican surgeons because he was not only a fast surgeon, but operated with a flourish and flair. We opened the chest uneventfully and performed the lobectomy.

As always, I looked with amazement at the heart. This organ undergoes a violent contraction and pumps blood through miles of arteries and capillaries. It rests only as the upper chambers fill with blood. Then contracts again. If we need more blood, it pumps harder. It never rests or goes on vacation. It pumps 60 to 160 times a minute depending on what blood we need--for a lifetime. Our body rests at night; the heart slows, but works on. And we are always one heartbeat away from death. Man cannot build a pump as small that does as much. And if we could, it wouldn't repair itself. *I am fearfully and wonderfully made* (Psalm 129:14.) How could there not be a creator?

I was thinking these things, as we were about to close. The patient suddenly went into ventricular fibrillation. At that time, one of the fears of chest surgery or heart surgery was ventricular fibrillation. There were no EKG monitors, but with an open chest we could see what was happening. We had a vague knowledge of fibrillation in medical school. Surgeons and cardiologists had come to understand sometimes what was called cardiac arrest was not stoppage of the heart, but improper contraction. There is no forceful beat of the heart. Nerve stimulation and motion of the muscle fibers are disorganized, ineffective, and there is a worm-like rippling motion of the heart. The heart pumps no blood. Survival is a matter of minutes unless fibrillation can be stopped. Intravenous medication will not reach the heart because there is no circulation. Medical knowledge of that day said that 110 to 250 volts at low amperage for .1 to .5 second could stop the abnormal stimulation of the muscle fibers of the heart in fibrillation. Every ER, OR, and nursing unit in any hospital now has a defibrillator unit that doesn't require opening the chest. Defibrillation is performed on the chest wall, as we see on TV shows. In those days, fibrillation usually meant death. There were units in large university centers, but not small hospitals like Jefferson. We didn't have constant readout of EKG for surgery. Our anesthetist took the blood pressure and checked the pulse every 15 minutes. If the pulse stopped in a closed chest, surgeons didn't know if the heart was in arrest or fibrillation. When I was in medical school, a few EKG units were not direct-writing. They had to be developed like a photograph. With the chest open, there was no doubt about fibrillation. We could see it.

"Pump, Mac, pump!"

I took the heart with both hands and compressed the quivering ventricles rhythmically. The anesthetist said that we were getting a pulse as long as I squeezed. We tried medications intravenously, without help. I stopped pumping long enough to inject 10 cc of 1% procaine hydrochloride directly into the left atrial appendage. We hoped that compression and medication would return normal motion of the heart. It didn't.

Dr. Albertson told the head nurse, "Get me that pack of stuff we put up last week."

"Doctor, are you sure you want to use that ... that thing?"

"If we don't, he's dead."

When she opened the package, Dr. Albertson lifted up this strange collection. I couldn't call them instruments, but they were sterile. Wires were soldered to two serving spoons from the kitchen. These were not even special wires. They were common twisted lamp cord with yellow and black woven fabric covering. One of the cords was cut and the ends soldered to a snap relay that looks like a child's cricket noisemaker. In this relay there is a small spring metal plate. When a thumb pushes down the plate, an electrical circuit is made. When pressure is released, the circuit is broken like the action of a telegraph key. The strength of the surge depends on the speed of the thumb. The nurse pushed the ordinary plug at the end of the wires in the 110 circuit in the wall. Once the spoons were in contact with anything and the circuit closed by pressing the snap relay, there would be an electrical surge between the spoons. If the thumb was slow, the charge was too much.

I held the spoons wrapped in a saline sponge on the rippling heart. Nobody breathed. Dr. Albertson pushed the plate. We saw the patient jump, and the worm motion of the heart stopped. We had broken the fibrillation, but now there was nothing. I took the spoons off and we watched. There was a flicker of notion. Slowly the intrinsic rhythm began and the heart was pumping again.

Our defibrillator cost less than five dollars because the spoons came from the kitchen. For a time, a man walked this earth owing his life to two pilfered spoons, a little wire, a relay, and a man with a fast thumb and the courage to use them. The treatment with the spoons appears as crude to us today as the surgery in the shade of the apple tree appeared to me in 1957, but aunt-tee lived, too. If civilization survives, how will the surgery of this day seem to those in the year 2057?

I saw outpatients in my tiny office and used the ER for any minor surgery. Late one day, I sat at my desk when a patient left. I told the nurse, "I think I've seen a little of everything today."

"Not quite. You have one more. She asked to be seen last. After her, you may have seen everything."

She brought the patient to the door, but didn't come in with her. I looked up from my chart, but couldn't stand before the lady sat in the chair across from my disk. I glanced at her, tried to look away, but couldn't. I opened my mouth to speak, but didn't get a chance.

She looked straight at me. "Go ahead and stare. Everybody does. I can't say I like it, but I accept it. I have no choice. People don't notice I am tall and have dark hair, but everybody with eyes knows I am blue." Her face *was* blue as a September sky, but her eyes showed anguish of a winter storm. Her lips trembled as she spoke. "You'll have to know about it sooner or later. For years I used silver nitrate nose drops every night. They helped or I wouldn't have used them so long. I knew my coloring was changing. I thought it was age and tried different cosmetics. A trip to Florida showed me the truth. I got bluer and bluer. As the years go by, my blue gets more intense. A doctor finally told me the truth. It is my fate to be blue forever. All that silver stayed in my body and when sunlight hit the silver in my skin, it turned blue. It will not go away even if I stay in a closet."

"Didn't the doctor try one of the therapies to try to rid the body of heavy metals?"

"Yes, and it didn't work. And I know all the cruel jokes about silver polish. I will be blue as long as I am on this earth. I don't want to wear a veil and I will not join the circus. I go out in public when I have to, like today. I had to quit work. Nobody wants a blue bank teller. I live on what my husband left. I am here today for this swelling because this is a free clinic."

I checked the lump in her cheek. "I can take that cyst out, but I have to tell you, I have no idea what the scar will look like. It may be a pale white stripe or even bluer. You are the first ... the first blue patient I have ever operated on.

I took the cyst out. When the patient left, the nurse said, "*Now* you've seen it all."

She never came back to have the sutures removed. I still have never seen a scar on a blue face.

* * *

As Chief Resident, I saw strange conditions--some said to be untreatable. I refused to accept this sentence and tried to help with whatever seemed logical. A man came in with phlegmasia cerulea dolens--clots of the deep venous system of the leg with massive swelling. I showed him to Dr. Trout. He said, "Too bad, we have no way to get all those clots out down the thigh and calf. You would have to make ten or fifteen incisions, but try if you want to."

I sat at the bedside, talked with the patient and told him what he had and what he could expect. I offered to try to help. Surgery could hardly make it worse. Without treatment, he faced permanent swelling or amputation. I let the systemic heparin wear off and took him to surgery that night. I made the usual groin incision. The vein was huge and packed. I opened it and coils of clots oozed out like a snake. With a short metal suction, I brought out more thick clots. I irrigated with saline heparin solution. We had a gush of blood from above, but nothing below.

I closed off the upper side with a rubber drain and asked for a sterile Levin tube.

"Doctor, *that's* for the stomach."

"I know that. If it's sterile, get it. There may have been vascular catheters somewhere, but we didn't have any. I passed the Levin down the vessel. When I applied suction, the end of the clot broke off and we got back small chunks. I couldn't get the tube beyond the row of clots. Still no flow of blood. I switched to the thinner and longer Miller-Abbot tube. The nurses reminded me that it was for the small bowel. I reminded them that if was sterile, I wanted it. I pushed the smaller tube past some of the clots, inflated the balloon on the far end just a bit and pulled back. Each pass pulled hunks of clots. I reached mid calf and still no backflow. The vein was still blocked. *Maybe Dr. Trout was right*. Another pass--this time all the way to the ankle pulled out more clots. Venous blood followed and poured down the drapes without irrigation. The leg was almost normal size in 48 hours.

Two days later I cut off the end of my left index finger. I had been taking an art class at a community college and was washing my glass palette in the shower of our apartment. It broke and severed the tip. I held pressure on the finger and went next door. People surrounded me, offering to suture it or graft it. I thanked everybody, took a student nurse to help and went to a corner of the ER. I irrigated with a local with adrenalin and held pressure until the bleeding slowed. I fitted the cut piece in place by matching the whirls on the tip and held it with butterfly strips. There were no packaged strips. I cut ordinary tape and flamed the small center part to sterilize it. We dressed it and I walked out like a left-handed Statue of Liberty. I canceled my surgery for the next week. I was in training to do all the surgery and crowd all the experience I could into the year and now I had done something stupid. I had cut off the end of the finger I run down knots with when I tie. I was depressed. There is no demand for one-handed surgeons. Three days later, I dressed it and the tip was blue. It might be gone. My depression was worse. On the sixth day the tip was turning pink. I glued a finger of a glove over the tip so it would be dry when I scrubbed my hands. I scheduled surgery. Now I had the problem of how was I going to tie. I tried using the left middle finger to push down knots. I could do it, but the index stuck out useless and in the way. I spent part of the night teaching myself to tie and run down knots with my right hand. The tip healed and I left it open in another week. The end was numb and the scar tender; I still couldn't use it in surgery. While I was waiting to heal, I tried to increase other hand skills. I had heard that surgeons should teach themselves to use the non-dominant hand by shaving with that hand using a straight razor. I wasn't that brave. I did force myself to shave with my left hand, but with a safety razor.

Six months later when the sensation in my finger was normal, I tied with either hand. Slowly I changed back to the left. I thought I had overcome a huge disability for a surgeon until at a medical meeting I saw a movie of a skillful plastic surgeon doing hand surgery. I suddenly realized he had Mickey Mouse hand--he *had* no left index finger. He lost part of it in an accident years ago and had the rest removed to get it out of the way.

I tried to get into the Berry Plan that deferred doctors in residency if they agreed to go into service after training. The plan was full and closed. The draft board drafted me again and relented only when I agreed to request active reserve duty as an artillery officer. Apparently the country needed people killed more than they needed them operated on. I took the physical and tests with the draftees. At the end of the physical, I was interviewed by Major A. Nonymous, commander of this district.

His question was simple, "What are you doing here? Don't you want to finish your residency?"

I agreed I did, but couldn't get in the Berry Plan. I didn't want to shirk my duty, just delay it. He said he had the authority to grant an administrative delay. The rules didn't say how long. We would delay until I finished training. The draft board was silent for months.

Toward the end of my second year at Jefferson, I began to look at my circumstances. I could stay another year as chief resident and do what I had been doing. But this was a three-year program. I would have to have a two-year preceptorship if I could find a Board Certified man willing to take me. I called Dr. Slaughter. His senior residents were not up to his standards. They were invited to leave. There was nobody for the third year spot. I could finish a full four-year residency at Lloyd Noland Hospital and become board eligible. I accepted. Life was more complicated than when we came. Our first child was due about the time we were to move.

We made plans to go back to Birmingham. We located a small house. It was not next to the ER and residents with big feet did not live upstairs.

When I notified the draft board of the new address, they discovered I wasn't carrying a gun and playing soldier. They drafted me again and notified me by a nasty letter I was to be inducted into the Navy as seaman third class. I called the major to thank him for what he had done. At least I had two years of training.

That night he called me at home. "Doc, would you still like to finish your training?"

"You know I would."

"This conversation never happened. If you tell anyone, I will deny it. Listen carefully. Put in a person-to-person call to Colonel I. B. Nameless at the Pentagon and tell him your story."

I had nothing to lose. I called the next day because I was to be inducted within the week. A secretary answered the phone and wanted to take a message; she transferred me to lieutenants, captains, then majors.

My answer was the same to each, "No, this is a person-to-person call. I must speak to Colonel Nameless." I did reach the Colonel and told my story. I was just trying to finish a surgical residency if the draft board would let me; then the government could have their two years--their pound of flesh.

His reply was short, "I see. I'll take care of it."

What could I say except thank you and good-by? I figured it was a waste of time, but I tried, though probably too late. I was due to go in the Navy in three days.

The day before I was to leave, a wire came canceling my orders. Papers came a few days later placing me in the Berry Plan, which was said to be closed. So the draft board left me alone for two years, though they may have ground their teeth because they couldn't touch me. I would fulfill my duty, but my duty would be delayed.

Duty Delayed Again
27

I finished the year as chief resident in my second year at Jefferson and moved back to Lloyd Noland Hospital to become a third-year resident in a four-year program. Betty almost created a scandal when she left Jefferson Hospital nine days after delivery of first-son Owen. New mothers were supposed to stay a full ten days. She went from the hospital directly to the airport. I drove the car with our few possessions. We lived in Fairfield Highlands in the first house we had all to ourselves. We had saved $1,000 from Betty's salary, so we figured that with this enormous savings Betty could stop work. As a junior resident I made $100 a month. In a year, as Chief Resident I would make enough for us to live on.

My status at Lloyd Noland was a comedown after operating almost autonomously as chief resident in Virginia. The main benefit was that I was assistant to Dr. Slaughter for all his cases. I was able to see a huge amount of good surgery, but did little on my own. Even at night, I was a junior resident and usually an assistant at surgery. I did steal a few cases in the daytime. The rule for the first case was the knife hit the skin at precisely seven-thirty each morning. Dr. Slaughter had a long drive and sometimes was late because of traffic, or he might have overslept. Nobody had the courage to ask. The first patient was put to sleep and I prepped and draped. I watched the second hand on the clock; at exactly seven thirty I made the incision.

If the chief came in huffing and puffing more than a few minutes late, the operation was well underway. Dr. Slaughter would say, "Oh well, just go ahead and I'll help you."

The next year, I became Chief Resident for the second time and had the responsibility of surgery for almost half the hospital. My pay increased, but not soon enough. When my year began, I was three months ahead on salary advances. Then, first-daughter Donna arrived in my senior year to add to our expenses.

I had been Chief Resident in Virginia, and this colored my thinking at Lloyd Noland. If I operated at night, I was supposed to call my attending surgeon. One afternoon, we had a patient with abdominal pain. The intern and I thought he had appendicitis. At 5 P.M., the attending staff man told us to watch him till morning. He left somewhat hurriedly.

As soon as he left, the intern said, "Whatar' ya going to do now?"

"Ask me in a few hours. We'll wait ‘til 10." I sweated gallons while we opened the abdomen. I couldn't believe I had done this--going against the advice of the attending. The patient did have appendicitis. Now I had the problem of what to say when we made rounds the next day.

Morning came and I sweated more. "Oh, Dr. Barron, he got much worse in the night. We didn't want to wake you. We were sure that you would want us to go ahead and operate."

The same method didn't work with Dr. Slaughter. I honestly didn't want to wake him at 3A.M., so we operated without calling. I spent the better part of an hour--or so it seemed--in his office being severely chastised. After that, I called at any hour.

I also spent time in Dr. Slaughter's office learning I was responsible for everything that went on with the house staff. If an intern or resident committed some sin, he never spoke to them; I got the blame. I learned to never give an excuse. I learned to say, "Yes sir." and hunt up the guilty party to make sure he didn't do whatever it was again.

There was still no ICU and no EKG or other monitors for the seriously ill or those under anesthesia. Early in my year, we were making rounds on Section D when a patient went into cardiac arrest. Nurses came screaming to get me. Whether he had true arrest or fibrillation made no difference. There was no pulse. There was no concept of closed massage. We opened the chest for arrest. There were no surgical instruments on Section D, and the OR was several floors and minutes away. The nurses offered a pair of suture scissors. I opened the chest with my one tool and pumped the heart with both hands until a crew came to take him to surgery to close his chest.

I caught my breath and washed my hands. My wrists were red and sore. We finished rounds and as I was massaging my wrists, I asked my intern, "I've been thinking about it and can't understand how I got between the ribs to the heart. In chest surgery we take out a rib and even then crank the chest open with a rib spreader."

"I can tell you how. You poked the sharp end of the scissors between the ribs, pushed the scissors to cut the skin and muscle, reached fingers of both hands in, grunted one time and broke the ribs. I heard 'em snap--sounded like more than one. You pulled the ribs down with the left hand and reached in with the right then the left."

A blast of adrenalin ... or more like when the man was in the well?

We did a huge number of thyroid cases in my fourth year because radioactive iodine treatment hadn't yet been developed. We did many gastrectomies because we didn't have effective medications for ulcers and cancer of the stomach was more common then.

I had my share of strange cases, as in Virginia. We once had a man with acute pancreatitis and developed a huge cyst. At that time, conventional wisdom said stay away from the pancreas unless forced to operate. We knew if we operated, we should wait until the cyst was mature. Then the wall of the cyst would then be strong enough to anastomose to stomach or small bowel for internal drainage. The man looked twelve months pregnant. He couldn't breathe. We operated, and the cyst wasn't mature enough to hook up to anything. We drained the cyst to the outside. He recovered and then began to fade away. He had what we called the 'dwindles.' The pancreas produces huge amounts of liquid with enzymes for digestion. All of the pancreatic juice and streaks of bile poured out through the tube. He could eat, but food increased drainage. He couldn't digest anything; huge fluid loss was hard to match with simple IV's. He was slowly shrinking. Today there is hyperalimentation and medications for this problem, but not then.

I presented him to staff men and got a reply of, "That's an interesting case; let me know how it comes out." They didn't know what to do either.

My junior resident and intern and I talked about the problem. If we didn't feed him, the drainage would stop eventually, but with nothing but IV glucose and saline he might not live that long. He needed good nutrition for healing, but food increased the flow of pancreatic juice. What his body needed was pouring through a tube to the jug on the floor liter after liter, and the nurse was pouring it down the drain several times a shift. I told the other two, "That stuff looks pretty clear. Doesn't smell bad.

Why not give .... "

The resident was horrified, "You can't do that! That's experimental treatment. You don't know what it will do to him."

"It's his own juice. What could it do? As it is, he's gonna die"

"Would you put it down a tube?"

"If we did, he would know for sure what we are doing."

We cultured the juice and looked at it under a microscope. Everything was negative. Two days later the resident and I took a jug of drainage fluid to the kitchen. We received strange looks when we made our requests. The cook assigned us a table and gave us what we asked for and went away shaking his head and saying something about three more years and he could retire. I mixed equal parts of lemon juice and lime juice with sugar and water until it tasted just right. Then I mixed pancreatic juice with it.

I looked at my resident, "Okay, I tasted the first batch. You taste this one."

"No way. I'm not tasting that stuff. It might turn me into a zombie or somethin'. Look, yonder comes our intern. Fat as he is, he probably eats anything. Hey Mike! Come'ear! We want you to taste somethin'."

"No way. The nurse told me what you two were doin'." I 'm not drinkin' that stuff."

We looked at that green mix with pulp swirling about. "It doesn't look too bad. Let's add a little more lime juice and sugar for good measure and give it a try." I took a pitcher of the chilled mix to the patient.

The three of us stood at his bedside. "This is a new ... uh ... sort of a high-energy supplement we want you to try."

We fled so we didn't have to watch. I was afraid my expression would give me away. As we sat at the nurses' station, we looked up to see our patient holding his tube round the corner, walking rapidly.

The junior resident turned pale and said in a whisper, "Oh my gosh, he's figured out what we did, or he's poisoned or... or worse! Anyway, here he comes."

The patient was a big man. He wasn't smiling.

He faced us and said, "That stuff ya'all gimme sho' was good. Could I have some mo'?"

He had a ring of lemon and lime pulp around his mouth. Our nurse became nauseated at the sight and left to solve the problem.

"Uh ... no, not right now. That's uh ... strong stuff and we have to wait a while. Maybe this afternoon."

By then, he produced enough juice to mix another batch. Over the next weeks he gained weight on ordinary food and our 'special high-energy supplement' and the drainage stopped. He never understood why he couldn't have his special mix any more.

I never knew what waited for me when my phone rang. One night late in my chief residency year, the phone rang at 2A.M.. The junior resident said that he had a patient in the ER with an ice pick in his heart. People fought with picks. Some carried them in a sheath in a pocket or purse. Sometimes, patients were brought to the ER with no apparent cause of death until we looked for the tiny pick-wound.

"And he's still alive? Are you sure?"

"Yes, in his heart. Come and see."

From Fairfield Highlands to Lloyd Noland Hospital there was little traffic at that hour.

The resident had started fluids and put the patient in Trendelenburg position. He and the nurses were gathered around the bed staring. The handle was lost in the scuffle. The metal part of pick was sticking in the mid-chest and waved up and down with every beat of the heart. There was no doubt where the tip was. I called Charlie Donald, our chest consultant, and explained the situation. At 3A.M., he wasn't as excited as I was.

He said, " Okay, take him to surgery, put him to sleep, prep him and take the pick out. If he goes into shock, call me, open the chest and I'll come in to help you."

"How do I take it out?"

"I'll leave that to you."

On the way to surgery, I passed the maintenance man making his rounds with a belt of tools that always pulled his pants halfway down his behind.

"Say, could I ask you something? Are you going to use those big pliers for the next hour or so?"

The nurses cleaned off the grease and autoclaved the pliers. After the patient was asleep, we prepped the chest and ice pick as if we were going to open the thorax. I stood on a stool so I could work level with the pick. I asked for the sterilized pliers. I stood watching the waving of the pick and trying to build my courage. If I pulled too slowly, motion of the heart could tear muscle or vessels on the pick. I couldn't take more than a fraction of a second to get a grip on the waving pick. I opened the pliers and moved them closer. I watched the pick move between the grooves. The anesthesiologist gave me signs for each beat of the heart. If I pulled fast enough when the heart was relaxing and filling, we had a chance., I saw the hand fall at the head of the table. I clamped the pick and pulled.

Dr. Donald got to sleep the rest of the night and the patient left the hospital two days later.

The next week, our patient shot the guy who stabbed him.

I did give the pliers back.

Several days later as I was about to wind up my day, they paged me to the ER. The doctor insisted that I come. The patient sat in a chair by the desk, holding an ice pack to his left jaw.

"What's the story?"

The ER doc said, "In a discussion with another guy, this man was hit in the jaw by a fist. He wanted to know if his jaw was broken. We X-rayed it and I told him there was no break, but the blade was still there. He didn't know what I was talking about. Look at the X-ray."

There was a two-inch pocketknife blade sticking straight in above the angle of the mandible. I took the pack off. There was an old scar on the cheek.

"He was in another dispute a year ago and was cut with a knife. He went to the big hospital across town and they sutured him and sent him on his way. When they took the stitches out, he told them he had trouble chewing. They told him it would get better."

I showed the X-ray to the patient and talked with him about surgery. I told him I didn't know what damage removal could cause.

I paged the maintenance man. He was protesting when I met him in the hall. "I need all them tools, Doc."

"If you promise to leave them with the nursing supervisor when you finish your shift, I'll get them back to her by the time you come back."

He reluctantly agreed to leave me pliers of several sizes. I took the X-ray and spent an hour or so in the library. It was frightening to think of what could be damaged by pulling the blade. The belly of the blade was wider than the broken base, which meant that even a straight pull had to cut something. Dissection would be through scar and could damage the same structures even more. The most remarkable thing was that the blade had not cut major nerve or vessel. It must have broken when it reached the skull. It seemed to have the tip in the bone but not through it.

The next morning, I checked with the nurses in the OR. My pliers were there. I ignored the offer of a screwdriver and wrench. I prepped the entire head and neck. I opened the old scar and dissected down to the blade and exposed about 1/4 of an inch. I picked the largest pliers I could fit in the hole and get around the blade. I reasoned that the blade went in without major damage; it would come out the same way--maybe. I pulled and almost fell in the floor when it came out. I slid a gelfoam plug in the hole and held pressure. After three minutes, there was nothing but small ooze.

I gave the surgical pliers back again, but the maintenance man avoided me the rest of my chief-residency year.

Duty At Last

26

All the while in these two years at Lloyd Noland, the specter of my military obligation hung over my head. In the late spring of 1959 toward the end of my residency, I hadn't received orders for active duty. I called the reserve unit office.

"Oh Doc, I sure am glad you called. We lost your records and didn't know where you were."

"You mean if I hadn't called, I wouldn't have to go?"

"Oh, we would've found you sometime, but we do have a problem. You should have been sent for a basic training program for medical officers--you know: marching, military courtesy, discipline, bivouac and stuff like that. It's too late for that. We'll have to figure something. We'll let you know."

A few days late, the FBI called Betty. They wanted to know where she and her parents were born.

The army didn't want me right away. I finished my residency and had no job, so Lloyd Noland let me stay for a month as a junior staff officer.

There was a little correspondence about where I wanted to go for my two years of duty. Since the government was paying, I wanted to go as far as possible. I chose Germany. If I would stay in an extra year, they would pay; otherwise, they wouldn't send my family. So I chose southern California.

The wire ordered me to duty at Sandia Base, Albuquerque, New Mexico. At least it was in the direction of California. I was due the fifth of July, so I left early because of heavy traffic on this holiday weekend. Our furniture was moved into storage. Betty and the two babies stayed with family.

I discovered Sandia was one of the most top-secret bases in the world There were buildings with three sets of barbed wire fences and machine gun towers at the corners. I managed to get by the guard at the gate and went to the hospital. Sergeants run the army. I saw one first, I told my story, and showed him the telegram.

"Sir, could I see your orders."

"I don't have any orders, just the wire."

"Could I see your ID card?"

"How about a driver's license?"

"No, sir, a military ID card."

"I don't have one."

"Could I see your 201 file?"

"What's a 201 file?"

Now, the Medical Service Major came out and repeated the routine. "And you don't have orders at all? This has never happened. No one has ever been sent directly to duty, certainly not to a high security base. I don't know how we will handle this."

"Could we maybe forget about it and I could go back to Alabama?"

The major ignored me and made calls to confirm that I had been ordered there. He shook his head, mumbled and finally said: "Okay, we'll get you in the BOQ. Then you come back in the morning, and we'll see about getting you a uniform so you can command a little respect."

I was glad to know respect was so easy to come by. I was dressed in slacks and sports shirt and commanded no respect at all.

On the next day in clean slacks and sports shirt, I met the Major and Colonel Healy, commander of the hospital. He said reporting to duty without even a uniform was unheard of. I was given detailed instructions about the location of the quartermaster building.

The quartermaster sergeant in building 201 was pleasant and smiling, "What kind of a uniform, Sir?"

"I don't know, just a regular suit."

"Sir, could I see your ID card?" He would not accept an Alabama driver's license either. "Sir, I can't get you a uniform without an ID card. You have to get that at building 601."

Building 601 was all the way across the base. Again there was a sergeant. I announced my desire for an ID card. "Oh, no sir, we can't do that today because we have to fingerprint you, photograph you and laminate the card. Please report here in the morning at 0800, in uniform."

By the time I drove back to building 201, I had time to build up a head of steam. The sergeant at the quartermaster building was still smiling. "Sergeant, I have been to building 601 and can't get an ID card without a uniform and you say I can't get a uniform without an ID card."

My first statement passed over his head, but he understood about the uniform. "Yes sir. That's right."

"Sergeant, I have a bulletin for you. If you don't get me a uniform right now, I'm going to have a triple revolving double duck fit right here in this office, and I will put your name on report as uncooperative with hospital personnel, and my colonel's wings are bigger than your colonel's."

"This is very irregular, sir."

"I *am* an irregular person."

I did get my uniform and with help figured where to put the insignia.

The hospital stamped me a dog tag so I could be identified if shot as a spy. I did get my ID card in uniform. Now that I had a uniform, an ID card and a dog tag, I had to go to work.

The surgery department had a small waiting room on the second floor. My secretary had her desk at the far end. My office was to one side of the waiting room and the one exam room on the other side with an adjacent procedure room.

One surgeon had been discharged and one was on a thirty-day leave. The lieutenant colonel Chief of Surgery was to be there another week. He had not seen the inside of the operating room in a year. The other two men who had one year of training had done all the surgery. They did the best they could. Since the colonel didn't operate, I was the surgery department for 35,000 troops and dependents. I was also temporary Chief of Orthopedics.

My office complex was adequate, but there was another story. The two doing surgery spoke with no authority. Standards had declined. The infection rate was terrible, especially to one just out of the residency. There had been 23 major infections in the last quarter. These patients had to stay in the hospital for weeks until they recovered enough to go back to duty.

Technically, as a captain I was head of surgery, but there were nurses in the OR who were majors, and one was a lieutenant colonel--an awkward situation. The old chief who never operated left. After my first week as Chief, I made a decision to try the army way. We had no scheduled cases on this Monday, and I found everybody in the OR lounge, drinking coffee, laughing and gossiping.

I said, "Today we're going to have inspection."

They laughed. I didn't. I went from room to room, pulled out all the packs from the shelves, opened them and dumped the instruments in the floor, piling up defective, even rusty, equipment. I cut the old rotten rubber T-tubes. I told the crew about the infection problem. I left, saying I found the whole unit unacceptable and would be back the following day.

The next day, I found my white OR shoes in my locker freshly polished, lined up perfectly, and laces tied. Everything was repacked, sterilized and defective instruments replaced. I never knew where they came from. In the next quarter, we had one wound infection after an appendectomy--not an unusual occurrence.

I learned that locked doors are a joke in the army. I had just done some operation for a man from Quartermaster. He asked if I had fatigues. I said I was told to buy them, so I had. He asked about a field jacket. I said no.

The next day behind two locked doors hanging on the coat rack in my office was a new field jacket.

A few days later I saw the sergeant. "Strangest thing happened: after we were talking, a field jacket showed up in my office."

"Is that so? Just go ahead and wear it."

"The problem is it's a size too big"

The next day, the first coat was gone and a smaller size was on the rack.

I did have a major problem at first. Toward the end of the day, I always ran out of energy no matter what I had done. At five o'clock, I would lie down and rest a little until mess hall opened at six. I learned to set the alarm clock for the next morning because sometimes I would sleep straight through. I had not known the altitude was so high. My hemoglobin built up in about in a month and I could make the day.

To add to my problems, I was expected to receive a training experience in my spare time to make up for what I had missed in the six-week basic course. I went to a few required movies telling me how to avoid VD or some other vital matter. I didn't think I should push my luck and complain about movies I had already seen in ROTC.

Three weeks into my tour, I was called to the emergency room late one night. A colonel and his family were camping in the Sandia Mountains when the teenage son developed severe abdominal pain. He had to carry his own pack and walk out. By the time he got to the hospital, the boy was dehydrated, had a high fever and rigid abdomen. I was working to rehydrate him to get him ready for surgery when I noticed Colonel Healy. Something was strange for the commander of the hospital to be out this late. As I talked with him, I began to understand his problem. The boy's father was a personal friend. Colonel Healy couldn't reassure the father because he knew nothing about me.

"Colonel, would you like to scrub in on this case? It's probably a bad appendix—maybe ruptured."

"Well, you know ... I uh ... I haven't been in an OR in twenty years .... on second thought, I believe I will."

I brought the colonel into the operating suite and received what-have-you-done-to-us looks from the crew. I assigned Sp 5 Hunkins, the best scrub tech I had, to baby-sit the Colonel. The Colonel was a thick-bodied man with military bearing and stern demeanor. Hunk was so short he always stood on a box at the OR table. He helped the Colonel dress, put a mask, hat and shoe covers on him. He then monitored and scrubbed at the sink with the Colonel. The surgery had just started when I looked up to see Hunkins leading the Colonel in the room. The Colonel followed close behind, taking stiff, zombie like steps--arms and hands held straight out with fingers spread, stiff and dripping. Hunk watched every motion as he dried his hands, was gowned, gloved and herded to the table. Hunk then placed the Colonel's gloved hands in the sterile field away from the surgery. He said, "Now, keep 'em right there ... uh, sir." I did the surgery; a scrub tech helped me; Hunkins did nothing but watch the Colonel to make sure there was no break in sterile technique.

Colonel Healy was in the mess hall the next morning telling everybody about the operation he helped with. I let him hold a retractor once. I couldn't resist the opportunity to tell a colonel what to do. That afternoon I was in Colonel Healy's office. After we stopped talking about the appendix, I told him about my problems.

"Colonel, I have to do the surgery for 35,000 troops and dependents. I am told I have to go to the movies and get trained in my spare time. I can't do both. And another thing, they tell me I can't get base housing for two years. I can't afford off-base housing, and if I could, how could I take call that far away? And they say there is a six-month wait for a phone. The MPs are going to complain about coming after me every night."

The medical service corps major called me to his office the next day to sign papers certifying my completed training. As we signed, he mumbled something about irregular and illegal. Suddenly somebody found a base house for me with a view of the mountains, a block away from the General's house. The phone was installed the next day. Betty, the babies, and the furniture came as soon as we could arrange it.

After the military training issue was satisfied, I began to do some serious surgery. I resolved to not be bitter as others were over forced service time. I would use these two years to get all the experience I could, so I would be ready for private practice. There is an active grapevine on most army bases. Word was passed that there was a young, but trained surgeon at the hospital for the first time in years. The volume of surgery increased.

Recurrent hernias came on a flood. Most had been operated on overseas in a small hospital. Regulations required elective surgery to be sent to a hospital in the States, with loss of time from their duty station. The hernia had been declared an emergency and done by the nearest doctor at the nearest hospital. In some patients, there was no scar in the area of the hernia. The first surgery never reached the right level. I did more recurrent hernias in two years than I have seen since.

A patient came in apologizing for not having a hernia I could see. He said in the Italian campaign he went for sick call with a painful hernia anybody could see. The doctor told him to come back when the battle was over and have it fixed. When he came back, another doctor found no hernia. He was pronounced a goof-off and sent back to duty. In the years since the war, he had gone on sick call at every new assignment to tell his story and say the doctor may not see the hernia, but it was there somewhere because he still had pain. After I checked him, I told him to stop with the sales talk; I would operate. "You understand, this will be an exploratory operation. I will do whatever I think is indicated. The reason for surgery is a long firm mass in your scrotum, too big to be a vas."

At surgery, the mass was an appendix plugging the neck of a large empty hernia sac. Appendectomy is not advised in a hernia repair, but I did it. The patient went home pain free for the first time since 1945. He asked for a copy of the operative report to send to all those other doctors.

Late one morning, my secretary, Rita looked in my office and said, "The ER wants you to check this patient from lock-up."

She escorted the patient into my office. Sgt. Ziger was two steps behind. The patient sat in the chair--ramrod straight, without his back touching.

"So, what's wrong with you?

"Fell down the steps in the Rec. Hall, Sir."

The knots scattered across his scalp were obvious. They were tender, but there was no break in the skin and I could feel no bone depression. Superficial neurological was negative. The X-ray was negative.

I gave them my report and Sgt. Ziger spoke for the first time since his first greeting. "Thank you, Captain. All right soldier, let's go."

A week later, an almost identical event occurred with a different prisoner, but same sergeant. The knots were scattered differently, but looked the same.

I saw the second one the day before I operated on Colonel Shazoski, commander of Element. The day after surgery, I told him the story. "What is the problem with those steps? How can a guy fall and hit nothing but his head?"

He looked around to be sure there were no listeners. "I was sent here to try to straighten out Element. They are the worst outfit in the army. We try everything we can to reason with those guys, Doc. Some of those jerks don't understand anything but something physical. Sgt. Ziger takes 'em to the Rec. Hall for a little entertainment, before he locks 'em up."

"What if that doesn't work?"

"It usually does. If not, we march the whole body of troops out in the desert. We stop and move the men around where they can see and hear. Somebody reads the proclamation. Another rips off all signs of rank or anything related to the Army. All the time, they are doing a number on the drums. The troops march away. The man stands alone, not only dishonorably discharged, but also drummed out of the service. Even his friends are forbidden to look back."

"How often do you have to do that?"

"One time should do it."

The next time Sgt. Ziger brought in a man, I looked at him a little closer. He wasn't tall, but the uniform hid the thickness of his arms and chest. I didn't know the army had shirts with collars that big. When he said, "All right soldier, let's go," he slapped the swagger stick in his hand. It was the large end of a decorated pool cue.

Several months later, this group of former goof-offs won several awards. The Colonel and Sergeant must have smiled.

I could tell something was coming by Rita stammering and clearing her throat outside my office. She opened the door and ushered in a bird Colonel. Even I knew not to salute inside. I stood and hesitantly held up my hand. The colonel put a chart in it and sat in the chair by my desk.

"I am here for my hormones ... Captain."

"Sir, if it's for a shot, that would be the medical department."

"It is all in the record you hold in your hand."

I did a quick scan. In the war the Colonel had lost part of his anatomy a little south of the navel—both of them—but the main member was intact. There was no explanation of why it was out of the way when the wound took place. Rather than have frequent injections, he had implantations of depot testosterone. I found descriptions of procedures at other bases. I made calls to the OR and purchasing officer.

"Colonel, I don't have the instrument to do that procedure. We can try to order it."

"I need my hormones this week. You are a *reservist* aren't you ... *Captain*?

"I *am* a reservist. I *am* here by law, but I *am* also the only fully trained surgeon on this base *and* Chief of surgery ... *Colonel.*"

"I know; I checked with your Commanding Officer. What day ... *this week* will you perform my surgery?"

"I'll have to see when I can get the instrument. Please leave a number where we can reach you. We will call." I stood and after a short hesitation he got up and left without a word.

Ten minutes later, the purchasing officer sat in my chair. "Doc, I can have the hormones by morning, but it will take a month to get that instrument. The cost is $80. I could go downtown this afternoon and buy the same thing from the poultry supple-house, but it has the wrong label.

"They use it on chickens?"

"It is the same tool made by the same company, but without the medical label and costs about $10. They use it to make capons--sort of a chemical castration."

I took the chicken tool and practiced that afternoon. We called the patient for the next day. I wanted to get it over with.

The next morning, I made a tiny incision in the area of the Colonel's choosing. I pushed in the thin four centimeter trochar to make a tunnel under the skin, wiggled it a little to make a pocket at the end, loaded the sterile testosterone tablet in the tube, and pushed the plunger to drop the tablet in the pocket. I did two other directions and closed the wound with a single suture.

When he came back a week later for suture to be removed, he had a tiny smile, but just one side. I could only assume the hormones had begun to work.

He had called me a reservist Captain with an upward curl of his lip. I was kinder; I didn't call him a

Capon Colonel and I didn't tell him he was my very first capon.

I never really understood the Army methods. A few weeks after I arrived, the purchasing officer came in to my office to ask if I needed any new instruments.

"I guess maybe a new retractor or two."

"No, Doc, I mean something for real money. We have to spend $65,000 by next month or we lose our allotment next year. If you don't spend it, I'll go to the internists. They'll buy something." I bought an electronic metal locater, heated hand-washing basins on a stand for every room, and all sorts of fantastic tools and toys I have never seen since, but I couldn't spend the $65,000.

Three months into my tour, one of the reservists in pediatrics, originally from New York, didn't show up for work. His house was empty and phone was disconnected. He didn't pass top-secret security clearance and was moved without notice. That day, I checked with the security people at the hospital. I had already passed.

We did have strange security procedures, but they were very specific. Men would come in the ER and say, "I think I've been poisoned."

"What with?"

"I can't tell you. It's a military secret."

We had to learn the names of the agents. Then the doctor took the patient to a secure area and asked, "Is it compound A; is it compound B?"

If we could name the chemical he could say," Yes."

As Chief of Surgery, I received pressure from many directions. As I was going into surgery one night, a breathless Lieutenant ran up, "Wait just a minute Captain, I need to talk to you." I stopped just outside of the OR and turned around.

"The man you are about to operate on is just a Private, but the General wanted me to tell you he is very interested in him. He wants him to have the best of care."

"Is the General implying I have two standards of care: one for officers and one for yard-birds?"

"Well no, but .... '

"It sounds like it to me. You can tell the General for me I *am* offended. I have one standard of care: the best I can do; if the patient is a Private or *even* if he's a pushy-Lieutenant."

I never heard from the General.

I applied to take the written part of the Surgery Boards and discovered I was not eligible, even though I had been a Chief Resident twice. I began in a three-year program and was bound by those rules. I was required to have a two-year preceptorship. After many letters and harsh words, the Surgery Board agreed to accept my civilian consultant as a preceptor. I took my exam almost at the end of my two years in the army.

We had strange cases I had never seen before. We did six thyroid cancers in my tour of duty. That was unusual enough, but one was six years old. He had radioactive iodine studies as an infant and again at age four. He was the youngest thyroid I have ever done. In the sun-baked desert we began to see increasing numbers of skin cancers. With large numbers of young men on the base, we had broken jaws, gun-shot wounds, skiing injuries, plane crashes, rodeo injuries, parachute troops dropped into a cactus jungle, and broken bones of all varieties. With many young wives on the base, we had frequent breast biopsies for fibroadenoma. Even without mammograms, physical findings were so typical I set up an outpatient program for excision of superficial tumors. We did cases under local anesthesia and sent them home after surgery.

When the regular army major came to replace me, he was horrified and stopped the procedure. According to him, all must be admitted and put to sleep. The world was not ready for ambulatory surgery.

Nobody warned me about common army scams. I was snared very quickly. Soldiers do not want to go on bivouac and sleep on the ground and eat from a can. They hate the exercise so bad they are willing to be circumcised to keep from going. A large healthy man showed up asking for a circumcision. He needed it, so I did it. According to army routine, he lounged around in the hospital for a few days while his buddies were roughing it in the desert. When I sent him home, I warned him not to use the affected organ for anything but draining his bladder and not to even think about anything else. That night he was in the ER with the stitches torn loose.

He was grinning from ear to ear and said, "Sorry about that, Doc. Just got carried away in a fit o' passion. Ya know I'm a busy man and I missed quite a few nights."

I explained to him again more graphically what he should do and not do. He was back the next night grinning and laughing. I repaired the damage. When I discharged him the next day, he said, "I'll try to be more careful this time, Doc."

"I am sure you will. I sewed you up with wire and left the ends long." I didn't see him for a week.

My secretary said, "There is a patient out here to see you. He's a little early for his appointment and he sure is walking funny."

The suture line was intact when I cut the wires. He had not been able to get any takers.

Other individual cases were unique and one of a kind. One guy was practicing for the quick draw competition. He might not have had the quickest draw, but he was the quickest shooter. A 45 makes a huge hole in a buttock.

Rodeo riders were as proud of the number of fractures as prizes they won.

Monumental cases came at intervals in the two years. In the first six weeks, I was making rounds when I overheard a conversation between a nurse and patient. The patient was in a body cast with a hip spica. His body and one leg were in plaster.

Before the nurse tossed her head and went off in a huff, I heard the patient say, "I'll talk with the doctor when he gets here."

"What seems to be the trouble? What wouldn't you tell the nurse?"

"Doc, I think I got the claps."

"What! You have been lying here in a body cast for two months and now have gonorrhea? How did this come to be? The incubation period is only a few days--which means you got it here! "

"Well, Doc, ya see, last week was my birthday and my friends, they wanted to do somethin' for me--to give me somethin' I really wanted--ya know I've read just about ever'thing in the library--so they sort of brought up this uh... lady of the evenin' an .... ."

"A floozy in an open ward of a government hospital right here in front of God and everybody?"

"You might call her that, but nothin' took place in the hospital. We knew better than that."

"Where then? Don't tell me you tried to hop on one leg."

"Well ... my friends sort of made this framework in the shop and fixed it to the window--actually the one in your office 'cause it was the closest--and rigged up a block and tackle and swung me out of the second story window by a rope sling and lowered me down to the back parking lot. Ya know the hospital back doors are locked and the lot's empty at night."

"And you went along with this: in a body cast with hip spica dangling by a rope from the second floor?"

"Uh ... well ya see, I sort of had to. They had already paid for the uh ... the party and they don't give refunds. Besides, I wanted my present. I have, uh . . . been out of circulation a long time."

"Did they bring the bed, too?"

"No, nothing that fancy. The, uh ... party took place on a mattress in the back of a pick-up. Ya see, I can't wear many clothes with this cast on an' all, so she ... ."

"Please, spare us the details. And where were your friends all this time?" "Oh, they hung out the windows on the second floor and sang happy birthday. Some cheered while, uh ... the actual birthday party was going on. After the party, they hauled me back up from the lot and through the window. "I looked around at the ward master making rounds with me, "Sergeant, you worked night shift a few days ago. What did ... . "

"Captain, I don't know anything about this. I didn't see a thing out of the ordinary, not a thing."

"Okay, Private Romeo, I hope you have learned something from this expensive lesson. We will start your penicillin after we do the smear. Just remember the first rule about gifts."

"What's that, Doc?

"What's important is not how much the gift costs, but the thought behind it. And what were any of you thinking?"

Some sexual activity was not tolerated. I lost one of my best nurses in the operating room. One day she wasn't there and nobody would talk about it. About the same time, a Chief Warrant Officer disappeared. I finally got the full story from the psychiatrist. They were discharged as homosexuals. I talked with an officer who had been, or who might still be, involved in counterespionage. Foreign agents involved these people or found out about their activity and threatened to expose them to force service to a foreign government. The officer told me, "Those guys don't come on our base; they get Americans to do their job."

"Where are all those agents?"

"Motels along the highway are filled with them."

"If you know about them, why don't you do something about it?"

"If we got rid of them, they would send others we don't know. It's better to have a spy you know than one you don't."

I never did figure out how a nurse in the OR and a Warrant officer in outpatient could do much spying. The Warrant officer had 19 years service.

One night, a motorcycle rider came in with severe head injuries. He would have been killed except for his helmet. It had a large gouge in it where he struck something hard. He was unconscious for days and took up much of the time of the unit personnel. When he woke up, he complained about having to wear the helmet, and complained with shouts and harsh words about the hospital and everything in sight.

One week after he was discharged, he was back in the ER unconscious from another motorcycle accident. He was out again for days. When he rejoined the rest of the world, he was more unpleasant than before and was frothing at the mouth to get out to his cycle. When he had sufficiently recovered, I discharged him again, but with new instructions. I took a witness.

"Sergeant, you can be discharged from the hospital today ... ."

"Great, I'll be on my bike tomorrow."

"Please, let me finish. Sergeant, do you know that while you are in the hospital you are under my command? I am your superior officer."

"I know *that*!"

"Very good. I don't have to explain it. Today in front of witnesses, I am officially giving you an order: you will never again ride a motorcycle either on duty or off duty. This is for the good of the service and for your own good, though you may not understand it."

"The army can't tell me what I do on my own time!"

"Yes, they can. This is not like a regular job. The army owns you, body and soul. We don't need to waste hospital time treating more head injuries."

"You can't do that!"

"Try me. I just did it. A copy of this official order goes on your chart and another will be sent to your company commander. Violate the order and risk court marshal proceedings."

Two days later, my bicycle-riding neighbor, a Judge Advocate General officer, came to see me at home.

"What is this crazy business about telling a guy that he can't ride a motorcycle?"

I explained the circumstances and told him, "I believe the order was the only reasonable thing to do."

"It may have been, but I don't know if it's legal or not. Your patient has come to me for an opinion. I'll have to check things out further up the line."

A month later the answer came from the Pentagon. My order was legal and binding. The patient resigned from the service rather than submit.

Another severe head injury disturbed everybody for different reasons. A seven-year-old came in unconscious from injuries. I helped my neurosurgery consultant operate on the skull fracture. After surgery the patient remained unconscious. He looked normal, but he just lay there with eyes closed. Now we have exotic materials to inject into feeding tubes and central intravenous lines to maintain the nutrition of an unconscious patient. Then, we had simple IVs. We watched this child fade away. The mother faded too. I violated hospital rules and let her stay with her son. Somewhere, I had read about a machine for this problem. The purchasing agent for the hospital was able to get an emergency shipment of a Baron food pump. We ordered a regular tray for the unconscious patient, took out any bones, cut up the food and dumped it into a blender and made mush of it. We mixed it with a little water and put it in the bag for the pump. The pump rotated double rollers for hours on end and pumped food through a small tube into the stomach. Color returned to his cheeks and he gained weight. Three weeks later, he woke up, apparently normal. I have never seen a Baron food pump since. It was worth whatever we paid for it.

I can't say I had no further problems in the service, but the army and the McGinnis family tolerated each other. One day, we were driving to the hospital, a friend said, "Did you know you just waved to the general?"

"He waved first."

"You knuckle head, he's a general. He can do that. You have to salute."

Saluting can be dangerous. As my JAG officer neighbor was riding his bicycle to work one day, he was holding his briefcase with one hand and the handlebar with the other. He released the handlebar to return a salute and hit a fireplug.

I remained a very unmilitary-like officer. But I did a huge amount of surgery and took calls every night for two years. The government had their pound of flesh.

At the end of my two years, I was offered two weeks terminal leave and early out. I refused, took my leave, and drove back from Alabama to sign the roster book. I spent the last day walking around the hospital talking to people I had worked with for the last two years. All the new equipment I had bought was being boxed up at the direction of the new chief of surgery so it could be "surveyed." Included were all my heated hand-washing basins that everybody loved and called "Dr. McGinnis' birdbaths." If there were fewer than twenty or thirty of something, they would be put in a ditch and covered by a bulldozer; burying equipment that would have lasted for years. The regular army major could order his own instruments and the hospital wouldn't lose its allotment the next year. The army was throwing away instruments and equipment I would have to buy.

A few months later, the Cuban missile crisis erupted. Friends of mine who took the early out were called back in. When I left, I was given a set of orders separating me from the service. I was warned to keep them on my person at all times. They didn't say how long. The shreds are still in my billfold. When I went in the army, I was told to have my dog tags on my person at all times. They are on a key ring in my pocket. I served two years and a day. I fulfilled my duty and carry the evidence.

False Start

Central City
29

In late spring of 1961, we saw a light at the end of the tunnel. After four years of college, four of medical school, a one-year internship, four years of surgical residency, and two years in the army, I was to be free of all obligations and could begin private practice. I am not sure I could have endured the first year of collage if I had known fifteen years of hard work lay ahead before I could begin a practice. It was frightening to look beyond the next quarter. In 1946, students were getting in medical school after three years of college and there was talk of reducing it to two. This leftover wartime logic disappeared.

We could hardly believe after all these years we could begin a practice. The problem was where. The desert was different and interesting for two years, but we didn't want to live where grass didn't grow without daily watering and trees didn't thrive. The army offered me a job, but that would mean moving every two or three years. We wanted to pick a place and stay the rest of our lives. Alabama was home, but we agreed we would consider anywhere in the southeast. I wrote letters in answer to ads in the *Journal of The American Medical Association.* A city in Louisiana sounded interesting, until I discovered that it was swamp country. I was not a swamp person, even before our years in the desert. We decided we had rather live someplace in Alabama. We knew there must be a city somewhere out there waiting for us with open arms. After all, I had finished my surgical training, been Chief-Resident twice, passed the written part of The American Board of Surgery examination, and had two years experience as Chief of General Surgery in a 250-bed Army hospital.`

Answers to letters didn't tell the whole story, so I decided to go on leave and look for a place to live and practice surgery. I drove our '57 Silver Hawk across Texas, Louisiana, Mississippi, and Alabama. Most of the trip was at night because the Hawk had no air conditioner, and part of the trip was through desert. Early on the first morning of the trip, I was making good time on flat west Texas roads. There was essentially no traffic, and just after sunrise, the air rushing in the vents still had the chill of desert night. I was startled by a white cloud that covered the windshield and hood. I pulled off the road onto the gravel drive of a tiny country store, the only building I had seen in miles. When I stopped, the whole car disappeared in a smothering cloud of steam.

A stooped elderly man came out of the store, "She's a little hot, ain't she?" After some of the steam cleared, he poured water in the radiator. It ran through the motor and made a puddle in the drive. My heart sank at the sight. I was on leave on a tight schedule as it was; and now I had a broken motor block. How would I ever get to Alabama and look for a place for us to go and how would I pay for a new motor?

The storeowner shrugged and said, "Thay ain't much I can do for ya. We do have a mechanic though."

There was no place to work on cars at the little store. "Where do I go to get him?"

The old man moved and spoke slowly and deliberately. He was in no hurry. I wanted to get on the road as soon as I could, if I could pay for repairs. I had a mental image of my car being held hostage for a huge bill. I had heard about travelers being victimized.

The man squinted into the sun coming over a rise in the distance. "I 'spec I better go get him. Late as it is, he's prob'ly in the hay field. You watch ma little store and I'll drive over and see can I find him."

He left in a pickup with waving fenders that could have used a visit to a repair shop itself. I saw him stop on the hillside at a hay bailer.

The mechanic repeated the process of pouring water through my motor. This didn't reassure me at all about his qualifications or the condition of my motor. He was thick-bodied with red face, wearing old jeans and a faded blue shirt with cut-off sleeves. Hay stuck to his sweaty arms. A stained ragged straw hat shaded his eyes. He went Texas style. Real Texans don't wear sunglasses. They squint. All this said farmer, not mechanic, but he was all I had.

He said, "Not much we can do here. We got to tow her to a garage." He hooked a chain to the front bumper of my car and the back bumper of his. I had to ride in the crippled car, steer and brake, and try to anticipate the tow car stopping. "I'll go sort'a slow. It idn't far; 'bout ten miles."

Distances in Texas are measured with a different ruler. To me, ten miles towed at fifty miles an hour in a crippled car was far. I made the entire trip with my foot over the brake pedal. We pulled into a little garage in a crossroads town. My hayfield mechanic had privileges to use a space for work. All the other people seemed to know him and came over to talk.

Nobody was in a hurry. A few gathered to look at my car, which was unusual in a small town. I visualized more charges for a strange car. I certainly didn't want them to know I was a doctor. All doctors are rich, or that's what most people think. There was nothing for me to do, but lean against the wall and watch.

Finally, the bad news came, "All you've done is blow a freeze plug. The bad news is that we don't have one and can't get one. Nearest Studebaker dealer is 28 miles east. Might get one Monday."

Somebody remembered the bus and after a phone call we had a 67-cent part on the way. The two-hour wait seemed like two days, but the bus and the part arrived. I had visions of the part breaking in installation, but the repair was made and the radiator filled. The mechanic cranked the car and announced that no permanent damage had been done. This was a shade-tree mechanic, but I had brought him out of his hayfield for half a day and was from out of town--to him a tourist. I thought about these things while he washed his hands and came toward me.

"I am certainly glad to have the car fixed. I do appreciate your help. Uh ... how much do I owe you?" I tried to say this with a steady voice, but I don't think I did.

He thought for a moment. I could almost hear a cash register going. "Well, les'see now, the part was 67 cents, so that'll be ... a total of $8.67. Some folks think ya oughta soak the tourist, but I don't. I won't even charge for the tow. I needed to come to town, anyways."

I was expecting ten times as much, which was all I had. There are people who victimize those in need, but there are others who truly try to help. They may be placed in our path and we see them not by accident. I handed him $9.00, thanked him again and left. I didn't have the energy to drive far in the afternoon heat. After a little sleep in a motel, I was back on the road at midnight. I hoped my near disaster did not foreshadow events to come.

I recovered from my trip and toured north and central Alabama, looking for the right place for us to live and me to work. I made phone calls. I visited any city I thought we might be interested in. I visited classmates. Betty had said she would go anywhere I would go. The pressure was on me to find a place. I awoke to brutal facts: every town wanted GPs, nobody wanted a surgeon. I visited classmates who seemed to be doing well in surgery, two years out of training. They might have used some help. They said they were happy to see me, but smiled and told me to try down the road. It was as if I had leprosy. For this I had worked fifteen years. At a class reunion, one of my classmates who gave me the brush-off told me his failure to invite me to practice with him was the biggest mistake he ever made. He desperately needed a partner within the year, but never got one.

After exhausting most obvious choices, I visited the little town of Central City. They desperately wanted a surgeon. The town had a Hill-Burton hospital of 23 beds with an operating room, and emergency room. I met with the hospital board and was assured of total cooperation in an unopposed practice. They assured me of an anesthetist, nursing and technician support and the cooperation of local doctors. They located a house I could afford. The community was smaller than we wanted, but they did want a surgeon. My practice would begin immediately, or so it seemed. This was important because I had no savings to fund a long startup time. With two children, we were about even financially when we went in the service and when we left. I never considered the implications of being the only act in town or the problems of a small hospital. I had never worked in one before. What could be wrong with a place called Central City, U.S.A.?

We moved in the heat of July: two young parents and children, ages two and four. The furniture shipment was delayed, shipped and unloaded into a warehouse at Metroville, 30 miles west, loaded again and sent to Central City. We arrived at a cavernous two-story house two blocks from the center of town. It was almost hidden in the front by two chestnut oaks. Inches away from the southwest corner of the house, was a hackberry tree. Three men couldn't reach around it. Nobody had ever seen such a tree. The tree towered above, wrapped around and was molded by the house. The house rested on the roots of the tree, and protected the trunk from the storms of winter. Even if the tree could have been cut, when the roots collapsed the house would fall. The house and the tree had grown old together. Each depended on the other. A 20-foot gully behind the house didn't add to the charm of the place. I cleaned the paint covering the windows around the front door exposing stained glass evidence of past glory of the old building. A little fresh paint made much of the rest of the house acceptable.

Board members and others tried to make us feel at home and part of the community. In our leanest period before any collections were made, the board took up a collection for grocery money: $62. I wanted work, not charity. Having a wife and two children and no income dulls pride. I accepted that money, but never again. We were invited to all social functions, a problem for Betty with two small children to care for. My office expenses were none. I used the hospital as home base for a while at no charge.

It hadn't occurred to me I had nothing to wear. For two years in medical school I wore jeans and sport shirt. In the last two I wore whites. As intern and resident I wore scrub suits, even to drive home from the hospital. The neighbors thought I wore pajamas to work. In the army I wore a uniform for two years. I didn't have any clothes because I hadn't needed any. I have fixed opinions about doctors, lawyers and other professional people. I believe they should look the part. Nobody wants to find his doctor in dirty jeans and t-shirt. My dad gave me a suit when we began practice. I rotated this with my two sport coats. There was not much variety, but I looked professional--sort of.

Word circulated about the new doctor. The article in the paper confirmed the gossip. Early after our arrival, Betty answered a knock at the door to find a strange-looking woman. I don't know if Neanderthals were black or white. She had the sloping forehead, heavy brows and thick stooped shoulders. She fit the part. She was not just ugly; she was frightening. She didn't ask; she announced that she had come to work for us.

When Betty was hesitant, she said, "You needs hep wi' dese chillun, and I needs a job. Now Miz Ginnis, I needs you and you needs me."

We discovered later she had beat up others in the black community to discourage them from applying for work at our house. Unemployment was widespread in the black community in this rigidly segregated town. I think Betty was afraid not to hire her. Angeline was a good worker, but one day she disappeared. At that time an organization offered to pay bus fare to the north for any black unhappy in the South. She took the free ride to De-troit. She was back in a week, at her own expense. She showed up as if she had never left, mumbling something about, "Dem yankees." She worked several months for us. She even brought us commodity foods at times. We discovered people on welfare sometimes ate better than we did.

We were unprepared for life and attitudes in this town. The first example was the arrival of a series of dump trucks delivering a mountain of topsoil to our backyard, filling to the edge of the gully. This was flat and the only part of the yard in full sun. A road grader then lumbered up to spread the soil for a large garden. The hospital administrator had heard me say something about a garden. All this was done at the direction of the county commissioner and with county equipment.

I got home as the last of the trucks and machines left. The hospital administrator explained how this had come about and with a wink said, "Won't cost a cent. We try to take care of people around here."

The hospital administrator's prior experience was owner of the tractor and farm supply store. J.P. Deer was a stocky talkative man with thick features, who prided himself in knowing people to call to make sly deals to get things done. He told me about the rich man who moved from the city to try farming. He and others had sold him equipment and material until he was ruined financially, gave up and left. J.P. was primarily a salesman. I had not understood that on my first visit to Central City.

Soon after we came, we visited new friends and admired their private paved road of at least 500 feet ending in a huge parking area by the garage. This was done at county expense. This man was proud of the fact that one of the commissioners was a close friend. Men of influence could accomplish much in this county.

The county was dry, but not bone dry. At several functions, men gathered in a group and invited me over. In a whisper, the local lawyer said, "You want a little drink?" They were sharing a bottle of inexpensive bourbon, straight. One night, I was invited to an annual event for men. One of the men cooked something like Brunswick stew, and the crowd went out somewhere in the country and stood around drinking and eating the stew with loaf bread. They brought a rural mail carrier, for entertainment. Whisky loosened his tongue. He babbled filthy stories and foul language. The men laughed and drank. When morning came, the mail carrier went back to his world and the others to theirs.

Like many small southern towns, Central City was a square with the courthouse and pigeon-abused statue in the center. Larger stores were on the streets around the square, or within sight of the courthouse. There were few industries in the town. The lumber mill was the largest. Much of the county was forested. Cutting timber, sawing and planing lumber dominated the town. The town and half the county woke when the whistle blew at 6 AM to call lumberyard workers. Several people worked at a garment mill. Those who ran the bank, lumberyard, garment plant, the local attorney, and owners of stores were respected and influential. Many were on the hospital board. All were white and male. A banker on the board owned much land in the area and sold me a lot near the hospital for an office, to be paid for when I could. I was being encouraged to make bonds I could not easily break. People were sent to visit, entice and entertain, probably by J.P. The local highway patrolman came by and took me out for a shooting lesson. He was in uniform, but said later in the day he would go to the main highway and "make" his cases for the day. That way he would not bother people in Central City.

Church activity is important in small towns. We attended the Methodist church. The pastor visited once. He was a dynamic young man and his sermons were animated. He explained his pulpit demeanor by telling me he went to Atlanta once a year and practiced preaching. He looked at himself in a movie so he could see how dramatic his sermon had been. I was more interested in truth than performance. I asked a question of spiritual nature about doctrine.

The preacher said, "I don't know about that. All I do is sell fire insurance." He laughed. I didn't. I never asked another question. I thought my insurance had been paid for long ago.

We did little shopping in Central City; I remember only groceries, hardware and gasoline. When I bought paint at the hardware store, the owner always discounted the bill. Poor blacks and lumberyard workers paid full price. I was guilty of an extravagance one week when I was feeling prosperous, and that is a relative word. I was in Birmingham to visit my folks and made the mistake of visiting Ann's Antique Shop in Homewood to sort through old furniture. The small shop had furniture and strange things literally stacked to the ceiling. A visit was always good for an hour's entertainment. In three separate places, I found parts of an old secretary of cherry and burl walnut with ebony drop drawer pulls. Behind the glass at the top, somebody had desecrated the inside with gaudy yellow paint. I felt sorry for the abused elegant piece. I splurged and bought the ten-foot tall secretary and a walnut hall tree delivered to Central City for $155.00. It is in our living room, minus the yellow paint. I do not relate it to Central City.

I could have endured the favoritism and elitism if I had been busy. I had been assured of total support of the medical community. The Hospital Board kept the friction among the doctors a secret. Two men supported me and referred an occasional patient.

Reed Bliss agreed to be my first assistant in major surgery. Some told me he was on drugs. Appearances at times said this might be true. The other doctor was a blind man I greatly admired for endurance through disability. When I visited in his office, I noticed the surgical instruments lying on the table. He said he didn't do many lacerations any more, especially when "leaders" were cut. He sent a few patients.

The other two doctors were younger and did most of the practice in the town. They had a disagreement with the hospital about obtaining a surgeon. They supported only themselves.

Dr. I. M. King had a large practice in a nearby community. When I visited him, he told me his son was in a surgical residency and would be back to take over his practice in two years. These three had the largest practices in the area and were sending patients out of town for operations, which could have been done in Central City. I did no minor surgery. The others did everything they could and sent out the rest.

I didn't do many cases, but some were spectacular. In those days I thought I was super-surgeon and was not afraid to tackle anything. The first was a man who slashed his arm and the brachial artery while butchering a goat. This vessel in the upper arm doesn't bleed, it gushes. He was lucky to make it to the hospital. I repaired the artery with one nurse, one anesthetist, and no blood. I never saw my first assistant that day. I did have the luxury of an assistant for a few gastrectomies and a rare gallbladder. I even did a few tonsils. For a general surgeon that's pretty desperate.

One morning, I arrived at the hospital to find an anxious doctor. Dr. Bliss had delivered a baby during the night, but had not called me. In small hospitals babies come, but little else happens at night. Recruiting an operating team after dark was next to impossible because there was one anesthetist, one or two OR nurses, and one laboratory technician, who was also the X-ray tech.

The doctor described the delivery with a look of horror. He was a slight man with halting speech, pale skin and paler watery blue eyes, frequently downcast–but not this day. He never smiled. His tremors were not due to drugs--at least not this time. I looked at the little baby and probably had an equally pained expression. The baby was perfect except for the abdomen. Most of the small intestine and some of the large lay outside the cavity on the abdominal wall surrounded by a thick membrane, indicating a condition that had been present for a long time in the uterus. I sent for the OR team and called Big John. I described the gastroschisis to Dr. Slaughter. He had never seen one either, but we both knew what had to be done. I suppose I called for moral support. We covered the exposed intestines with a towel moistened with saline to move the baby. When the cover was removed, the OR crew was repulsed by this tragic sight. After the baby was asleep, I told the circulator nurse to prep the entire baby below the chin.

The anguish was obvious, even behind her mask. "Dr. McGinnis, I just ... I can't do it."

I prepped the baby and swollen intestines as gently as I could. We draped and began the surgery. I hoped the membrane would peel away easily from the normal bowel, but it didn't. The thick membrane on the bowel came away with great difficulty, if at all. The thickened bowel was stuck together in a lump as if glue had been poured over it. I heard the noise as the circulator nurse hit the floor. The scrub nurse went next. Now, there was no communication with the outside world. We had no intercom. I looked up to ask my first assistant, Dr. Bliss, to break scrub and go for help. The green color showed through his mask. Within seconds he was a crumpled pile on the floor at the other side of the table. My anesthetist, Imogene, was built like a varsity tackle and sometimes talked like one, but nobody is immune to something like this.

I looked over the ether screen. "Now it's just me and you and God to take care of this baby. So help me Imogene, if you pass out, I will find ice water somewhere and throw it on you."

I managed to get the bowel covered with a thin layer of skin using every trick I knew and some I invented. The fainters never revived to help, or at least never acknowledged being awake.

Sometimes the answer is no. The baby died three days later. Most do, even in the best of circumstances. I had warned the parents, but the event was still tragic to us all. Some of the nurses cried with the young parents. I did my usual wondering and soul searching about whether or not I could have done something else, or if somebody somewhere could have done better. In this case somewhere else was out of the question. The parents could barely afford basic needs. I am sure they never paid the bill in Central City.

The next week, I got an early morning call from a classmate, Isaac Norris, in general practice in Clear Springs, a little town 30 miles east. I had not spoken with him since medical school. He had tried to get help from his usual consultants in Birmingham, but they wouldn't come.

He was always a laughing, happy person. This time he sounded breathless and anxious, "Say, Mac, I delivered a baby last night, her first baby, too. The baby's okay, but the mother has been ... well she's been in shock all night; and uh ... something is hanging out between her legs."

"What do you mean, something hanging out? Is it the uterus? Did you pull a lot on the cord to loosen the placenta? Even I remember Dr. Garber told us to never pull on the cord."

"We can't tell what it is. We've tried to push it back in, but we can't. And no, I didn't pull on the cord at all!"

"How low is the pressure?"

"Pretty low; we've been giving blood all night, but it hasn't helped much."

I agreed to come and bring an anesthetist. They didn't have one, even though their hospital was larger. We made a quick trip and found a pale young woman in deep shock. Hanging from the vagina spreading her legs apart was a huge inverted uterus. There was drying of the front side, weeping of the backside and a meat market odor. Replacement was out of the question. Their operating room was about like the one in Central City. I talked to the patient and then privately with the husband. Surgery on a patient in deep shock is high risk, but without it she would die within hours or even minutes. I had never seen an inverted uterus, but the diagnosis was obvious. I knew the condition usually happened in women after many pregnancies. It most often happens after vigorously pulling on the cord. Cause was not the question; the problem was treatment. We moved her into surgery with the last bottle of blood running. As I did a quick scrub at the sink in the hall outside the OR, I thought for the first time how foolish I was. I was about to operate on a condition I had never seen and on a patient rejected by surgeons with more experience and better judgment since they refused to see her. Somewhere in the world, this problem and solution was described in a book. There were answers, but no time to look. My hope was that the course of action would be clear at the right time so I could improvise an operation I had never done for a condition I had never seen. A surgeon can't depend on a force from above to direct his every action if he works in total ignorance. He must be trained and prepared as completely as possible, but nobody knows it all or has seen it all. Sooner or later surprises come. The totally unknown appears. I hear you Big John!! The surgeon must draw on experience and knowledge of the past and improvise. Direction may be indicated from above, but the surgeon must have the skills. As I walked in the room and looked at the pale patient on the table and the grim nurses and doctor, my mind was filled with course of action. We couldn't go below; we had to go above. I had done hysterectomies, but nothing like this.

When I was gowned and gloved, Imogene

induced anesthesia rapidly and with frightening calmness in her red-neck speech, said, "Dr. McGinnis, I sure wish you would get in soon as you can. She has no blood pressure and I can't hear her heartbeat with a stethoscope. I don't know if she's alive or not."

Imogene was rough around the edges, but she was good or some of my patients would not have survived. I am not a fast surgeon, but her words gave me quickness I didn't know I had. We made a lower midline incision. There was no bleeding--a sign of deep shock or death. I slipped a hand in the abdomen and felt the aorta.

There was a faint pulse. "*She's alive*!"

We packed the bowel out of the pelvis with the patient in a deep Trendelenberg position with the head down and legs up because of shock and to let the bowel to fall away from the pelvis. The nurse and doctor held retractors on the stretched and loose abdominal wall. The pelvis was the strangest sight we had ever seen. Where organs should have been, there was nothing except two large ovaries pulled deep in the pelvis. The uterus, big enough for a baby, had been pushed, sucked, or pulled out of the abdomen and turned wrong side out and was hanging through the vagina into the outside world, pulling with it the ligaments with the thumb-sized blood vessels enlarged by the pregnancy. I shouted for: *"Heaney clamps, Kochers, 00-silk and 0-chromic sutures, now!"* There was no please or thank you. The ligaments of the uterus were pulled tightly against the wall of the pelvic outlet. Somewhere in there were conduits for urine: the two ureters. There was no time for identification. The distorted swollen tissues made that impossible. The only hope was to clamp close to the uterus and try to push aside the tissues with ureters; but I was working wrong side out. Not only did I have to work that way, I had to think wrong side out. The ligaments were too tight to get a clamp on.

The two circulator nurses, one scrub nurse and doctor helping me were almost as pale as the patient. I picked the circulator with the most color, "Run your hand under the drapes and push on the uterus, up toward the pelvis. No, push harder! I've got to have slack on these ligaments."

Slowly the slightest looseness appeared, and I clamped, cut and sutured, trying to push the ureter away, but never knowing where it really was.

"Doctor, the uterus is ... it's moving!"

Each time I cut a ligament, a little pull was released and the wrong side out uterus descended, just a little. Finally, when we severed the cervix from the vagina, there was a sudden squishing sucking sound like a cow's hoof pulled out of the mud. Now the pusher nurse was the same shade of pale as the others. She was holding with both hands a bloody, wrong side out uterus.

The loose abdomen came together easily. We did that entire operation in twenty minutes, skin to skin. When we finished the pressure was 120/80.

I looked at Imogene, "Please tell me there is pee in that bag."

"No, Doctor, it's bone-dry; like when we started."

I talked with the husband, thanked the crew, wrote up my charts and waited. An hour later a few drops of urine appeared. We knew she had not had irreversible shock, and at least one ureter was intact. I told her doctor that I wanted an IVP done early the next day and I wanted to be called the very minute that he saw it.

The call came. Both ureters were working and the patient was fine. A week later, she and her husband came to Central City. I am sure the new father would have paid if he could.

I still believe the doctor pulled on that cord.

Slowly we began to collect enough so that we were not fearful about grocery money. I rented an old house for an office and hired a part time secretary, so I could feel like a real doctor. That's not quite true; I needed a place to study for the second part of my boards. I didn't know there are two-week review courses for this, but I couldn't have afforded them anyway. I read five years of five surgical journals. I read Christopher's *Textbook of Surgery* through twice. I made trips to Birmingham to the medical library and read books on physiology, other basic science subjects, and texts in my own library. I had the time. We had a minimum amount of office furniture. As usual J.P. knew how to find items at little or no cost. We furnished the office with heavy oak office chairs, an oak table as a desk, lighter weight chairs with plastic covered seat and back and a 1942 operating table. These used things came from Northington Hospital where I first started to college. I built a bookshelf to hold books for my review work. I had no office surgery. Patients never came in for simple cysts, moles, or skin cancers.

I continued to be pressured to do general practice, but I was determined to be what I was trained to be: a surgeon. Board members and the administrator arranged for me to make house calls at night to see influential people. I tried to explain that I was a surgeon and didn't do general medicine. The administrator took me to shacks where poor blacks lived. As a surgeon, I could do little except make a diagnosis. The hospital did admit emergencies in spite of finances. At times I thought patients might have known more about the hospital than I did. If I saw them at night, when the sun came up they went to the city for surgery. Quality of care was a constant worry. It is difficult to attract good nurses to small hospitals. Only one person was qualified to do specific jobs such as anesthesia, laboratory work, X-ray, or postoperative care. I did much of the post-op care myself. I had time to see patients several times a day. I was in constant fear of a break in sterile technique and was forced to watch the nurses set up the table of instruments and did simple tasks that should have been routine. There were breaks in technique. Surgery was a last resort in this town. People would say with resignation, "He's give up to the knife!"

In the late fall, I left for Duke University for the oral part of my board exam. I spent the night in a motel so I could have a good night's sleep and do a little last minute cramming. I had reduced the practice of surgery to a stack of three by five cards. On these cards were bits of information difficult to remember, but might be asked. I had listed diagnoses and uncommon tumors and laboratory values I would ordinarily look up. The examiner was not limited to surgery. I was expected to know everything in medicine.

Fifty worried budding surgeons gathered in the assigned building. We had all passed the written portion of boards. Half passed the year I took mine. We were assigned a sequence of rotation of rooms. Long benches or chairs lined the hallway outside each room. We were given a two page mimeographed paper. This described a surgical case. The patient had been operated on at Duke twice. They missed the diagnosis, but we were asked to do better.

My name was called and I went into the first room. I recognized the doctor's name as the author of several books. Some of the examiners were well-known authors. I glanced at the wall as I entered.

There were hundreds of pictures of all sizes.

After I introduced myself and sat down, my examiner smiled and said, "Dr. McGinnis, look around the room and point out all the pictures of Dr. William Halsted."

I had spent four years in college, four in medical school, a year in internship, four years in residency to say nothing of two in the army and six months of reading everything I could get my hands on *--for this*!

I didn't look up, "Sir, I know a little about his work in surgery, but I really don't know what he looked like." I didn't care either, but I didn't say it.

He dropped that subject and asked about Dr. Billroth who lived even further back in the nineteenth century. He wanted to know who he married and who his father-in-law was and what that had to with surgery. By the time we got around to the case, my composure was lost. I left the room after my ordeal and sat on the bench in the hall.

As I waited, others staggered out with a look of terror, sweat running down their face, saying things like, "My gosh, listen to what that clown asked me," or "I really blew that one; I'm a goner for sure now!"

There was a delay between sessions in the inquisition rooms, by design, to add to our anxiety. These examinations lasted several hours so we were exposed to a number of men, each with a different approach. One asked me something about an obscure pancreatic tumor. I tried to bluff my way through. He led me down the path to destruction with more questions. When I was hopelessly lost, he looked right through me and said, "Nothing takes the place of knowledge, does it, Doctor?"

You cannot snow men who wrote the book. All through the day we kept coming back to the case they had given us. It could be used as a basis of discussion even if we totally missed the diagnosis as they had at Duke. I decided early in the day this was a case of obscure bleeding from a small bowel tumor, probably duodenum or upper jejunum. Several men tried to shake my diagnosis. If I backed away, I would be seen as inept or wishy-washy. If I persisted and were wrong, I would be seen as hardheaded, stubborn, or obstinate. I decided to be stubborn. I stuck to my diagnosis and my nature. If I went down, I would go in flames. I didn't want to appear indecisive. Somehow all of us managed to finish the day and slink away. I sat on a park bench and talked with a surgeon from Florida. He was ecstatic. He knew he had passed. I later heard he didn't. What is the one about the man who knows not and knows not that he knows not? I slept at least ten hours that night. I went for breakfast before my drive back to Central City. I couldn't eat. I could not physically chew because of pain in my jaws. I had sat on that bench listening to the anguish of others on the day of inquisition. I was all bunched up in a knot with my teeth so clenched, I has actually strained my masseter muscles. Even my shoulders were sore.

I drove back to Central City and told Betty about the exam. I didn't feel good about it because I knew I had missed some questions, and I couldn't identify Halstead's pictures. I went back to my practice. Even without board qualification, I was so-called board eligible. I kept reminding myself that many didn't pass, and they were still good surgeons. Only twenty-five percent passed both parts the first time. I was not sure I could endure the agony of another try. There was even less to do without having to study for boards. The hospital board was supportive, but there was nothing they could do with the other doctors.

Agonizing weeks later, the letter came. I had as much trouble opening the letter as I did with the one from the medical registrar's office when I was a senior in college.

I told Betty two words. "I passed."

She said five words, "Great! When are we leaving?"

"As soon as I can figure out where to go." We never openly discussed our intense problems or leaving. When two people are close, conversation is unnecessary or even painful. Knowledge is there and understood without words or even better than with words. We wanted to protect the children from our problems. They have essentially no memory of that episode. They were happier than we were. They entertained each other.

There was little time to rejoice over passing. We felt that every day in this town was a day wasted and lost. I began a series of phone calls. I now had an extra credit; I was Board certified. Stubbornness sometimes pays off. I got word that only two of us made the right diagnosis of the case they gave us. Both had written a paper on the subject.

I made calls over north and central Alabama. As far as surgeons elsewhere were concerned, I still had leprosy. Working in partnership was out of the question. I began to understand the concept of turf protection. If a surgeon were doing well in an area, he would do what he could to protect his interests and avoid competition. We had come to an area where people said they wanted a surgeon, and that hadn't worked. Maybe I should go where I wasn't wanted. After many calls, Dr. Paul Saulter in Birmingham told me about Anniston. There had been a big argument among the staff in this town. Dr. Horace Ash, the senior surgeon in the town, wanted to give full surgical privileges to his nephew, who had no surgical training. Dr. Ash said he would train him. The staff had a split along specialty lines: surgeons on one side and general practitioners on the other. A surgeon just out of training had seen this problem and started a practice that benefited from the dissension. There was still a draft law. To avoid the draft, this surgeon, Dr. Henry Hawk, joined the National Guard. Others doctors did also for the same reason.

A few months after he began his practice, the Cuban missile crisis happened and the Guard was called to active duty. Dr. Hawk left his practice. The discontent still festered. I also don't believe surgery should be done by those not trained. After a little-soul searching, I decided I was not above taking advantage of the situation. I made visits as I could. I did have some surgery to do. I visited Dr. Frank Caffey, Jr. at his home. I visited Dr. Bob Simmons and Dr. Chilton. There was a strange set of circumstances in their hospital. When the sun went down, there was no doctor in the building. There was a call roster for the emergency room, but nobody wanted the calls. Doctors were busy in the day and tired at night. Nurses had to beg or threaten doctors on call to get them to come. I saw a practice waiting in the emergency room.

* * *

After our leanest Christmas ever, we moved in the dead of the winter of 1961. I didn't know this is the worst time of the year for a surgeon. Surgical practice is directly related to the temperature. The movers loaded our furniture in their van, and we loaded the children and our clothes in the car. My mind was filled with the trials of the past and fears of days to come. I had failed and was defeated. Through my Irish nature, I am stubborn, but I was leaving. Was this weakness, or could it be a sign of strength? Failure should not be the end; it *is* painful and depressing. It should be educational, and followed by a new beginning. I convinced myself I could have stayed, fought the system and slowly built a practice. I did leave through fear. I was afraid the struggle against elements in the community would cause bitterness in me and hardship to my family. At times, the strongest course is change. It is far more difficult. It is easier to stay in a situation even if it's not ideal. Change causes fear of the unknown. I was concerned about losing surgical skills through inactivity. My few months experience convinced me it is difficult, if not impossible, to have quality surgical care in any hospital under thirty to fifty beds. Well-meaning citizens in small towns get funds for a Hill-Burton hospital and put up a building. The townspeople gather and say, "Just look at our fine hospital!" The theory was good; a local hospital for every community, no matter how small. The little hospitals looked good, but the problem was qualified people to staff it and expensive equipment to run it. How does a tiny hospital attract a trained administrator or a surgical nurse? Men and women work in small hospitals if they want to live in their hometown or a town of that size. Physicians were suddenly handed a hospital they were expected to fill even though they hadn't worked in one in years. If three guys in a staff of five get mad, the hospital slowly dies. Dissension destroys it. If three guys on a staff of fifty get mad, it hardly makes a difference. If a surgeon is the only act in town, what happens if he gets sick in surgery? I have seen it happen since, but when we went to Central City I thought I would last forever. What about time off? I took call every day and night for two years in the army and my entire time in Central City. There might come a day when I wanted time off.

I did not want to be molded and shaped by the town as the hackberry tree was molded and shaped by the old house. I could never fit that town like the tree fit the house. We could never grow old together. We left that place and shook the very dust from our feet. We never looked back. We took nothing but experience from Central City.

Second Chance

Sink or Swim

30

We got to Anniston too late in the day to unload furniture, so we spent a night in the Van-Thomas Motel. We had rented a house from Bob Simmons near the shopping center in Lenlock. Bob said pay him when I could. The next day, Betty supervised unloading of the truck. I supervised the unloading of what little furniture I had in my office, rented on credit from Dr. Chilton. He owned three old buildings on East Tenth beginning at the Quintard corner. Dr. Maurice Richard, a G.P. with full surgical privileges, was in the west side of my building. Dr. Chilton's office was a few feet east of our office.

I had one office, one exam room, one waiting room, and a workroom for supplies. Dr. Hawk had worked in the office a few months. The facilities were sparse, but the rooms were large and the price was right. There was no air-conditioning. The ten-foot ceilings helped and I put an old window unit in the treatment room. I hung my plastic shingle on the front of the building. There was a sign painted on a front window: "Colored entrance in the rear." I didn't want to rock the boat at this early stage in a new town, so I left it. I still had the old furniture from Northington Hospital. I bought surgical instruments and an autoclave from General Surgical Supply in Birmingham, also on credit. We might be short financially, but I had to have good equipment and supplies to do surgery. I bought a desk kit for a reception desk, also on credit, and put it together in the next few days.

I went to the hospital that first day. I had temporary privileges, but wanted to be put on call. I was anxious to do what others didn't. When I walked in the hospital, I was being paged. I hadn't been exposed to a loudspeaker in years.

When I answered the page, a smirky voice said, "This is Frank Caffey. I don't need a thing. I thought you needed the advertisement."

I arranged for real advertisement: a simple announcement of small size. The man at the paper said with a little grin, "We'll help you by doing a feature article on you and tell how good you are."

I thanked him and told him the announcement for three consecutive days was adequate. That was the ethical standard. In the years that followed, there were many of those feature articles. Once, ads in the phone book, newspaper or billboards were thought not in keeping with standards of the profession and unethical. There are no standards for advertising in today's world. One of my first calls and correspondence in my new office was a letter and call from Dr. Hawk, telling me he would be back; all of his friends would send their patients to him and I didn't stand a chance. I should have saved and framed the letter, but I didn't.

I was the last to perform another ritual. I was told the new man should visit and introduce himself to surgeons, internists, or family practice doctors. This was an interesting and sobering experience. It identified friend or foe. I received a cool reception from surgeons. One told me I wasn't needed, wasn't wanted, and would never make it. I told him I was glad to know exactly how he felt and left his office. Another surgeon, Joe Henry gave a halfhearted welcome. Turf protection is a knee-jerk reaction. After Joe thought about the situation a bit, he called to suggest we might rotate calls. He had been unable to swap calls with other surgeons. I elected to take off on Thursday afternoon since Joe took Wednesday. We began rotating off-day calls within the week. This lasted until he retired. He asked me to take his calls and make rounds for him the first week. I was attempting to see patients on Unit 20 when the head nurse, Sara Green, told me it was not visiting hours and I would have to leave. She was a good nurse, but wasn't known for diplomacy. After this rocky beginning, she became a good friend.

I visited family practice docs. Except for the two with surgical privileges, they were more congenial. I had something to offer; I was willing to take any or all of their ER calls. I signed up some as I visited, and others began to call. In the first year, I once worked 13 nights straight. Sometimes the emergency room was crowded, and no doctor wanted to come after a busy day. There were drunks and bums, and the doctor on call was expected to see them. I sorted through this collection of humanity, kept the surgery and referred medical and pediatric problems. The nurses discovered I was willing to come, so there were a few unofficial referrals. My office practice was essentially zero at first until patients began coming in for suture removal. Betty was my only employee. She was the only one who would work on credit. Because she had no experience in a doctor's office, we practiced our routine before the first patient came in so we wouldn't look clumsy. When there was blood in minor surgery, sometimes she had to go to the alley for a breath of fresh air. There was little time for home life.

One courtesy visit to a doctor brought an unexpected result. Dr. Batson said he would take his own ER calls, and then asked if I would help him in surgery. He was part of the problem. In his late 70's, he had full surgical privileges through a grandfather clause. He was allowed to do surgery, but had never had training. He added, "I pay cash--$25 for an appendix." I admired him for continuing to provide a service for his parents of many years, but I couldn't agree with once-in-a-while surgery by a general practitioner. I understood his problem: he had to have another doctor in the room when he did surgery. Surgeons wouldn't help and he had to call on doctors with no more training than he had. What he offered wasn't fee splitting, but pay for services. The patient needed to have at least one surgeon at the table. I agreed and helped him fumble through two appendectomies.

One day he called with a strange request. He asked me to see a patient the day before surgery. She had had abdominal pain for several weeks, tenderness over a vague mass, and a history of irregular, scant periods. I had no clear diagnoses, but agreed she needed surgery. When she was asleep, prepped, draped and both of us scrubbed and gowned, Dr. Batson said, "Why don't you go ahead and do this one?"

When I recovered, I said, "Dr Batson, this patient went to sleep thinking you would do her surgery, She signed the permit for you to do it. For me to operate in secret is ghost surgery. I can't do that." I could see him taking a deep breath to begin a tirade. I said, "If her husband is in the wafting room, I will talk with him and tell him you have asked me to do the surgery. If he agrees, I will operate and tell her when she is awake."

Her husband agreed. When I came back in the room, Dr. Batson threw down his gown and gloves and left without a word, leaving me to operate without an assistant. When I opened and sucked out the blood, I found a ruptured tubal pregnancy. This happened weeks ago and the placenta had implanted in the mesentery of the transverse colon. It had partly separated to cause the bleeding. I added to the flow by peeling off the rest of the placenta. There was no choice; almost half was loose. I finally got everything out without taking the blood supply of the colon. I tied and sutured what I could, but blood was still coming from the whole raw area. Anything I put on to stop bleeding floated away. I held layers of gelfoam with abdominal packs and closed the abdomen over them. I left a small opening in the center of the incision and brought out corners of the packs. I scheduled her for another surgery the next day.

I didn't breath easily until I pulled the packs 24 hours later. I saw no bleeding and closed the center of the incision. I called Dr. Batson both days. His answer was little more than a grunt.

Dr. Hawk came back to town and did his referrals.

Dr. Batson still did trauma in the ER. Some months after we came, one night I watched him suturing a face. He sniffed and wiggled his nose. I have had to resort to wearing a mask or twisting my neck to use a shoulder when I had the sniffles. Dr. Batson grabbed a sterile sponge off the Mayo stand, blew his nose, threw the sponge in the kick-bucket and took another stitch without changing gloves. The patient left with his entire left eyebrow shaved and sutures in place.

It's hard to stop something you have done for a lifetime. He eventually did stop ER and surgery and limited himself to his office until he died. He provided care to a huge number of patients for years. Many of the office visits were at no charge.

I was assigned a monitor to oversee my surgery. The rule may still be on the books, but is not carried out to the degree mine was. Dr. Henry, ol' eagle eye, was there for every case, reviewing the chart and first assisting. He finally announced further supervision was unnecessary.

When we came, Anniston Memorial Hospital was a collection of units or blocks connected by long halls: a cantonment type structure built like Northington Hospital during World War II. The old OR was a collection of drab and dismal small rooms. I heard all the stories about the days gone by when an administrator had pay air conditioners installed in each room. Nurses said if they worked with a cheap surgeon who wouldn't put a quarter in the machine, everybody roasted in the summer. In the midst of difficult surgery the quarter might run out, and the circulator would be sent for change amidst a shower of harsh words.

I scheduled my first real case, referred by Frank Caffe, in this dreary unit. I was glad it was a hemorrhoid; they're painful, but always do well. The surgery in the old OR was uneventful. I made round the next day; with only one patient I couldn't say rounds. Pain is expected after a hemorrhoid operation, but not like this patient. I turned her over and couldn't believe what I saw; the skin of the buttocks, thighs and the back all the way to shoulder level was swollen, red, and hot. Within minutes I had her on intravenous antibiotics. I tried to get telephone consultations with everybody I could think of who might help. Nobody had ever heard of such a thing. In each new day, I lived in hope the antibiotics would work their magic. Nothing changed; she didn't get better. In my mind, I heard Dr. Slaughter's words again about something taking the wind out of my sails at unexpected times. I didn't know he meant something like this. I had other admissions to the hospital. Word hadn't gotten out about my first case. Other patients came and went, and my hemorrhoid patient stayed as my albatross. After what seemed an eternity to her and to me, all findings cleared. She had a good result after so long a time. I was fortunate she was an understanding patient.

A new south tower OR opened shortly after we arrived. It was officially opened at three in the afternoon. I did the first case in the unit and then two others that night--all trauma dredged from the ER. I saw little of my family on nights like that.

The old ER was one large room with small areas along the edge with curtains, which could be pulled if the patient must be exposed or too much blood spilled. It reminded me of a busy bus station with constant pacing back and forth of nurses and patients with all sorts of complaints and injuries. If possible, doctors examined patients with their clothes on as they sat in a chair. There was a waiting list for a cubicle with curtains. A constant babble of voices in the room, mixed with an occasional grunt or yell, added to the confusion. Doctors repaired lacerations while visitors and other patients watched. The ERs began as a place to bring patients for admission and limited trauma care. People began driving faster, climbing higher, cutting deeper, and shooting more. Rich and poor alike demanded care at all hours for any illness, even if self-limited. The ERs in community hospitals became areas of bedlam faced with tasks they were never designed for.

The new ER opened with two rooms of two beds each, separated by a curtain. Between the two rooms was a dental room with chair and new equipment. We couldn't entice a dentist to come to the hospital. Eventually the hospital sold the dental equipment. After an experience in the old Tower of Babel, the unit seemed great. Rooms were big, bright, and cheerful. Men who design buildings don't live there. The ER was an improvement, but inadequate the day it was built. There was no work area for nurses and doctors to write on charts. In the past twenty years, technology had given us a vast array of supplies and equipment to treat patients. We had little storage space. The concept of quick availability had not yet arrived. Many of our supplies were stored in central supply.

We made a makeshift work area and stole a room from physical therapy. The unit became a familiar place. I saw derelicts and drunks, but others were transients with injuries or good patients whose own doctor wouldn't come. Some older doctors advised me to "Get paid while tears are in their eyes." One always carried a hundred dollars in change for the smart guy who said, "Oh, I can pay you, but all I have is a hundred. You don't have change? Too bad, I'll see you next week."

I couldn't do it. I couldn't hustle people for money when they were sick or hurt. I took money from those who offered to pay.

Unlike Central City, I had few visits from local citizens. Toward the end of the first month, a vice-president of a bank visited me. He was after an account for his bank. I almost laughed. On our first day, I had gone to the nearest bank--the Anniston National Bank--and deposited our entire savings: $264. At this stage, only a few dollars were left. Even desperate vice-presidents aren't interested in accounts of less than a dollar. He had not considered I might be in dire financial straits. After all, doctors are rich. He smiled, shook hands and left, still encouraging me to open an account. I smiled too, but not for the reason he thought.

After he left, Betty left since we had seen our few patients and the office was empty. Bob Simmons called to apologize for not sending any surgery. He said in the last month all referred for surgery had their own surgeon. He allowed patients to make their own choice. He later sent those who asked his advice. Frank Caffey's patients expected to be directed. I sat in the empty office and began to look at our situation. In the first month in Anniston, I had done more cases than the entire time in Central City. They were not as spectacular, but they were cases. I had also done what I had not done in Central City: seen large numbers of patients in the emergency room. This was great, but I was broke. I had a dollar or so in my pocket and less than ten in our account. Collections were almost nothing. Those with insurance didn't want to pay until their insurance paid, and we had received no insurance payments.

A call to Frank Caffey about turnaround time convinced me something was terribly wrong. I called Blue Cross and after going through fourteen offices, found the right one. They were sending my checks to Lloyd Noland Hospital, as they had done when I was chief resident two years before. They ignored my new address. The Blue Cross lady gave a limp promise to correct the error. After I hung up, I looked at my desk and thought *promises don't help*. I was looking at bills for over a thousand dollars. I had begun on credit, but credit had caught up. I had heard stories of doctors who didn't break even for a year. Who did I think I was to make it from point zero in a month? Just because I was willing to work hard, I thought I could begin on a shoestring and survive. At least there was security in the army. There was none in Anniston. For a change I did not have call in the ER so I drove home slowly while I brooded.

I arrived to another crisis. Betty had heard Owen talking to a neighbor across the fence in the back yard, "Yes, ma'am, Mother works in Daddy's office, and she's going to keep on working 'til he can afford to get somebody better. "Betty fussed at him--just a little. He pouted and said he was going to run away from home. She said, "Okay, buster, don't forget your toothbrush."

In a few minutes, she took a break from the

kitchen and discovered Owen and his toothbrush was gone. She didn't really think he would go. Betty was madly searching the house and yard and down the street and toward Lenlock Shopping Center where all the traffic is. Owen was nowhere to be found. He had wrapped his toothbrush in Kleenex and left through the front door. He walked toward the street, thought for a minute at the curb, and then walked down the sidewalk until he came to the corner, then thought again. His mother had told him to never cross the street so he didn't. He turned right and walked the next block. At the next corner he turned right again and walked farther. At the next corner, he turned again because he couldn't cross the street. At the next corner, he suddenly realized he could see his own house and smell supper cooking. He decided maybe he wouldn't run away, at least not until after supper. His appetite saved him. His mother was too glad to see him to scold him much.

I should have enjoyed my time off, but I was haunted by the specter of a thousand dollars in bills. Was I about to fail a second time? I sympathized with Owen, but I couldn't run away. I had to face my problems on Monday.

After I finished surgery and rounds on Monday, I made the dreaded trip to the office. A patient had come in and paid a sizeable bill. Then another came to pay. On Tuesday--wonder of wonders--the Blue Cross check came. Sometimes, the check-is-in-the-mail story is true. I made my deposit. I still didn't have enough to pay the bills, but I had enough to do what I had done when we went into the army. Moves bring unexpected expenses and I couldn't pay all our bills then either. I wrote a letter to each creditor and sent a partial payment. I told them we would pay as soon as we could. I shuddered a little as I mailed the letters. This was not the way a new surgeon makes a good impression. Maybe that banker would get the message and understand why I couldn't open an account. As the months moved on, we paid our bills, but stayed about even financially

In midsummer, it became obvious we needed different housing. Owen would begin kindergarten somewhere. The school had to be convenient since we had only one car. At Lenlock, there was too much traffic so close to the shopping center. Owen might run away again. We had rented long enough. But without a down payment, what could I do? Young families have the greatest needs when they have the fewest dollars. Hard work and good intentions don't count. Banks wanted securities in some form to loan money for houses.

Frank Caffey's brother-in-law, Emmett Freel, was in the real estate business and in the process of opening up the Golden Springs area for new homes. We picked a large corner lot in an area with only one other house. Emmitt "gave" us the lot and took a second mortgage to be paid off in two years. We used the lot as a down payment for the construction of a home by the real estate company. All this was necessary, but probably illegal. We picked a plan and the house was built to our specifications, up to a point. This was an interim house and had compromises such as small rooms and no air-conditioning. We learned a lot. I didn't check closely enough on the contractor and sub-contractors. I learned how quickly shoddy work can be covered up. Toward the end of construction, I did catch mistakes such as windows of the wrong size, but the field lines for the septic tank were covered before I saw them. They went out 18 months later. Sub-contractor work is guaranteed one year. Hoyt Fair came to do the landscaping work and had planned to do the usual stripping of the lot to plant grass. I walked with him and explained that we wanted our yard left in its natural state as much as possible. We left all the sugarberry bushes, haw trees, muscadines and trees except for blackjack oaks. We did clear and plant the front yard in grass, but the back and sides were left wooded. We planted grass in all but one area of the front yard toward the west edge. I told Hoyt I didn't want grass there, but I did want the soil worked.

"Well, whut do you want planted if ya don't want grass?"

"Peas."

"Oh, you mean something like sweet peas. Yes, they are pretty."

"No, I mean crowder peas. I would take purple hulls if you can't get crowders."

"*Peas* in the front yard?"

"I like peas, and besides that's where I'll have my garden next year, and I don't want grass in it."

Hoyt left, shaking his head and mumbling something about, "Crazy doctors." He planted the peas.

When we moved for the fifth time in three years, the kids asked how long we would stay there. I told them a long time, but Betty and I agreed on five years.

I began to take stock of my status in the office. I was working over eighty hours a week. I had surgery most mornings, and some office practice. All through the day and night I went to the emergency room. On occasions, I spent the night in the hospital. I had picked up some good patients; some are still my patients. However, nobody warned me that the new doctor collects rejects from the medical community. We saw patients whose bellies looked like a road map. There were scars from every surgeon in town and some from Birmingham. They think one more operation will make them like new. These patients take a long time to work up. They usually don't need surgery, but there is always the fear that something will be missed. We saw a few true hypochondriacs. Some become angry if I didn't furnish them a disease to fit their complaints. I did see a patient in her 60's with a history of admissions for abdominal pain and obstruction every few years since surgery as a child. She and her doctors knew the appendix was gone because of the scar in the right lower quadrant. I agreed to operate to try to free adhesions. I also took out the appendix. She had only drainage of an abscess as a child. I could not restore the years she lost.

The new doctor sees drug addicts. I was taken in by a paregoric addict. Who would have thought anybody would like that stuff?

Addicts are good actors. Once a man came in my office without an appointment and demanded to be seen immediately for severe back pain. He was told if he waited we would work him in when we could. After a few minutes, he stood in the middle of the waiting room and screamed, "AAAAAAHHHH."

They brought him back to the treatment room. He gave the classic story of being from out of town and not having his medicine. He gave a history of many admissions for back problems, and he did have apparent muscle spasm and pain. He was willing and anxious to go to the hospital, but wanted a shot to ease the pain until he could get there. I told him I would not give a narcotic to a man who had to drive himself, but I would give a muscle relaxant. We had a few sample ampoules of a new drug. He still wanted the shot for pain and reluctantly took the muscle relaxant shot. He walked well as he left. I thought, *That new stuff must be pretty good.*

After he left, I called the hospital admissions office and gave the man's name and diagnosis. There was silence at the other end of the line and then a confused answer, "Doctor McGinnis, what must I do? He's already scheduled for admission by two other doctors." I checked; he did get narcotics in those offices.

The new doctor collects bad-pay patients. Not true charity patients who need help and can't pay, but those who have no intention of paying, even though they could. The identity of these people was a surprise. I was flattered that a man who owned a business with several employees and lived in a big house on the mountain had come for surgery. In short order, I saw several members of his family. He told us his business was self-insured. When we finished the surgeries, he disappeared and ignored the bills. I did a little checking and found he owed everybody in town. He had a big house because he didn't pay for anything and had no insurance. There were others. I checked my collection rate and found it less than 50%. Over half my work was for free. My medical school didn't teach economics. I didn't even know what to charge patients. For doctors to discuss fees is a violation of the restraint of trade laws. I talked to Joe Henry and Ray Taylor. They gave me a list of their charges. I didn't feel like a law-breaker. I set my fees a little lower since I was the new doc.

I sent a final notice statement to my patients whose bills were overdue. If we received a reply, promise, sad story, or an outright lie that sounded good, we didn't pressure them. I have always been a sucker for a sob story. The rule in the office is to take the stories at face value. I had rather be taken advantage of by some than push others who are truly having troubles. All who didn't respond in some way, we turned over to the collection agency. My practice dropped 50%; I thought I was ruined, and we had just moved into a new house. The next months showed me I was doing half the work, but my income was down only 10%.

Another crucial decision was forced on me about this time. Sam Singletree, a prominent physician, had asked me about the Country Club. He pressured me to join a second time. At this stage in my life, I didn't feel like country club material. I didn't have time for social life. I didn't play golf and wasn't interested in learning. A nice place to eat Sunday lunch was great, but there was the matter of money.

While I was thinking on these things, Sam said, "One thing's for sure, a doctor just can't make it in Anniston unless he belongs to the Country Club."

"Sam, I just made up my mind. I appreciate the invitation, but I don't believe I will join."

I didn't enjoy free time now that my practice was reduced. I began to look for more things to do because I was a new doctor and I didn't want to catch "The Disease"' I learned of the disease when I was a first year resident in Virginia. A new surgeon had come to town fresh out of residency. I had finished helping him do a case and was talking to an older OR nurse who was wise in the ways of men and medicine. The new surgeon had been curt and surly with everybody in the room. He complained about the anesthetic, the instruments, the lights, and I didn't hold the retractors right. He left storming down the hall in the direction of a nursing station to complain about the preparation of the patient for surgery, saying something about not being able to build a practice if he couldn't get any help. I licked my wounds and made an unkind observation to the nurse. She said, "Oh, he's okay, He's a good surgeon; he's just got 'The Disease,' and in time he'll get over it. Right now, he's got Doctoritis. He may wound a few of us, but it's not a fatal disease. It will pass."

I didn't understand that day, but as I saw men begin their practice, I began to appreciate what that wise nurse said. Doctors, especially surgeons, finish eight years of college and medical school and five years of residency and internship, and maybe two years in the service and come to a town to try to begin a practice from point zero. If they join a group on a salary, 'The Disease" may be mild. If they begin alone, it can be severe. If they have climbed a long way up the educational and social ladder, pressure and anxiety is greater. These men see friends earning a living ten to fifteen years before their practice begins. The new surgeon is consumed with the pent-up pressure and frustration of the past years. Somebody has supported him financially and emotionally for years and he is goaded and driven to succeed, not by family, friends, or colleagues, but by a fire within. The great push is not just financial, though finances are part of the problem. There may be debts. There is usually a family to feed. The pressure is on the new surgeon to build a practice that didn't exist before. In times gone by, he couldn't publicly announce his availability and training. There was such a thing as ethics. Besides, such a thing would have been in poor taste. He must create a practice within ethical standards. The new surgeon was under pressure to make it, to succeed, to build a practice in his chosen field; he was years behind when he began and driven by pressures within. Now I *might* have had a symptom or two.

My advertisement came from the ER. I treated severe facial injuries: the banker's son with lacerations across his entire face, the contractor's grandson with even worse lacerations, the professional guitar player with all the extensor tendons cut in his left hand, and the teenager who took my scar on her forehead across the stage in Atlantic City in the Miss America Pageant. Good results are worth more than ads in the paper. A satisfied patient sends five more. A disgruntled patient keeps ten away. In the first year, I also took on two burns: a child with 55% burn and an adult with 85%. They took much of my time. I grafted the man's entire body from the right shoulder. In his six-month stay he wore out a Striker frame. In three months the child said one word to me. When I told her and her mother she could go home, she said "Bye."

Because I did facial trauma and the hospital was too cheap to buy what I needed, I bought my own plastic surgery instruments and kept them in a soak pan in the ER. My scrub-nurse of 38 years worked for the hospital at the time. She says they always tried to hide when I came in to do a case. Invariably, some other doctor had complained about the instruments in the ER; they looked like leftovers from a hysterectomy. A bright young nurse would say, "Oh, I know where the nicest little scissors and pick-ups are." So she opened the pan with the label that said 'For Doctor McGinnis Only.' I arrived to find my tools in use, sent for reprocessing or in the laundry. Now, I *might* have said a word or two about my instruments. Is it my fault I wanted everything just right? If you had your nose half cut off, you wouldn't like it put back almost right or just close would you? You would want it put on just right *wouldn't* you? I wanted my instruments and my help to be just right.

South to Randolph
31

I made a few calls to doctors in nearby towns. That's ethical! I drove up to do a case in Piedmont. The surgery went well, and I had forgotten about it when the referring doctor called a month later. The voice on the phone said, "That appendix you did up here ... have they ... did they pay you?"

I had to admit I had no idea if they had or not. I offered to check. He stammered, stuttered and hung up. Green as I was, I didn't figure it out until the line went dead. He was looking for a payoff--a split fee. He never called again. I wouldn't have gone, but others did. I did one case in Heflin. The OR technique was clean, but not sterile. I eliminated two small hospitals. I next tried Wedowee, thirty miles south. Willis Israel ruled the hospital like a medical monarch. He started in my class in medical school and dropped out a year to teach. He had a huge practice and was interested in having surgery done in the Wedowee Hospital. I told him from the first, some operations shouldn't be done in a small hospital. He agreed to refer difficult cases if I would do the others there. The hospital was a little over 30 beds, but adequate for uncomplicated surgery. The OR crew was reasonably trained and pleasant. The atmosphere was low-key and relaxed. The staff was always happy and eager to help. Willis told the families they couldn't expect a surgeon to come from Anniston to operate without paying that day. This wasn't my idea, but I couldn't argue with it. Thursday was my afternoon off and sometimes day off. It became my day to operate in Wedowee. I spent many lonely hours driving crooked Randolph County roads. Some nights, as I topped a hill and dropped into a bottom, I sank into a sea of swirling fog, hiding everything but a few feet ahead. Trips home were slow.

Willis did send a few patients to Anniston, and came to scrub in when I operated. Most of the cases he called me for were appropriate for a small hospital, but not all. He once called for a hernia; nothing unusual he said, but they couldn't reduce it. I arrived to find a red faced man of 65 who weighed at least 300 pounds and was short of breath at rest. The hernia was monstrous and had been out three days, long past the safe period for taxis or reduction of the hernia by pressure. Willis was as jovial and unconcerned as the patient. He was almost as round as the patient. There had to be something in the Wedowee water.

Willis knew I would operate once I had driven down. We opened this hernia at surgery to confirm my worst fears. The sac was filled by the cecum dilated to the size of the man's head, with early gangrene on the side. It was too big to reduce through the small hernia opening to the abdomen where it belonged. I couldn't get around it enough to consider resection. Even simple pressure might rupture the thin gangrenous wall in this first part of the colon and turn this into a disaster. I was faced with a condition I had never seen. He would not survive a blowout of the gangrenous wall. I had to invent an operation I had never heard of. I hear you again, Big John!

I made a small incision in the lower abdomen just above the hernia incision and pushed a Foley catheter into the abdomen. I threaded the balloon end down the abdominal cavity and out the tight hernia opening holding the bowel. I pulled it until several inches lay by the distended cecum. I made a purse string suture around the gangrenous part. We packed everything in case of spillage of liquid feces. One nurse held constant suction to the Foley catheter. I am sure everyone silently prayed as I put a quick stab wound in the balloon-like bowel. At the same instant I pushed the Foley catheter through the hole in the bowel, I tightened the purse string, and the scrub nurse inflated the balloon. All the while, the suction was making sickening slurping noises in the liquid doo. The cecum collapsed around the catheter. I put a reinforcing suture about the catheter and inverted the area of gangrene. We pulled gently on the catheter, and the collapsed cecum fell back in the abdomen. We had deflated the cecum, reduced the hernia, and created a cecostomy--not in the usual way, but a cecostomy nevertheless. We had no spillage, but we had entered the colon so there was a chance of infection. We used wire sutures for the hernia repair and gave post-op antibiotics. The catheter would decompress the bowel and could be pulled out when the tract was established.

With his size and the risk of infection, I worried about healing. I shouldn't have. Our patient had lived with the nagging hernia for years and avoided surgery until it was forced on him. After he discovered his hernia was gone, he was up the next day wanting to get out of the hospital to go fishing.

Willis called once for a gallbladder case. He didn't tell me about the jaundice and length of illness. He asked me to make arrangements for my own anesthesia. His usual people were unavailable. I asked Sandy Best, our only anesthesiologist. I never liked him since the night I asked him to give an anesthetic to a 350-pound woman who was bleeding to death from an ulcer. He refused because she was a poor risk. After I threatened to record his words, he did the case, but made major charges for extra risk. He rarely smiled and when he did, it was a smirk when he told a junior high dirty joke. He was a pompous, arrogant know-it-all surrounded by southern ignorance. He was competent. He told us he was. He told us he was the best. Besides, he was the only one I could get that day.

* * *

A mile south of Highway 78, 431 South makes long sweeping curves through a section called the Narrows. It's a deep cut through rock at the foot of a mountain. Walls are weathered and worn to shades of gray. As the sun moves, shadows twist and change along the wall. Rivulets of water trickle from cracks in lower rocks. In winter, trickles turn to icicles. In cold dimness of early morning they hang white like a giant's gloved fingers, a startling contrast to the weathered walls. At midday, icicles are translucent, wet and glistening.

In summer, moss, ferns and wildflowers grow from gaps in the rocks. Off to one side, a branch winds through swampy areas. Patches of deep woods filled with poplar, oak, sourwood, gum, and big leaf magnolia almost hide the little stream. Laurel, azalea, hydrangea and wild flowers fill the under-story.

Shades of fall almost demand a stop at one of the parking areas to see the colors and listen to sounds of the stream. Nature's big fling before the drabness of winter brings on a touch of sadness.

Beyond the Narrows, the road winds through rolling hills then drops through low areas shaded by old hardwoods. Houses, barns, fields and upland woods are scattered along the road.

In this drive there is beauty in any season.

* * *

Sandy saw nothing, but drab asphalt leading him to a case when he had nothing else to do. To him, a trip down 431 South was a trip into wilderness. To him this scene implied ineptitude. We drove into the town and to the little hospital. Sandy's eyes got wider and wider. I saw the patient, heard the full history and had my own worries.

With a worse than usual frown, Sandy called a conference in the OR, "When has this anesthesia machine been standardized?"

Willis said, "I don't know, always seems to work when Ivory Suit uses it."

" If it hasn't been checked recently, I can't trust it. I cannot judge the amount of nitrous oxide with a machine I am unsure of. We will use cyclopropane. I can judge that without a machine. This floor is conductive, isn't it?"

"I don't know. It's the only one we've ever had. We've always thought it was pretty nice."

"That's not the point. Cyclo' is highly explosive, one spark and we blow out the end of the hospital. Everyone will just have to operate barefooted. We can wet the floor a little to make sure there is no spark."

"You mean take off our shoes?"

"No, shoes and socks, down to bare feet."

"Sandy, are you going to check the nurses' underwear? Sometimes nylon causes a spark." He huffed and mumbled something about *him* being in charge of this operation. *He* would give the nod for the surgery to start.

So we gathered in this little OR: Sandy sitting on his stool at the head of the table with his lip stuck out, still warning us of the dangers of the smallest spark, well-fed Willis sweating and complaining about the cold floor, a scrub nurse, a circulator nurse with fresh polish on her toenails, and a worried surgeon; all with rolled-up pants legs so Sandy could see our bare feet on the cold wet floor. I had worries of my own. I couldn't use a cattery because of the explosion hazard; we had to tie even the smallest bleeder. This wasn't a simple gallbladder; I had to explore the common duct and take out stones. Finally, I was ready to close and asked for the T-tube.

Willis said, "T-tube ... T-tube ... I think I saw one

of those a month or so back ... somewhere."

I had a sinking feeling. The lump in my throat was cold as my feet. They found the tube--the only one they had. It was rotten and the wrong size. I was left with an open duct 35 miles from any supplies. We improvised with a straight catheter. That's not the way the book says drain an opened common duct, but it worked. As we closed, in spite of cold feet both literally and figuratively, we began to relax a little. Sandy looked around the room for the first time. His eye traveled over the shelves on the inside wall to the window unit air conditioner in a cutout space high up in the outside wall. Suddenly, Sandy began to choke and sputter, gasp, stammer and point. We thought he had been breathing his own gas.

"Look, just look! It can't be!"

We followed his trembling finger down from the air conditioner along the wire down the wall to a huge naked splice just before the plug in the wall. Willis said, "Sandy, don't worry about it. It hardly ever sparks anymore. Just don't jiggle it."

Sandy became a little cyanotic. He was afraid to breathe. As he extubated the patient, he kept turning to look at the splice. He had us walk on the opposite side of the room as we moved the patient out.

As we left the little hospital and drove north into shadows of afternoon, Sandy was still visibly shaken. He did collect his fee; he wasn't that shaken. Sandy looked back at the hospital and said, "Never again."

"Don't worry, Sandy. I won't ask."

Sandy stayed several years and then suddenly left to go back north. I hope he is happier wherever he is, but I doubt it. I always thought our trip to Wedowee helped him make his decision to leave.

The patient did well, the machine *had* been standardized and the floor *was* conductive and my feet are *still* cold.

* * *

I made many trips to Wedowee over the next few years. As suddenly as he began sending patients, Willis stopped. Monarchs do things like that. Several patients came to see me for an opinion and said they were sorry they couldn't come for surgery, but they had to go where they were sent. He was the only doctor in the town, and if they made him mad they couldn't get treated any more. Another doctor had offered to do all cases at Wedowee Hospital, even complicated ones. The Randolph County practice did fill the gaps until I became better established, especially in the dull days at the end of the year.

Nobody warned me about the doldrums of winter. To one newly in practice, it is discouraging to have nothing to do but sit in the office and look at the wall for most of three months while the bills keep coming. The longer a doctor is in practice, the more this smooths out, but winter is always relatively slack. An unexpected event helped. Asa Lloyd called me to come to Lee Brothers Brass Foundry to talk about doing workman's compensation cases. They had 1,500 employees at their high point.

What Next?

32

The flood of patients in the ER continued. Most were appreciative, but not all. I was once called for a man involved in a car accident complaining with chest pain. I asked for a chest X-ray and left for the hospital. As the X-ray was made, the patient suddenly became short of breath. I walked down the hall of the ER and saw an anxious X-ray tech' running behind the stretcher toward a treatment room. The patient was not just cyanotic, he was black and making gulping motions like a fish out of water, but with no sound. The X-ray tech' put up the chest film. The film couldn't be, yet was. Both lungs were totally collapsed. The usual situation prevailed; the nursing supervisor had staffed the ER with nurses pulled from units thought to have extra help. The nurse was wringing her hands and said, "Dr. McGinnis, I will be glad to help you, but this is the first time I've been in the ER and I don't know where a thing is."

"A chest tube, a chest tube, any size, now!" I *might* have asked a little harshly. The nurse didn't know what a chest tube looked like. They weren't kept in the ER. We sent the orderly to central for supplies. He left as if riding a snail. By the time "molasses-in-January" got back, our patient would be dead.

"Get me the biggest needle you can find. Surely you can find that. Get several, and IV tubing and a pan of water. No, not sterile water--just wet water! No, don't use oxygen unless you can put it in a poultice; he sure can't suck it in his lungs."

I wiped the chest wall with alcohol, stabbed the big needle into the chest cavity, and fitted the IV tubing on the end. The nurse held the tubing and needle on the chest wall. Very carefully, I applied the wall suction to the end of the tube, theoretically creating a vacuum in the chest to expand the lung. How much suction for how long? I don't know, just some. When I thought the lung might be expanded, I put the end of the tube in the pan of water. A column of water came up the tube when he breathed in and bubbles came out when he breathed out. We had a chest tube and a water trap of a sort, but they worked! The patient's color began to improve. *Now* we could use oxygen. The snail express brought every tube he could find in central supply. He didn't want to get yelled at or have to make another trip. I put on gloves and put a real tube in the other side and connected it to a water trap while the nurse held my "Rube Goldberg" apparatus in place. I replaced the needle with another real tube. Now the patient had both lungs expanded and had a healthy pink color. We were feeling proud of ourselves that we had a live patient when he discovered he could talk again. And what were his words of gratitude? He cussed us out because I wouldn't let him go out in the hall to smoke! I wrote orders and left him arguing with the nurse.

Members of the knife and gun club arrive in various stages of inebriation. Alcohol can bring out the worst in people. We had no security force in the hospital and a nurse would have to beg the desk sergeant to send an officer to help with an unruly patient. A big man with a full load might throw nurses, orderlies, and doctors all over the room before we could get help. If lacerations were to be repaired, when the officer came, he had no choice but to restrain the patient with leather straps. We had such a patient one night. He had all four extremities strapped, a sheet across his chest and was still writhing about, slinging his head and making the air blue with his language. I was trying to repair a facial laceration while the nurse and orderly held his head.

I stopped my repair and tried reasoning with him, "Now listen to me; you are not so drunk you can't understand me."

He raised his head as far as he could and shouted, "Drunk? What do you mean drunk?"

"I hope you *are* drunk. I hope you wouldn't act like this sober."

He failed to appreciate my logic. The air continued to be blue with the foulest of language. I reminded him that ladies were present and, in addition, such language offended me. I thought that we had made him understand and I began the repair again. He came out with a torrent of unbelievable words. He even intimated our parents were never married and we had canine relatives. There are times when patience snaps. The only reason I tell this now is statutes of limitation have run out. I gave orders to the nurse. She thought I was crazy, but got the stuff. I took a sponge stick, fitted a folded sponge on it, and soaked it with pHisohex. We prized open his mouth, and I carefully swabbed out his mouth with the soapy sponge. I then packed his mouth with sterile gauze packing. We heard no more curses; about all he could get out was, "Gaaa and uuh and duuu."

We finished and time came to turn him loose. I began to realize what I had done. We took off the straps and pulled the packs from his mouth.

He smacked his lips and I thought he was cranking up again. He discovered he could talk and apologized for causing any trouble. He said "Yes, ma'am to the nurse," and then said he really loved everybody for their work. He got the treatment he needed, but in this litigation-prone climate, I would not do it again.

Humor, Both Light and Dark

33

From the flood of humanity in the ER, I picked up assorted OR surgery. Gallbladders and appendectomies came and went, but few were memorable. I saw local people and transients after wrecks. Unimaginable carnage can happen in a high-speed crash. In those years, there were no airbags or shoulder straps, and windshields broke with knife-like shards. In a head-on collision a patient might go through the windshield then fall back after the car stopped. I once sent a patrolman back to a wreck to find a section of cheek hanging on the glass. It did take as a graft. On busy nights, surgeons and nurses saw broken bones, torn faces, blunt trauma to the abdomen or chest in a constant stream. Doctors handle stress differently. Some curse, scream, shout or throw things to vent frustration. Nurses try to tolerate these explosions, but they can't do their best in these episodes. When circumstances are tight, in my room silence is the rule. Wise nurses have to know how to deal with both extremes.

The non-medical person would find it difficult to understand humor after tragedy and injury. The human spirit can stand intense pressure for a finite period of time. Humor is better than curses to reduce tension, but only when the pressure is over.

When life hangs by a thread, conversation is serious and formal, but when stress is past, sometimes there can be vacations from tension. In the operating room, events happen and words said that might be ignored in the light of day, but not when the burden is lifted after a tight case.

A heavy and chesty nurse named Mary Ann became bored during a long late night case, and with nothing to do as circulator, dropped a book in the bottom of the folding linen hamper, sat on a stool, and leaned over the hamper to read. This was against the rules, but we couldn't see the book. It must have been dull because she went to sleep. As she relaxed, her considerable upper body weight pulled her down and sucked her in the linen hamper headfirst. In those days, nurses wore dresses. After the muffled cry, we looked up to see her trying to do the impossible and wriggle straight up out of the hamper. It rocked back and forth, fell over with a clatter and splat. The hamper snapped, collapsed and ate her like the whale ate Jonah. The hamper rolled and jumped; with grunts and gasps she squirmed out like a big snake in reverse. She sat by the flattened hamper, with dirty linens on her shoulder, and tried to pull down her dress and restore dignity, while we tried to control hysterics. As far as I know, the boring book left with the dirty linen.

* * *

Once a young man from far away was in a car wreck and thrown from a bridge onto a railroad track. He was in severe shock from a total body crunch. We took him directly from the ER to surgery. I put in a chest tube. Dr. McCrimmon did the orthopedics and left. We worked most of the night under tremendous stress and pressure while I did the abdominal and facial surgery. The nurses questioned why I would take such abuse.

Agnes said, "At least we have a few days off. You're crazy as a road lizard to do this night after night!"

After hours of patching torn parts, four of us

took him from the OR with the endotrachial tube in place, being pumped by the anesthetist. The scrub tech stayed to clean the room. We were headed for the intensive care unit, three floors up. All of us felt totally drained as we rolled the stretcher down the hall to the elevator.

Mary Kay, our circulator nurse, had discovered our patient was Catholic and called for a priest to come and say the right words over him, since he might not live. She couldn't get the priest from Anniston, but one came from Fort McClellan. He met us in the hall in front of the elevators outside the operating room doors. I had never seen him before. All I knew was that he had a white collar.

He asked, "Can we do this right here?" At least, that's what I thought he said. We were anxious to get this guy to intensive care, but we had to respect his religious customs. Mary Kay and I both nodded and said, "Yes."

So here we waited. Mary Kay and I stood side by side at the head of the bed, looking toward the foot. Agnes was to one side, looking at the patient and bagging him by pumping the portable unit. There was a constant swish-scrape -snick, swish-scrape-snick as she squeezed the bag to push air through the tube into the lungs. Two intravenous lines were going, and a chest tube was connected to a water trap. One leg was in balanced traction. The orderly backed away from the proceedings, pressed the elevator button and leaned against the wall.

We watched the priest at the foot of the bed turning pages in a little black book. He turned them front to back, and then back to front. He was mumbling, "No, that's not it. Let me look in the index." He looked in the back, then the front; turned more pages in the little book. "Here it is! No ... that's not the right one either ... but it'll do."

He said it. He really said it! He said, "That's not right, but it'll do!" He was at the foot of the bed and I couldn't smell his breath, but I have my opinion. He read some words in Latin--I think--waved his arms, closed the book, and with a little fumbling, managed to get it back in his pocket. He looked up and said, "Well that's it."

Mary Kay was aghast; she had arranged this event. We were still standing side by side looking over the headboard with the priest facing us at the foot of the bed. I whispered from the corner of my mouth, "Mary Kay?"

She turned toward me, "Y-yyes doctor?

I said a little louder, "Mary Kay, I think we're married!"

The priest opened his mouth, but said nothing and left toward the stairs. We rolled the stretcher in the elevator as quickly as we could because we laughed so hard people were looking out of rooms on Unit 20 to see what was going on–and it was 3 AM.

As the elevator went up, Mary Kay managed to stop hysterics long enough to say, "I'll tell ya one thing, ol' boy, there ain't gonna' be no honeymoon!"

We never again saw the priest who couldn't find his place in the little black book. The one from Anniston did come and say the right words before the patient died three days later. I never did find out what service was performed that wasn't right, but would do. I may *be* a bigamist.

* * *

Sometimes the patient sees humor in disaster. Early in my practice, I saw a meat cutter with an injury. Few remember the days when a butcher took down a quarter of beef and cut a slice to the bone and the cut the bone with a cleaver or handsaw. In this day when everything is done in a hurry, meat is cut and prepackaged for sale. My butcher patient was cutting meat in the modern fashion by pushing the quarter of beef into a band saw. The saw cuts through meat and bone. In this case it also cut off the butcher's thumb. Replantations were not yet done, so there was nothing to do but close the stump as smoothly as possible. One year later he was back in the emergency room. He had cut off the other thumb. I told him that I was sorry for his injury and I was surprised he was doing the same job after the first disaster.

He said, "Well, Doc, I'm sorry I done it too, but butcherin's all I know. That's just the way things is. I told the wife when I left the house, just don't gimme me no pocket knife for Christmas this year."

* * *

A doctor must not take himself too seriously. He must be willing to see humor in himself. When I arrived in Anniston, I was thirty-two years old, and, considered myself prepared and mature. I once saw a man of 70 or so in the
ER and proposed surgery for bowel obstruction.

I had come from surgery and was wearing green scrubs. He looked me over up and down and said, "I don't know about that. You sure are a young lookin' feller to be acuttin' on folks."

My dignity was wounded, "Well, just how old do you think I am?" He studied me a little more, "Well, I don't know. You ain't much over 40.

If I looked 40, maybe I was crazy to do all this night work.

Even at home a doctor's ego may be deflated. One summer morning, the phone rang about 5:30. I expected to hear the emergency room nurse. Nobody else would call at such an hour. Instead, I heard a disgustingly happy voice, "Say Doc, I got the piles sompin' fearse. Whut time can I come see ya in the office today?"

I struggled to prop up on one elbow and looked

at the clock again. "Man, do you know what time it is?"

There was silence at the other end for a bit. Then he said, even more cheerfully, "Why, look outside, Doc; hit's daylight. "

I groaned into the phone. "Oh, I see. If you are up, everybody from here to east China should be up."

"I don't know about them folks in Chiner. I didn't call 'till I milked the cows. I'm fixin' to get to the field now, so's I can get ma work done before I come see ya."

By that time, I couldn't have gone back to sleep anyway. I told him to come at 9 o'clock, since it was Thursday.

When I said good-by and hung up, he was saying, "That late, huh?"

Not too many days later, I was sewing an involved wound on a lady's arm when she made a request, "Dr. McGinnis, I sure wish you would make your bill cheap as you can, 'cause I'm tryin' to save up enough money to let Dr. Ash take out my garter."

I looked up to see she did have a large thyroid. When I knew him a little better, I told Dr. Ash the goiter story. He grinned a little and said, "Yeah, and I got it, too."

I learned very early to never try changing a patient's mind about the choice of a surgeon. If they begin talking about Birmingham, I offer to take them to the bus station.

However, it is deflating to a doctor's ego to do a complete work-up and advise surgery and have the patient say, "Dr. McGinnis, I don't mind you atreatin' me , but if thay's any surgery to be any done, Dr. Ash will do it."

What else could I do but retire as gracefully as possible? Her surgeon of choice operated and she died. I shudder to think what would have happened to my reputation if I had pushed her to let me do the surgery.

A doctor must never give the impression he is laughing at a patient. The rule causes problems at times. There are times when a patient says something and I would like to run around the corner, have a laughing attack and then come back. It never works out that way. We have to hold it in and get a hernia. I'm sure that's how I got mine. An older man was admitted the day before he was to have a hernia repaired. We did that in those days.

He asked how much I charged for the surgery. I told him, and he thought a moment and asked, "Are ya agonna come back tonight?"

"I could."

"Well, come on back. I wanna talk to ya after I call ma wife."

I came back at five. He untied a handkerchief and took out several slightly damp and musty bills. "Now I'm agonna pay ya half ya bill now. If I live, I'll pay the rest. If ya let me die, I don't know if the ol' lady will pay ya or not."

He may not have heard the words "job incentive," but he knew the principle.

My worst experience at hiding hysterics happened while I was taking a past history, something usually mundane and boring. I thought I had heard him say it. It couldn't be, so I asked again.

"Like I said, Doc, I ain't had no problems except I had VD of the lung onct."

"VD of the lung?"

"Yes, sir, I never did tell ma wife. Don't know how I got it till yet."

"Are you sure? How do you know?"

"A doctor tol' me. I had this turrable pain in my chest and couldn't get my breath and went to the 'mergency room. They give me a X-aray and then poked a big ol' tube in my chest an' just tol' me, 'Man, you got claps of the lung.'"

It was hard to keep a straight face long enough to convince him that the word was "collapse" and had nothing to do with sex. In the south, we tend to slur our words; obviously one doctor did.

Humor can be shared with patients, but they must never sense they are being ridiculed or laughed at. Sometimes the line is narrow. With serious illness, severe trauma or long hospitalization, humor is needed to restore perspective and sanity. If a man can laugh in the face of illness, injury or tragedy, or better still if he can laugh at himself, he will not cry.

A couple in their 20s from out of state had a serious wreck. The wife had a few lacerations, but her primary injury was a fractured hip. Dr. Veach operated on her while I did the

Mr. Robinson was in deep shock. I thought we might lose him before we got him to surgery. I opened the abdomen to find a rising pool of blood. As I did a quick exploration of the abdomen, the left lobe of the liver fell off in my hand. Blood was coming in a torrent from the torn surface of the remains of the liver. All I could do was put lap-packs on the liver to stop the flood temporarily and throw away the loose lobe of liver. We cleaned out the rest of the abdomen and found no other major injuries. Vessels in the liver are too fragile to tie and too large to cauterize. In the last few days, I had picked up a sample of Avateen at a medical meeting. Now was the time to use it, if ever. We took the soaked pack off and put the contents of the jar on a pack and slapped it on the torn surface of the liver. They only gave one sample since it cost $35.00. We would win or lose on these few ounces of fluffy white powder. We repacked the liver with moist abdominal pads and waited. I have learned not to try to guess at time. What seems to be an eternity to me in the heat of the moment may be less than a minute. I watch the clock.

After six minutes I peeled the pack from one edge. Still a little ooze. More packing while the anesthetist pumped blood. The second time I took off the pack there was only a little bleeding from one area. We had no more Avateen, but I found a little piece overlapping the raw surface and used it on the last bleeding area. There was some ooze from the trauma to the entire upper abdomen, but nothing he couldn't survive. We closed the incision and continued fluids, blood and antibiotics.

The postoperative course was not smooth. He did well for a time, and then developed an acute abdomen and I reoperated a few days later. We drained a pancreatic abscess and dipped out chunks of necrotic pancreas. The gallbladder was involved; we took it, too. After this, he recovered physically, but not emotionally.

Five weeks after the wreck, both were on Unit 8 East, in separate rooms. He was on the north side, and his wife on the south. She had done well and could have been discharged, but in those days we could keep patients for long stays. Their home was in North Carolina and she had no place to go. He was eating, exercising and walking, when forced to. His vital signs were normal and his laboratory studies were normal or what was to be expected after his injury. He was down-in-the -mouth, solemn and mule-faced. For him, there was no light at the end of the tunnel. He had a pained and troubled expression. He never smiled.

Happiness cannot be written as an order. We had no psychiatrist. Therapy was up to me. I don't know if he had true depression or not. I just called it 4+ bad mulligrubs. I tried to convince him that recovery from such an injury took months. I was glad to have a live patient, and thought he should be glad to be alive, but he wasn't. I couldn't reach him.

His wife was a contrast. Opposites do attract. She was pleasant, and after the first few days, always smiling. I talked to her about her husband and his attitude problem. She said he was moody and had episodes of the blues. One of the unit nurses said they had done all they could do.

Mrs. Robinson smiled and said, "Maybe I could help him with an attitude adjustment."

"I had assumed that you have talked to him."

"Oh, I mean more than talk, but I don't know if we should or not after the surgery and all. We're young and ... and it has been a long time, but I don't want either of us to injure ourselves. Do you think we could ... well, you know! It's always seemed to help before. Could it be dangerous?"

My nurse was looking out of the window, trying to stay out of this conversation.

"Mrs. Robinson, a young man asked me a question like that when I was about to discharge him after a hernia repair. He was still on his honeymoon and was interested in my answer. I said, 'That depends on how athletic you are'." He looked confused and said, "What do you mean?"

"No kinky stuff. You can't drop down off the chandelier or anything crazy. You can resume those activities when you can do such and not put yourself in a strain or injure yourself. I leave the exact timing and methods to your own ingenuity."

He nodded and said, "Uh ... okay."

I finished rounds and passed his bed again. He was sitting on the side of the bed grinning ear to ear. "Just talked to the wife, Doc. She said come on home. She'd have sompen' figured out ... time I got there."

Mrs. Robinson laughed and seemed to understand the comparison and what I was telling her. The nurse and I left and walked toward the nurses' station.

The nurse said, "Dr. McGinnis, shall I write 'may have sex' as an order?"

"Hey, come on! That wasn't an order. It's legal. They have a license."

"Dr. McGinnis, you know full well we can't have treatment carried out on this unit without an order. Shall I make it a P. R. N. order for sex?"

"What?"

"Can he have the treatment repeated if he needs it?"

As we rounded the corner at the nursing station, she told the whole crew, "Guess what! Dr. McGinnis is ordering sex for all our patients! His practice will double overnight."

"Now wait a minute, that wasn't an order. It was more permissive than directive." The nurses would have none of this logic. I left in a flood of giggles about what was about to take place on their unit.

I stepped back to the door, "Now listen, I know some of you will be working tonight and pass the word to others; no peeking and no listening at the door. Don't even check vital signs. You can write that as an order. See that they have privacy ... just in case."

I walked the few steps to 8 West. A nurse ran out with a prescription pad in her hand, "Dr. McGinnis, that treatment you're giving on east side? Could you write me a prescription for it? Some of the other nurses might like one too." How can gossip travel that fast? I had to endure more smirks and giggles so I made a quick note in the charts and got up to leave.

One of the nurses said, "What's your hurry? Aren't you going to stay to evaluate the treatment?"

"I have to go. You know what they say?"

"What's that?"

"Physician, heal thyself. After all this talk, I've

got to go home. Hey, I need to prevent the mulligrubs." I could hear laughter and giggles all the way down the hall as the elevator opened.

On the next day as soon as I finished my morning surgery, I walked to Unit 8 East to make rounds. A few terse greetings were offered as they looked up from their chart work. They glanced at each other. Their mouths were controlled straight lines. There was no doubt as to what had taken place in the night. "Surely you didn't peek?"

"No, we didn't, but third shift saw him slip down the hall to her room after visiting hours. He stayed a long time, too!"

I started out to make my rounds, and for the first time in history all of the nurses got up to go, too. The charge nurse glared the others back down in their chairs and took over the duty. She wouldn't have missed this for the world. We went to Mrs. Robinson's room first. Her husband was there. He knew we always went to her room first. As usual she was smiling--in fact she was radiant. Mr. Robinson had the longest face I had ever seen, with an anxious pained expression.

We never even had time to make a cursory greeting before he started, "Dr. McGinnis, I've got to ask you something. Last night I came up to my wife's room and ... and I got kinda frisky ... you know, it has been a long time ... and I uh ... I mean we uh ... Dr. McGinnis what would make a man's semen red?"

I looked at these two: one anxious and one glowing, and my mouth opened before my brain got in gear. "Mr. Robinson, it could be several things. In your case, it's probably rust."

No matter how hard I tried, I couldn't get the words back in my mouth. What had I done? I was afraid to look, but I could hear her laughing. I looked at him, and he had a little sickly smile on one side. More would have cracked his face. I offered reassurances that the color was probably old blood from the severe trauma to his abdomen and should clear.

My nurse was no longer with us, and I heard a commotion in the hall. My nurse had leaned against the wall to have hysterics, had slid down and was sitting in the hall. Not only was she laughing hysterically, at intervals she made whooping noises. The other nurses were gathered around her. She couldn't stop long enough to tell the story. They were considering calling for the crash cart. They finally got her up and sent her on break to recover. She was really no good for the rest of the day. When a patient is in various stages of exposure and her nurse remembers an earlier event of the day and breaks out in irrational laughter, explanation is fruitless.

The treatment must have helped. Mr. Robinson did recover. Three years later they came back to see us. Both were smiling. I assume Mr. Robinson had further treatment. They had a small child. I'm sure he has red hair.

* * *

Some nurses delight in deflating a doctor's ego and composure, especially pompous doctors or those who seem to be bothered by unexpected events. I had been warned about a certain nurse, but I forgot to be vigilant. We were about to do some hand surgery. Since I am basically lazy, I planned to sit on a stool to work. Cheryl Tidwell had just prepped the patient with a Betadine sponge, making the arm a deep brown. Afterward, I remembered seeing her standing there with the sponge stick in her hand. I walked around to sit on the stool as somebody held it for me. As I settled down on the stool, there was a sudden squish and a terrible wet sensation. She couldn't stand the temptation and shoved the soggy sponge under my behind as I sat. Betty never accepted my story of how I got brown stains on my shorts.

My treatment was minimal compared to that of Dr McCrimmon. The same nurse who wielded the sponge stick happened to be going down the hall one day as Dr McCrimmon finished scrubbing for surgery and was walking toward the operating room with dripping outstretched arms. At the time, he wore his scrub pants low slung on his hips. On impulse she gave his scrubs a little tug and Herb was standing in the middle of the hall in his shorts with his pants around his ankles. He couldn't grab as they fell because his hands and arms were scrubbed and sterile. He certainly didn't want to call for help. Thereafter whenever Cheryl was around, he leaned against the sink when he scrubbed and looked all around when he walked to his room. Some of the nurses autoclaved a rubber snake and put it in the instrument pack for one of his cases. A real one couldn't have been more effective.

Cheryl was also guilty of putting KY jelly on the commode seat in the nurses' bathroom. Cheryl pulled the tug on the scrub pants routine on Dr. Veach. Later he slipped up behind her when she was scrubbing and returned the favor. He made a vigorous pull and got underclothes too. That ended the tug-on-the-pants tricks.

The other episode was an accident, as far as we know. One night Herb was called to the psychiatric unit for a consult. Most of us are not wild about having to go behind locked doors to see patients. Doors are locked for a reason. Herb was alone at the end of the darkened hall about to go into a room. He didn't see the woman in the corner. All of a sudden, she sprang from the shadows, said "Hahyaaah", jumped on Herb's back and wrapped her legs around his waist and her arms around his neck in a stranglehold grip. To his credit, Herb didn't scream, shout or run, but it's hard to run with someone not playing with a full deck, riding piggyback, and hard to scream through a stranglehold. Much as he tried, he couldn't dislodge his passenger, and he couldn't breathe well enough to call for help. He struggled to walk down the hall into the light of the nurses' station. Two startled nurses looked up from their chart work to see Herb. The strong specter had a death grip around his throat, and he could hardly breathe. With a gargle in his voice, he said, "Do you think you could do something about this?" They prized her arms off and pulled her away. Herb had not been able to see who or what had him, but his first words were, "Whatever that is, it's crazier than a striped-ass road lizard."

Herb no longer does consults on that unit. We never knew if that was a put-up job or not.

When We All Got Naked in the OR

34

On a spring day long ago, at eight in the morning, a sixteen-year-old boy was brought to the Emergency Room pale and shivering, though wrapped in a quilt. After we started fluids and covered him with warm blankets, I got the full story. With a new driver's license and a rebuilt '34 Ford, he went to visit his girlfriend in the late afternoon of the day before. On the way home, he ran off the road and into a drainage ditch. He woke with dirty water lapping at his chin. He was upright, but his shoulder was pinned between metal. When he struggled, he slipped deeper in the water. He concentrated on staying awake with hope and faith that help would come. When there was no sign of the boy at midnight, his father began a search of the back roads. He found him at daylight.

I cleaned the wounds, cut away dead tissue, packed them, gave fluids and loaded him with antibiotics. He improved enough to grieve over the loss of his car. Just as rapidly, on the second day he became worse. He had a high fever and was stuporous at times. I moved him to isolation. His wounds became dusky red with foul smelling gray-tan drainage. Greenish black patches lay along the skin edges. Light touch in these areas gave a sense of crackles. The culture was positive, and there were small dark spots on the X-ray of the wound area.

When he had a lucid moment, I sat and talked with the boy and his parents. "I'm sorry you are so much worse, but now I can tell you why. Your shoulder and upper arm were crushed and torn under dirty water for several hours--a setup for what you have. There are clear signs of gas gangrene. It's a serious condition. As big and deep as the infection is, standard treatment calls for amputation--in this case the arm and shoulder."

All three turned pale and stammered a few words about what else could be done.

"If I were sixteen-years-old and faced with this, I would choose to have the diseased tissue cut away and keep my right arm. I will have to cut until I see normal tissue. You will lose part or maybe all of some muscles of your upper arm and shoulder blade area. It will make a huge hole, but I can graft that later. You must know: that course of treatment is a calculated risk. We are risking your life to save your right arm."

We agreed to try to save the arm. To avoid exposing others, I scheduled him that night, after visiting hours. To get him off the table as soon as possible, I asked Dr. Robert Elliot to help me.

Agnes Black, the anesthetist, Linda Small, the circulator, and Jane, the scrub tech, were quieter than usual because of the stress of the case. We cut away the diseased tissue and a margin of normal skin and muscle as we would in cancer surgery.

As we cauterized the last of the bleeders, Ag said, "Dr. McGinnis, he's already better. Everything is stable now. You must have cut away all those evil spirits."

As we put on the dressing, Linda said in her high squeaky voice, "Now, you know the new rule about gas gangrene, Dr. McGinnis." She held up a copy of the directive from the bulletin board. "This is such a bad contagious infection everyone has to strip and leave everything in this room."

"You mean gowns and scrubs?"

"No! I mean gowns, scrubs, hat and mask, shoes, socks *and under clothes*--every stitch on your body--everything! Then everybody has to take a pHisohex shower."

"You mean together?"

"No! You go to your dressing room first and we better not see your faces until we call you."

"Okay, if that's the rule about gangrene, nurses first, and we'll stay with the patient. Hey, that's only logical. According to the rules, the captain of the ship leaves last. We'll just sort of look at the patient while you peel."

Ag said, "There's also one about the captain going down with the ship."

It is difficult, if not impossible, to win an argument with three women faced with nakedness. The docs had to go first and three nurses stayed with the patient. Linda had anticipated the nudity and banished long-tall John the orderly to Outer Mongolia. As John left, he was to barricade the door to the OR suite and was threatened with his life if he came back before he was sent for, even if the building was on fire.

Linda said, "Now, Dr. Elliot, I will hold up this sheet and you can step behind and undress."

We heard fumbling, muttering, an occasional curse, the swish of falling clothes and the clatter of kicked-off shoes.

Then in typical little boy fashion he said, "Now, ya'all, I'm standin' here naked as a jay bird!"

Without thinking Linda said, "Yes, Doctor, I know, I know."

I stripped and left a few minutes after Dr. Elliot, amid more discussion and threats.

Nothing takes away any semblance of dignity like walking down a long well-lit hall totally naked. Over the years, I have had dreams like this. The door at the far end was closed, but it *could* open and giggling visitors stream in. I didn't run. I was afraid my bare feet would slip on the slick floor and I would fall, hit my head, and be found unconscious and nude when the OR opened again.

We agreed to stay in the doctors' lounge at the end of the hall until all the nurses had taken the patient to the recovery room directly across from the docs' dressing room and streaked back down the hall to their lounge for fresh scrub suits. Bob was in the shower when I got to the lounge. I finished mine before the nurses extubated the patient, moved him to a stretcher, and peeled. They shouted one last warning as they started down the long hall toward our door. We didn't want to endure the wrath of three angry nude women, so we didn't peek. We didn't have to. We heard the slapping of feet and who knows what other fleshy parts. I had clear mental image of three stark-naked women rolling an unconscious patient on a stretcher down the hall at a dead run. We could only imagine what the patient might think if he woke up. The stretcher is about hip level. If the patient looked up--or if he looked down--either way would be startling to a sixteen-year old boy blinking through the fog of anesthesia. We heard them round the corner across the hall.

The startled recovery room nurse jumped up from her stool, looked down at herself, then up at three nude women rolling in a stretcher. She said, "Oh my goodness, is this a new dress code? I don't think I'm qualified."

Ag said, "Shut up and react this patient."

Before the stretcher stopped rolling, the three pushers turned tail and ran.

Across the hall we heard everything.

Bob said, "Give ya a hundred dollars to rattle that door and open it an inch or two."

"Not for all the tea in China. I can see the

headlines now: *Assassination of local doctors by nude women ruled justified."*

After our forced isolation was ended, I walked to the nurse's desk to get the chart. I had on a fresh scrub suit and seemed to function without underclothing. Girls are different. Some are more different than others. Jane was hugging and supporting her ample chest with one arm as if something were about to get away and holding the phone with the other hand.

She was speaking angrily, "Never mind why, just bring 'um--*right now*!"

By morning, the story of nakedness in the OR had spread through the hospital. Dr. Henry Hawk did another case of suspected gas gangrene the next night. He benefited by our experience. Not wanting to be without his white operating room shoes for two days, he conveniently borrowed a pair from Dr. Reynolds' open locker. By the time he got back from a three-day trip, the shoes would have been gas sterilized, back in place and he would be none the wiser. Gas wouldn't hurt the shoes and it would even help by killing off any fungi. John, the orderly, became confused, or in revenge for being banned and not allowed to streak with the others, didn't put the shoes in the gas sterilizer. He put them in the autoclave at the usual high temperature and pressure. Dr. Reynolds' shoes came out the size of the first baby shoes with the toes curled up. They looked more petrified than bronzed.

A few days later, Dr. Rush Smitherman had a case of gangrene. As he began to peel without the benefit of a sheet, his scrub tech' Jean Penny turned her head.

With a smirk Rush said, "What's the matter Jean, afraid you'll be embarrassed?"

"No, Doctor, afraid I'll be disappointed."

After Dr. Smitherman's case, when everybody

had peeled and redressed, the circulator, Pat Board, couldn't find her husband to make a delivery. "Whatever can I do? I can't go home like this."

Jean said, "That's no problem; we're about the same size. My son's at home." She made the call and said, "Please go in my room, look in the top drawer of the chest and get two pairs of under britches and two bras and bring 'em. Yes, *two* pairs. What do mean you don't even want to know what's going on?"

Through all this, my patient survived and became a productive citizen. Betty did discover that I came home without my underwear.

I am the only one left in the hospital who remembers the night we all got naked in the OR. Dignity has returned. Because of these three cases, rules have been changed. There is no more nudity in the OR ... that we know of.

Proper Behavior in the Operating Room

35

Conduct in surgery is not what the non-medical person might expect. Conversation and events rarely take place with the pompous formality of movies and TV. Some customs and conventions in the operating room are strange and confusing to the newcomer. There is no course in medical school and no manual to teach budding surgeons how to behave. The resident or intern blunders ahead, commits sin, is chastised, suffers remorse and tries to change his ways. A training period should not only teach a surgeon how to treat patients and operate, but also how he should conduct himself and relate to others in the medical field.

When I was an intern, a hundred years ago, the doctor was exalted to the status of monarch. When we made rounds, the nurses stood as the doctor approached and gave their undivided attention. The head nurse made rounds with the doctor and his retinue, carrying her pad of notes. She reported on every aspect of every patient: medications given, drainage amounts from whatever tube from whatever orifice, temperatures, diet consumed, and of course, graphic documentation and description of bowel function. There is no privacy in a hospital. Woe be unto the nurse who was asked about a test or procedure that had not been done. The intern or resident was just as culpable. Our responsibilities were different. We performed many procedures now done by nurses: inserting Levin tubes or Foley catheters, starting IVs or changing dressings. When the attending physician made rounds, the intern presented a detailed history and physical report on new patients. On established patients, we reported on procedures we had done. There was no excuse for not completing a task. Everybody huddled around the doctor answering questions, carrying out commands, running in every direction if asked, as if they were in the presence of a king. We listened to every sound as if his words were truly *Apples of gold in settings of silver* (Prov. 25:11.) When an intern or resident came down the hall toward the nurses' station, nobody looked up and acknowledged their existence. I never knew how nurses could hear footsteps and tell if they were those of a real doctor who deserved respect or ones made by an intern who deserved none.

If the real doctors on the medical units were monarchs, surgeons in the operating room were regarded as near deity. Each surgeon set the tone for behavior in his room. The most strict require no spoken word unless necessary for the case at hand. Even instruments were requested by hand signals and passed in silence, and passed promptly or the nurse was chastised. Then we heard the standard lecture about how delay of a few seconds each time an instrument was passed in the course of an operation added up to minutes of lost time. Orderlies spoke when spoken to and never to each other in the presence of the surgeon. Nurses spoke to each other in hushed tones in the far corner, when absolutely necessary. The intern or resident who spoke a word about a subject other than the case at hand or about another patient was severely chastised.

This surgical tyrant, whether benevolent or intemperate, didn't actually say, *Who is this that darkens council by words without knowledge?* (Job 38:2) The implication was evident. We knew that for every careless word spoken, we would *render an account for it in the day of judgment* (Matt.12:36). Our judgment was now. See, like deity.

Dr. John Slaughter, our chief of surgery when I was an intern and resident, was this type, a very single-minded person. I respected and admired him as the best technician I have ever seen operate and a superb clinician in the care of patients on the ward, but at times I suffered his wrath by speaking about some other patient in the OR. If I hummed a tune while I worked at my trivial jobs, I was reminded of my musical ineptitude. I admired him, but long cases could be stressful. Still, he was the surgeon. Ours was but to comply.

Other surgeons were not so strict in control of the mood of the room. All had the same authority, if they chose to exercise it. They were captain of the ship. They were responsible for all they surveyed. Everything revolved around the surgeon in the circle of light. Discussion of other cases, trivial conversation or even laughter was permitted. The atmosphere may change from one extreme to another with the same surgeon and same patient. During surgery, if there is casual conversation or music in the background and relaxed atmosphere, the case is going well. If there is icy silence and palpable tension, the operation is not going well, or it's difficult or dangerous. Some surgeons are always uptight and those around them are tense. Wise nurses and assistants know which rules apply.

The surgeon selects the temperature and attitude for his room. If he chooses, he is the only one to speak. He is also the only one who is allowed to have gas--not the anesthetic kind, the personal kind. I didn't know this until my first year of residency in

Virginia. I was helping Dr. Hugh Trout, Jr., do some sort of abdominal procedure. The senior resident was the first assistant. We had no interns. As the junior man, I was consigned to the retractors--the idiot sticks. I don't know what dietary indiscretion I had committed, but I began to have agonizing gas pains. The more I pulled on those dumb retractors, the worse the distress became. The pain became more acute. I knew what would relieve it, but what could I do--ask for a break to go ... well, what could I call it? I was new and I couldn't ask for special favors. I thought maybe I could relax on those dumb retractors a bit and be very controlled and careful--Ahhhhhh. I felt much better immediately. Control was excellent--not even a whisper of sound.

I didn't take into consideration the lack of air-conditioning of that day. Also, warm air rises. In grade school we always said the silent ones were the most deadly. This event was especially wicked.

Dr. Trout had a tendency to be somewhat spastic in surgery. Suddenly he came to full alert, straightened up, and gasped, "We've perforated the bowel! Did you smell that? We've perforated the bowel. Mac, pull harder on those retractors. We've got to run this gut and look for the hole." He sorted through the loops of bowel and his voice went to a higher pitch, "Pull harder, it's getting worse! There must be a huge pool there somewhere."

"Dr. Trout, I, uh ... that is I ... "

The words wouldn't come. I couldn't think of a way to say it. After he ran and reran the bowel and found nothing, he relaxed and we finished in silence. The futile search took minutes, but seemed hours to me. I never knew if he suspected what happened or not. He never made any accusing glances my way.

After Dr. Trout finished the inside work, the senior resident and I closed the abdomen. He was fat and was sweating as he sutured and I tied. After the last suture, we went into the lounge and he sat very carefully in the chair with a pained expression on his face.

"You know, that problem about the bowel and all ... that ... that could have been my fault."

"What?"

"I've had this gas problem all day, and I was straining trying not to ... but I could have ... you know, slipped ... and all that might have been my fault. I'm going to have to watch my diet."

"Oh, I think you should! Don't worry about it. Every thing came out fine. See ya!"

When I drain an abscess and there is a stench in my operating room, I usually say, "Something really smells. Either one of you girls *do* something?" I don't want them to think I did it.

Many years later we live in a different world with different rules. The surgeon is still captain of the ship--to a degree--and he is still the only one permitted to have gas. Once during an operation, a surgeon, who has been known to be crude at times, suddenly put his weight on one leg, lifted the other and relieved himself, audibly. Even under the mask, the grin of a grade-school kid on the back row was evident.

The circulator nurse was aghast. "Doctor, how could you? This is a sterile room!"

"You know these gowns are good filters. Besides, 'tis better to toot and bear the shame than hold it and bear the pain."

"I'd be ashamed, doctor; this patient is awake!"

"It don't make any difference. He's older'n dirt and deaf as a post. He hadn't heard thunder in twenty years."

About that time, this gentle white-haired man, under a spinal, raised his head slightly, looked at the anesthetist, the only one he could see, wrinkled his nose, and in that loud expressionless, inflectionless manner of the totally deaf, said, "Somebody--jist--let a fart!"

He might have been old and deaf, but he wasn't stupid, and there was nothing wrong with his nose. The nurses never convinced him through frantic handwritten notes the aroma was from a hemorrhoid case across the hall.

Nurses are not permitted to have gas. I was doing a case in Room A Mini-surgery one day when my circulator nurse disappeared. She knew full well the rule about gas and ran through the connecting sub-sterile room to the Room B operating room. Her pain could be eased just beyond that second door. Relief was achieved magnum cum loudness with echoes as she entered the room. She expected an empty room, instead she saw in the other doorway two nurses pushing a stretcher with a patient. The patient sat up. All were startled by the eruptive greeting. What could the nurse say? In the outdoors, she could say, "Uh-oh, I just stepped on a frog." Frogs don't come in the OR much any more, so she turned and fled. Shirley, my nurse, and I knew nothing of the events. As we were finishing our case, we noticed half of the nurses on the unit had gathered at our door, were peering in the small window and had broken out on a rash of silly giggles. They could hardly wait for our patient to leave to give a graphic description of the event.

The deflated nurse was defensive, "Everybody does that sometimes. Don't ya'all ever do that?"

"Yes, but not with an audience."

More shrieks and giggles. Discussion rapidly descended to a grade school level. The nurse was renamed and suggestions were made for the renaming of Room B. On a higher plane, I "sent" a message to the administrator notifying him that we had had an explosion in Room B. Two nurses and a patient were overcome by fumes, but would recover.

Nurses shouldn't have gas, but rules were relaxed for one of the senior nurses in the main OR, probably because her control was not as good. She sometimes used her privilege as a threat.

If the surgeon tended to dawdle in his surgery, she said, "Doctor, if you don't hurry, I'm going to have to go over here and rattle those pans on the back-table. You know what that means, don't you?"

When doctors make rounds today, some nurses look up and speak. Some keep writing. Certainly none stand. No one listens to the doctor's words as if they were apples of gold in settings of silver. At one time, the doctor represented a body of knowledge and diagnostic ability, the patient's hope for diagnosis, treatment, and healing. There was a day when the wise doctor talked with the patient, examined the patient and rendered an astute diagnosis with nothing more than basic tests. He had a discerning glance, a caring heart and a healing touch. Doctors today are more knowledgeable, but more removed from the patient. The two are separated by people, tests, and machines. Doctors, of necessity, delegate much of the treatment to others. We don't deify the doctor, but the CT scan, the magnetic resonance and a thousand other tests and machines. There is a tendency to treat tests and not patients. Nurses today are well trained, efficient and considerate in the OR, but there is no more whispering in the corner. Perhaps all have discovered what should have been known all along; doctors have feet of clay like everybody else. Respect must be earned. Respect does not require one to grovel.

Recently, a doctor was performing abdominal surgery with the help of some of these nurses. As usual, a nurse was across the table, one at the Mayo stand, and the circulator was across the room. A nurse was giving the anesthetic at the head of the table.

The surgeon looked up from his surgery with a serious expression and said, "Uh-oh ... poot alert, poot alert!"

"Doctor, don't you dare!"

The doctor turned to his work again and said," Too late, too late! "

Actually, he was considerate. He didn't want to cause an uproar like I caused so many years before. He didn't want them to think the bowel had been perforated. Besides, it was his right. Much of our status as doctors is tarnished or gone. We may have only one special privilege left. In the OR, only the surgeon may have gas.

Anger

36

We don't always see laughter and happiness in the medical field, but a range of emotions. Patients show concern or even anger with disease and surgery, anxiety with injury, fear of cancer, and anguish over death. There is pain or fear of pain, depression and dread of disability and death. All who deal with patients must develop a degree of emotional shell or we couldn't function. But we can't be callused, jaded, distracted and unfeeling. We need a balance of empathy with objectivity. We identify with the patient's pain and anguish, but to a degree that doesn't sway judgment in managing disease or injury. Each doctor or nurse works out their own solution to this problem. There are times when rules don't apply. There are patients who affect us all and are remembered always.

There was a man who had endured hardships as a prisoner of war. He had retired from the army and moved to New Mexico with his wife and child to live and enjoy life for the first time. They brought their daughter to Sandia Base Hospital when I was chief of surgery in 1959. What I thought would be a simple appendectomy became a horror show. This healthy appearing twelve-year-old girl had advanced cancer throughout the abdomen. I could do nothing but biopsy the tumor. I didn't know then, and I still don't know a good way, to tell such news. I did the best I could.

The poor parents exhibited classic stages, which I could not change: first disbelief and denial. "This terrible thing cannot be. You must be mistaken. She was playing ball with the boys last week. She's a bit of a tomboy, you know. She's just a child--our *only* child. She can't have cancer. She's always healthy. You need to talk to another doctor."

"Sergeant, I talked with my civilian consultant during surgery and the pathologist. There is no mistake. No, I don't know why things like this happen to people who don't deserve it."

In surgery, I cut away a patient's problem or repair it and life goes on. When I can do nothing, what should I do, call the Chaplin, walk away and never look back? That may be legal, but it's not moral. I tried to help the best I could.

In the days that followed, anger replaced disbelief. Families may become angry with the healthiest person they see. They became hostile and angry toward me. I had what their daughter did not: health and life. The chaplain couldn't help. The psychiatrist couldn't help. I could do nothing, so I withdrew. I transferred her to a larger hospital. In those days chemotherapy offered little, but the parents might better accept their bitter fate in a setting filled with doctors with leaves or eagles on their shoulders and more gray in their hair.

Tears

37

A wailing, moaning family surrounds a desperately ill dying patient. Even if she's in pain of terminal illness or unconscious, they demand, "Keep Momma--or Daddy--alive every minute you can." The bitterest tears ever shed are those spilled over words that should have been said and things that should have been done but were left unspoken and never done. The door of opportunity has closed and will never again open. The mourners know what they have not done, and desperately want to do something, even if it's wrong and too late.

This does not have to be.

I was finishing rounds with hope of eating supper with the rest of the family when I heard the page. I knew the number well. In the emergency room, I found a nurse and two ambulance attendants standing by an old woman lying on a stretcher.

The nurse looked up. "You're on call for surgery tonight. They could have sent this lady all day long, but they waited 'till now. This is Ida Bell Higgins from the nursing home. Her belly's blown up and she's vomiting. Doesn't know she's in the world."

I examined her abdomen. It was distended and silent but for a few rushes and tinkles. I thought I felt a mass. Her lips and mouth were dry. There were stains on the sheet by her head. She had no expression, no awareness of anything.

I leaned over so she had to see me. "Ms. Higgins, where do you hurt?"

The nurse smirked, "Told you so."

I tapped her forehead with my finger. "Ida Bell Higgins, are you in there

. . . somewhere?" Her eyes moved toward me. "Blink if you hear me."

The eyes looked away. I stayed to see the X-rays and lab work. I put in a Levin tube and started fluids. I talked by phone with her daughter in Oklahoma.

The next day her hydration was better and the abdomen down enough for me to be sure about the mass. There were hard nodules under the right rib margin. Another X-ray showed haziness in the area where I felt the mass and clear signs of obstruction.

I met her daughter that afternoon. She had taken emergency leave from her job. Her husband couldn't leave his business. She had no children to call on.

We sat at her mother's bedside. "I'll tell you all I can about your mother. She has almost complete intestinal obstruction. I feel a mass in the left abdomen. I can't be certain; it's probably cancer. There is blood in her stool and returns from an enema. The only way to know is surgery. There are no other tests. If we are lucky, we can remove the tumor--whatever it is--and hook up the intestines. If we can't take it out, we may have to do a colostomy. That requires a bag and a lot of care and she won't understand it. Either way, we will put her through pain she won't understand, and the most we can hope for is to take her back to whatever life she had before. Her nurse at the nursing home said she ate when fed, but never spoke."

"Yes, it's been like that for some time. It was hard to put her there. I left her here because this town is her home and her friends were here. Lots of them have died. The ones who are left don't come any more because she doesn't talk. I come when I can and call the nurse once a week. It would be next to impossible to move her to Oklahoma."

"I *will* operate on her if that's your choice."

"What is the alternative?"

"Not operate, let nature take its course and make it as easy as possible."

"Are you talking about *giving* her something to put her out?"

"No, that's active. What I offer is passive. Give her something for pain, enough IV fluids so she's not dry and a little water on her mouth and lips. Then take what follows."

"Don't we have to have a court tell us to do that? Is it legal? Will we get in trouble?"

"Only if you broadcast it to the world or tell some judge or lawyer. If your mother can't make this decision, who better than her closest living relative? It's far easier for me to operate than not operate. I have been taught to fix a problem or cut it away. The loss of a patient is always a personal defeat for me, but I have thought about this situation and can live with your choice ... either way. *You* have to decide if *you* can live with it. Do what you think she would want done if she could tell you. There is more to life than a moving chest and beating heart. We don't want to look back and regret what we do. I will not accept an answer tonight. Think about it, pray about it, call your pastor or your nephews if you like and I'll see you in the morning."

"How long do you give her--without surgery, I mean?"

" I don't give time. It's not in my power and not my responsibility to give time. As thin and frail as she is, I think she would last four or five days ... maybe a week. But understand, that's a pure guess. We should make a decision by morning. If we operate, we should do it before she gets weaker."

The next morning, she was sitting at the bedside holding her mother's hand. She looked up as I came in the room. "No surgery. Yes, I'm sure. You're right; it's my decision alone."

Over the days that followed, she didn't leave her mother's room. She slept on a cot when her mother slept. The nurses brought trays of food for her. She ate little. When her mother was awake, she sat at the bedside and held her hand or arranged her hair and talked. She smiled, laughed and told stories from her childhood, sang songs, childish at first, then those of teen years. She shed tears when she spoke of the loss of her father and death of a brother.

Sometimes she tired and stopped to watch the slow drops of the IV–the ticks of life's final clock. I made rounds twice a day, some days a third time between cases. Ida Bell Higgins was shrinking. The tumor seemed larger, but her eyes looked bigger. The door to the room was closed, but the nurses stopped in the hall to hear soft words, songs and at times laughter.

At five in the morning of the fifth day, the nurse called. Ida Bell Higgins was gone. I looked at the clock and said," This is not unexpected, please ask the ER doc to pronounce her. I have a 7:30 case."

As I walked through Unit 20 toward the OR, I glanced at Mrs. Higgins' room. The bed was empty and freshly made. Her daughter sat at the bedside. She met me at the door.

"I thought you would be gone. I know you have a lot to do."

She smiled and took my hand. "I could not leave without telling you how much I appreciate your helping me make the most difficult decision of my life. I *can* live with it. Thank you." She gave me a hug and turned to leave.

The nurse at my elbow said, "Too bad your mother couldn't hear you."

The daughter looked back and said, "Oh but she did. I looked in her eyes and she told me she heard my every word and that it was all right."

The nurse said, "Did you hear what she said? That's not possible."

I watched the daughter step in the elevator. "Do you remember--her mother's eyes were almost the same color as hers--just a little faded. Yes, I heard what she said and *I* believe her."

I was late for surgery.

Victory
36

I will remember there is an art to medicine as well as science, and that warmth, sympathy, and understanding may outweigh the surgeon's knife or the chemist's drug.

Hippocratic Oath (Modern Version)

When I opened the peritoneum, there was a rush of cloudy fluid spilling down the drapes. We suctioned it away and I explored the abdomen. Implants were scattered over the omentum, mesentery, and bowel wall. I reached a hand in and moved my fingers gently along a mass below the greater curve of the stomach: the area of the pancreas. I felt lumps in the liver. I biopsied several places and closed the abdomen.

His wife stood to meet me in the waiting area. "Your husband is in the recovery room and doing well. I took fluid out and left in a drain. He did have a growth. I can't be sure until we get the pathology report on the biopsies."

I got by with this half-truth that day and the next morning. In the afternoon, I saw them last on my rounds. His wife moved from the chair at his bedside so I could sit there. After all the operations over the years, I had no good way to tell a story like this. I looked in his eyes and told him the findings directly and honestly.

"You can't take it out?"

"It's too widespread."

"X-ray or chemotherapy?"

"X-ray is out of the question. Chemotherapy is a consideration. You can go to an oncologist in Birmingham, or I could treat you here after I call for a consultation. The tumor is aggressive. The most we can hope for is to buy you months or weeks at the cost of side effects of the drugs. They are quite toxic."

My patient turned toward the window, stared at evening shadows and said nothing. I could hear muffled sobs from his wife behind me. This retired Methodist minister in his late sixties turned back with a smile, "I have had a good life; I have spent most of my years in God's service, and I have known wonderful people in those years. I have my memories. I will rejoice over what I have had, and still have. My God and my wife will not leave me, no matter what. I will make the best of what time is left."

I made rounds twice a day, sat and talked with my patient and his wife. Churches where he had been pastor were not nearby, and he had no close family other than his wife. He had few visitors. We didn't talk about his tumor except to agree we had faith in total and complete healing, if not in this world, then the next. He talked about his years in the ministry, places he had been, experiences he had, and his regrets, though they were few. Other than the day after surgery, he never asked for a narcotic. In my mind's eye, I saw the tumors in his pancreas and liver. As they grew, organs were stretched and there had to be pain. At least, there is in others. God must grant special favors to special people. My patient never complained. He still smiled though he was weaker each day.

On the last day I saw him, he thanked me for what we had done for him. I said, "Oh no, you do more for us than we can do for you."

He frowned for the first time, just a little, "What do you mean?"

"The lessons you have taught us. The way you have accepted this part of your life, the way you conduct yourself, the way you smile as you face the end."

"Oh, but I must. These are principles I have preached these forty years. I have tried to live by them. Now, I *must* try to die by them. There *is* no other way. I cannot mourn my thorn of the flesh. I want to die as I have lived."

I turned to leave and found my nurse had gone. This big tough talking nurse was in the hall crying softly.

That night he died. The nurse called to say another doctor had checked him and I did not have to come. When I could get awake enough, I went in to see his wife.

She said, "I have been waiting for you. I wanted you to know. We talked until the very end. In his last hour, he spoke of the nature of people and how great it would be if man could see the goodness of his fellowman and not his faults. He watched the sunrise though the window and quietly passed into the next world."

She showed me his words she had written as he spoke--the poetry of death. Her eyes were wet, but she smiled. Her soul mate of forty years had no more pain. He did die as he had lived. Few make such an exit. God does not promise to protect us from disease or death, but I am convinced, at times He takes his own in a special way. He took Elijah in a whirlwind. He took my patient in a sunrise while talking of others.

For special people, death comes as a thing of grace and beauty and victory.

The Last One
37

I finished the subcutaneous repair and was beginning the skin closure. The breast biopsy was benign. Our circulator, Jean Pearly, had nothing to do and casually felt the patient's right wrist.

"This patient has no pulse!"

The patient was young and healthy, but there was no pulse in the neck either. I began external massage. We got a pulse when I pushed, then a weak spontaneous pulse. On pure oxygen, she still didn't move. She didn't breathe. She had standard anesthesia of the day. She was put to sleep, a machine breathed for her, and the anesthetist took her blood pressure every fifteen minutes. Sometime in the last fifteen minutes, her heart stopped. It was almost time to check the pressure again so she might have had no circulation the full quarter hour. When I see dark blood, I know there is poor circulation, but there was no bleeding when I closed. As we moved the patient to a stretcher with the endotracheal tube in place, two other anesthetists consoled and took out the weeping lady who gave the case. I had to talk to the husband and nobody consoled me. How do you tell a man his wife in her early thirties died during a breast biopsy she delayed until Christmas vacation? What can *he* tell their children?

I spent most of the next two days in the ICU. The Administrator and others came. There was little they could say and little I could do. This was like a 48-hour wake. I could discuss and reminisce, but I couldn't change events of the past. The weak heartbeat was her only sign of life. Then it stopped and I had to talk to her husband again.

On Monday morning, I sat in the OR supervisor's office. I described this tragic case in detail. I said, "She got standard care and standard wasn't good enough ... she died. I want to be very clear about this: there is a new standard for me. Don't ever ... *ever* put a patient of mine to sleep without a monitor of some kind. I want one I can see or hear."

"But Dr. McGinnis, We only have one and it's for cardiac patients."

"Then buy some. I won't do a case without it."

"But they are so expensive!"

"What *is* the value of a human life? What is *your* life worth if *you* were on that table?"

She looked at the schedule book. "You have a case January 2. We'll have some by then."

* * *

Years later, I was doing another left breast case with several monitors going. Bobby Burford jumped up from his stool at the head of the table and said, "You've got to help me here. I've got a straight line." I glanced at the EKG monitor as I began massage. She had no circulation for less then twenty seconds.

She reacted like any other patient, but when fully awake in her room, she was mad. "You told me this would be an outpatient procedure. I thought I was going home."

"I thought so, too. The hospital has a very firm rule; if you die during surgery, you have to stay overnight." I pointed to the cardiac monitor. You did die; that stopped for a few seconds. I made up the rule. It seemed reasonable to me.

I explained the episode, but didn't tell her that she and others lived because another died so many years ago. The death I remember so well had new meaning.

Life Outside the Hospital

First Funeral

40

As my practice increased, we could afford things beyond food and shelter. The first of these was help for Betty. We never had the luxury of having family members who could even help with baby-sitting. I was undependable with my irregular hours and trips to the ER. Sylvia Thomas came to work for us. In those days, black women commonly worked in homes. She became increasingly important to us when Evan was added to the family. At times, her husband Frank worked for me.

Sylvia's mother died. We discussed the circumstances. If Sylvia were white, wouldn't we go to the funeral? Things like this weren't done in the mid-sixties, but we don't always abide by custom and convention. Betty got directions and we left early enough to arrive a full half-hour before the funeral on this summer Sunday. The little church was out in the country south of Anniston. I accused Betty of giving me the wrong time. We had to park a quarter of a mile from the church, and cars were still coming. We walked to the little white church surrounded by a sea of black faces. Some looked our way in disbelief. We spoke or nodded to those by the door. We got in the line that led into the church. We assumed the line was for seating. It passed down the right aisle, across the space in front of the church by the casket and then up the left aisle and out of the church. This was the line "to view th' co'pse." People were elbow to elbow in the pews. There wasn't room for a songbook between them. People were hanging over the rail in the balcony, others sitting in chairs by the wall at the end of the pews and some were standing at the back. Chairs in the choir loft were filled. There was not an empty seat in the church.

People were dressed in their Sunday best. Children were fresh scrubbed and shiny in their finest. I have never seen humanity so closely packed except when the mob crowds the gate after the home team loses. There was no place for two white faces in this church, so we made our way up the second aisle and into the narthex, visually asking each other what to do now.

I was startled by a voice from this sea of faces, "Dr. McGinnis, don' you want a seat?"

I didn't recognize the orderly from Unit 5, now dressed in a fresh pressed dark blue suit. I had never seen him in anything but the scrub suits at the hospital. "Hello, William, we did come for the funeral, but I didn't see seats anywhere."

"Oh, Dr. McGinnis, you go back up front. Time you get there, I'll have you somp'n."

We had no idea where we could sit besides somebody's lap, but we went. William ran out of the church and came back through the choir loft, , bringing two folding chairs. He put our chairs in the left aisle next to the front row, right under the preacher's nose and in front of the casket. The chairs filled the aisle. Like those in the pews, we were sitting elbow to elbow with those in the front row. On my right side, I had a little problem. The lady sitting next to me barely fit the pew front to back, and from side to side she overlapped into the aisle--considerably. She must have occupied three seats. She had to sit at the end; she could never have made it to the center. Fat women are supposed to be happy, but she scowled in total disapproval. I assumed she didn't want to sit by two white faces. As we walked down the aisle, I had looked around the packed room as much as I dared. I recognized some faces. I realized I had never seen these people all dressed up, but only in working clothes. We saw one other white face half way back in the middle of a pew. Sylvia's mother had worked in Alfred Caro's restaurant for many years. Alfred must have gotten there a full hour before the funeral to get a seat in a pew. There were then three white faces.

This was a three-preacher-printed-program funeral. At the beginning of the service there were few flowers in the church. Only the casket marked this as a funeral. At the beginning of the observance, flowers were brought down the right aisle and arranged at the front of the church. The giver was announced and the card was presented to the family. The flowers were then not arrayed by strangers. The "flower girls" were mature women friends of the family or a friend of the departed. There were tears and a degree of sadness, but this was not a depressing event. The preachers smiled and spoke with enthusiasm, each in his turn and each with increasing fervor.

Then they began to sing; and did they sing! The first song was by the choir. The lady overlapping into the aisles frowned with disapproval at the group and muttered, "*That* ain't no singin'."

She took a deep breath and helped them. I had to hold my program when she took that breath. I looked to see if the windows were going to be blown out. That was the most powerful voice I have ever heard, and she didn't need a songbook. She must have been kept out of the choir for fear she would dominate it. Even in the pew, she was louder than those on the stage. As the last note faded, I was happy to discover she did not discriminate. She looked at everything with disdain, and not just me. Then everybody sang, not just one song, but several with increasing enthusiasm. There were no funeral dirges. I felt in the presence of a celebration, not like the somber funerals I had known. I don't know how long this went on. I lost track of time listening to the singing. We must have been the only ones in the church not singing. Even little children were trying. After the first two preachers spoke, the main preacher began slowly and then increased volume and tempo.

Then at a critical point, in a sing-song chant he said, "Why-don'cha-say-amen?" Many did. After he spoke further, at another point, he said again, "Why-don'cha-say-amen?"

The same response came louder and longer. He didn't have to ask again. The participation of the congregation was infectious. Replies spread over the crowd. There were spontaneous courses of "Amen--Glory hallelujah--Yes Lord--Thank you Jesus" or just, "Oh, yessss." The walls seemed to throb with each response.

I wouldn't have been surprised if somebody had shouted, "Roll Tide!" This was like a giant pep rally or celebration. I never saw anything like this growing up in a Methodist church. I whispered in church of the past, but I had never said anything out loud. In the church of my childhood, few but the preacher spoke. The congregation watched and listened. After the event was over at last, we spoke to several people and waved to Alfred and walked the quarter-mile to the car.

As we pulled away, I told Betty, " I hate to admit it, but I enjoyed that funeral."

Betty said, "Yes, I did too. It probably does us good to find ourselves in the minority position for a change.

* * *

Years later, we went to the much larger New Prospect Church in Choccolocco to hear Doris Gilbert sing. She was working for us at the time. Her family had banded together as a singing group and bought an old school bus to tour northeast Alabama and Georgia for concerts in churches.

After we parked and began walking toward the church, long before I could recognize anybody, I heard the piercing voice of Sealey who had worked in X-ray forever, "Ya'all looke yonder. Here come Dr. McGinnis!"

They offered us a front row seat. After our experience in the past, we asked for a space farther back. We saw the same enthusiasm in singing we had seen before. Again, little children were singing or were on the stage with their parents trying to sing. The final number was "Twelve Gates to the City." Doris sang until she had to be helped off the stage.

Twice, we went to a church with a black congregation. Each time, members tried to make us feel welcome. I wondered if they came to our church, would we make them as welcome. Though people are different, there is no dispute when they walk common ground.

Land

41

Time passed and my practice grew enough so we didn't fear for survival. I bought a little office and hired secretarial help and a nurse. My office was small, but efficient. We had segregated waiting. There was one waiting room. I put a bench on the porch. Smokers were required to sit there. Times were changing. Betty did work when we first married. After the first baby, we didn't consider her working as a viable option. We had an unspoken agreement. I made the living and she made the living worthwhile. After two years in practice, we paid our bills and had some left over. I couldn't splurge and live high. The stock market fell a few months after I was born. I was not a child of the depression; I think I caused it. Those who lived through the dark years in the 30s have a different view of finances and security. Anything beyond food, clothing and shelter is extravagance. Years passed before I could bring myself to buy things that might be considered indulgences. I still can't throw away any piece of equipment. I might need a part or use it to build something else.

Our house in Golden Springs was modest, but better than we were accustomed to. We agreed we would keep it at least five years. At this stage, I had no intention of buying a bigger house or buying luxuries. Possessions are not the mark of a man, but there is a degree of security in owning a home, and even more in owning land. A man can be judged by what he does with his possessions, especially his land. There are those who are takers. Some strip-mine land and leave gullies and ponds of stagnant water surrounded by dead and dying trees. Others cut timber, leaving treetops, brush, and scrub trees. They abandon the land as worthless. The forest struggles to recover. Thirty years later, another taker comes and cuts the now smaller amount of good timber. After the third cutting, little is left but blackjack oak, brush, and hickory. The land has been high-graded by man as a predator. These men have taken everything and given nothing. What right does any man have to destroy land, nature has taken eons to develop? We have possession of land a few short years--a mere nothing in the history of the earth. We never truly own land. We hold it in trust. When we are gone, others will walk the land we called our own. If we have abused it, they will ask, "Why is this a desolate and destroyed wasteland? Who has done this thing?"

My own grandfather and great-grandfather were takers. They cut trees, but never planted. Nobody gave a second thought to this practice. The forests of virgin timber were thought inexhaustible. After they were all cut in North Carolina, my great-grandfather moved to Guinette County, Georgia, then west to Rome. My grandfather moved to Slackland, Alabama and then farther west to Springville as the trees were depleted. The moves followed the shrinking virgin timberlands. I have no wish to be a taker. I have never had an ambition to win the lottery, to derive gain I did not earn, probably because I have never won anything but a tacky party and a sack race.

I would like for those who follow to look at land I called my own for a few years and say the land is better for my presence, that I made a difference, even if the difference is small.

I began to look for the worst land I could find. As farmers say: that way you can make a good showin'. I met Jim Cleveland, who became my timber advisor. Randolph County offered the best opportunity for timberland. Coosa River Newsprint decided to sell all of their land east of the Tallapoosa River. The company wanted to sell to one person. The price for 1,600 acres was more money than I had or could imagine. I had just gotten out of debt and said I wouldn't borrow for anything except a house or car. Besides, I didn't know anybody could borrow that kind of money. The land I didn't buy would be worth millions in current value and timber harvested. In my defense, I did buy the largest single piece of land: 256 acres in Pinehill. Even this amount was frightening to one who had so recently been in debt. I was told to buy land for growing timber at $25 per acre. I had to pay $28. I had it cruised by a forester. There was enough standing timber to pay for the land the day I bought it. Never again would I see this kind of opportunity.

Pinehill was mostly scrub, but had some growing timber, so I left it undisturbed for 18 years. I had land, but nothing I could work on. Within a year I began to look for more worn-out land. Word came to me about a farm in Swagg, which was about as far out in the sticks as you can go. This farm of 498 acres was the only occupied farm at the end of a dirt road three miles long. I had only general directions, so I had to search for the place. I took with me Charles Jones, an anesthetist.

We made the trip on an Indian Summer Saturday. Early cold weather had turned a few leaves, but warm weather had come back. The sky was clear and blue. We drove Highway 431 south through Hollis Crossroads and Chulafinne then off the main road at Folsom School near Pinetucky onto a narrow paved road, then south on an even smaller road at Foster's store. After several miles we turned on a dirt road marked by a clump of canes. Country roads have no signs. We crawled along the rutted road, leaving a cloud of dust. We saw abandoned tumbled-down houses and crumbling chimneys wrapped with vines, marking the site of burned-out homes. They stood like tombstones against the sky, marking a resting place of life that once was. A few barns were barely standing with loose rusty metal flapping in the wind. Plows, broken hay rakes and rusted car bodies were sinking in a sea of vines and weeds. Fields were covered with scrub trees, weeds, and kudzu. Most of the woods showed evidence of years of high grading. A few acres had been cleared and planted. There was proof pines would grow.

As we made the last turns in the crooked road, I warned Charles, "Do not tell this guy I am a doctor. Call me any thing you like, but don't call me Doctor, Doc or even Mister. Try Mac or just wave. If he finds out, the price goes up. If he asks, I won't lie, but I won't volunteer."

We found the dirt drive and drove through the gap in the fence a half-mile from the house. The house was a tin-roofed white building. Mr. E. L. Major and his son were on the porch. They knew we were coming by the dust and sound of our pick-up. We introduced ourselves and stated our business. "I understand you are interested in selling your farm. We would like to look, if you have time."

Mr. Major said he didn't want to sell his family farm, but he was getting old at 55 and was afraid something would happen to him and his unmarried son would have to ride a mule to town to get help. The son had never learned to drive.

"Mr. Major, I see power lines. You can't get a phone?"

"Naw, them sorry phone people won't put one in. That's why I got to move closer to town so I can get one."

I knew the company would put in a phone anywhere there were power lines, but they charge mileage for the line. The charge would be less than the cost of a move, but I didn't argue with him. Mr. Major left his son at home and we drove and walked across much of his farm.

As we walked along the road, I could see Mr. Major silently measuring me. He looked me over from head to toe. I had worn old clothes, boots and a farmer's straw hat. He was a thin wiry man with wrinkled burned skin and was an enthusiastic talker. He spoke in explosive bursts and tended to fidget as he talked. He was dressed like I was with hat, shirt, pants and boots. He had searching, questioning, darting gray eyes. I could see his confusion as we talked. He couldn't see my reaction. He squinted, but I wore dark glasses. He pointed out any good feature of his farm as we passed. We walked by fenced pastures, abandoned fields, wooded ridges, and bottomland by the river. We stopped to look at a small bog he had fenced in to keep cattle away. He pushed a stick in the ooze and we watched it slowly sink out of sight.

Finally, he could stand it no longer," This here is a cattle farm. Ya in the cattle business?"

"No sir, I'm not in the cattle business. Might try it, though."

We walked a little farther, "Ya in the farmin' business? We usta raise lotsa corn and cotton on this place." Each time he gestured with his hands.

"No sir, I'm not a farmer."

Each time he asked a question, Charles looked the other way as if truth would show on his face. He was afraid he would say the wrong thing, so he said nothing. Twice he ran into briers while trying to look sideways and walk straight.

"Ya in the construction business? Lots of houses bein' built up the road."

"No sir, I'm not in the building business."

"Just as well. They've been saying they wuz gonna build a dam on that ol' river there for thirty year, but I don't see no sign of it till yet, and I don't b'lieve I ever will."

He limited our walk to the south end of the farm, which had most of the 130 acres of open land. This and much of the wooded area were fenced for pasture. When I asked about the other part, he assured me it was just the same, and we didn't need to see it. I didn't tell him I had seen the aerial photographs and knew the north and west were rolling hills covered with scrub, certainly not the same.

He had showed us what was left of a once thriving row crop farm that supported two families. As we walked the east road, we passed by a rock chimney, an open well, walnut trees and stunted yucca plants as evidence of the second home. This farm had been converted to a cattle operation, but they gave it little care. They didn't even own a tractor. Many of the fields and pastures were covered with scrub and weeds. Some fences were straight and others crooked as wires stretched tree to tree with only an occasional post. Here and there, terrace rows pushed up through the weeds in old fields like monuments of days gone by. When the two needed money, they sold a few cows. The cows wandered pastures, old fields and woods almost as free as the deer they shared the land with. The woods showed evidence of high grading in the past and one area had been clear-cut within the year. This was a good farm stripped of value. It was land and it could grow trees. The farm filled the inside bend in the Little Tallapoosa River where the Wedowee Creek empties.

The lot south of the house had three weathered barns and a large spring for the stock. Huge beech trees along a ridge surrounded the lot. They were old enough to have a thousand initials carved in the smooth bark and strange symbols, which could have been Indian signs. A little spring near the house joined the larger spring in the lot to form a branch that meandered, almost hidden by trees, across the southern part of the farm and emptied into the river. The branch and its genesis belonged to the farm. The bottom along the stream had not been cut. On either side of the crystal clear water were river birch, oak, poplar, gum, bay, big leaf magnolia, crabapple, dogwood, sourwood and a tangle of muscadine, wild grapes and plants I couldn't identify. The takers had missed this and another drain, because of difficulty in hauling timber from low areas. This was the center of the farm. We were so isolated and quiet, except for sounds of the birds and the buzzing of insects, it seemed as if the rest of the world didn't exist.

"Any sign of Indians living here, Mr. Major?"

He shook his head, "Been livin' here man an' boy 55 year. Ain't never seen no sign of injuns livin' on the place, though ther is a place called Injun Bathtub to the west."

We walked to the strange area. A rapidly flowing branch had made a six-foot deep cut in solid rock. We could walk up the stream and look up to the moss-covered layers of rock and get the impression of being in a huge elongated tub. I picked up an arrowhead and several chips along the trail above the bathtub. I said nothing. If he had not seen these in 50 years, why try to change his mind now?

As we walked along, Mr. Major began to tell about the loss of his wife a year ago. "Yessir, she took sick an' I done what I shoulda done. I taken her to the doctors right off. An' they put her in that hospital, and give her a lot of medicine an' she got worse an' worse, an' just plain died out. After they let her die, they still charged me a fortune, an' I had to pay it--them blood suckers. Ought to be a law agen' them folks."

We heard sudden coughing, gagging, choking sounds.

"You okay, Mr. Jones?"

"Uh, yessir. I must of ... ah ... I guess I sucked a gnat down my windpipe. That's what it was."

I took a quick look. Charles didn't have on dark glasses. He was looking away toward the woods as if somebody could read his mind through his eyes. Mr. Major continued to condemn doctors and hospitals until we reached the house. I was walking ahead at one point, but I could see the other two out of the corner of my eye.

He looked at Charles carefully and under his breath said, "Ya'all two ... ya in partnership?"

"No *sir,* I just came for the ride."

We said our good-byes at the house and drove the narrow drive to the dirt road and back to the paved road. Finally Charles said, "I thought I would bust."

"So I noticed. Remember, he never asked what I did, or what you did, for that matter. He only asked possibilities he thought of."

I asked my friend and timber expert, Jim Cleveland, to give an opinion. Mr. Major tried to pry information from Jim without success.

Jim's opinion was clear, "It's a good farm, but it's twice what you ought to pay for timber land. It's too much."

The final decision belongs to the man who pays. That much land almost surrounded by a wild river doesn't come on the market every day. The land had been stripped of timber, but it could grow more. There was open land to plant and scrubland to improve. I drove back one night to make him an offer for the farm, a little less than he asked. Mr. Major wasn't fidgeting. I could see from his eyes that the offer was reasonable.

"Well, I'll have to see if I can buy a farm toward town fa that much. Ya know we have to have someplace to move to. If ya bought this place, we couldn't stay a single day. I'll call ya from town one day if I can find somethin'." For the next few weeks, we answered the phone with a simple "Hello."

He called to accept the offer. I refused to wait for lawyers to clear the deal. I wanted money to change hands. I drove down the next night. I wrote a hand written bill of sale and had Mr. Major and his son sign acknowledging the sale and receipt of money. I gave him a check. You would have thought I had handed him a snake." Why ... why you're a doctor, says so right here! Why'n't you tell me?"

"You didn't ask me. Besides, would that have made any difference?"

"Well ... ah ... why no, I reckon not. I just never sold a farm to a *doctor* before."

"That's okay. I never bought a farm like this either. Things will be fine."

Jim shook his head in disbelief when he heard about the purchase. Three months later the soil bank program was announced. I agreed not to grow cotton, corn and tame hay for ten years and got half my money back. I wasn't going to anyway. A year later, the lake was announced. I had rather it had never happened because I lost 90 acres of bottomland. We did gain four and a half miles of shoreline on the lake. It is now the last large undeveloped piece of land on Harris Lake. Sale of land and timber on the flooded shoreline returned the purchase price several times over. The remaining 400 acres are planted in pines and in production. We have made major cuts three times and several smaller cuts for a return of many times the purchase price. I never mention the place to Jim Cleveland. I don't have to. Whenever I see him, he always moans about the worst advice he ever gave anybody.

Our Last Move
42

After we lived in the house in Golden Springs our agreed five years, we began to feel smothered by houses on every lot. With three children, we needed more space. If the kids were to have a home to remember, we needed to move. We never had air-conditioning, but thought it might be nice. We wanted to live on the far side of the mountain from Anniston and not on the mountain looking down at the rest of the world. Land along Choccolocco Road was unused and looked to be available. The land *was* there, but nobody wanted to sell. I even knocked on doors to find out who owned each piece of land. Each time I looked at property, I clocked driving time to the hospital. I didn't want to live more than ten minutes from the ER. After looking for a year, the only land I found was a steep hillside or farms beyond Choccolocco, over 15 minutes from the hospital.

I had not considered one piece of land because it belonged to Arthur Lee. He owned Lee Brothers Brass Foundry, the largest brass foundry in the world. He never sold anything but brass castings. Driving time to the unused land was nine minutes. What could it cost me except more disappointment? I called Mr. Lee, reminded him I did his workman's compensation and told my needs. I told him I wasn't looking for land to develop. I wanted a place in the country to build a home where we could raise our kids and a few acres for cows. The next Thursday, he drove me around his farm and the unused land across the road. Mr. Lee was cordial and spent most of the time showing me his farm. His land on the north side of Choccolocco Road had a house, swimming pool, and barn. The pastures were mowed like a golf course, and the little branch was lined with cement blocks on the sides and poured concrete on the bottom to prevent flooding. We did a quick drive through on the land across the road. It looked terrible. Shacks, sheds and old buildings were tumbled down. The fields had seen no care in years. Brush and weeds were everywhere. There had been fences once. A few strands of rusty wire hung on posts, more horizontal than vertical. All merchantable timber had been cut except one area around an old house site: a two-room house built on poles, several sheds, a leaning barn and a privy. The source of water was a spring 20 feet from the house. Remains of three other houses were scattered about. One house at the southeast corner was occupied. It looked like grade school kids built it at recess. There was a three-acre swamp along the branch to the south, and the north end was under water most of the year. Mr. Lee said he had tried to give it to Donoho School. They refused, saying the land couldn't be drained. Before the visit, I checked the soil map and a topography map. There was a 26-foot fall corner to corner of the land. As I looked at the map I thought, *I am no engineer, but if I can't drain 35 acres with a 26 foot fall, we will give up and move to the mountain.* Arthur Lee's farm looked great. The land across the road looked awful. No wonder the school wouldn't take it as a gift, but it was land, and land was what I needed. I thanked Mr. Lee and left. You can't make an offer of money to a millionaire. What would he need with a few more dollars? I went home and dismissed the events, even though this piece of land was my last resort.

Events of the day did not dismiss me. Scripture tells of prophetic dreams and visions. I have no reason to doubt these stories. Wild dreams come at times.

There may be meaning to some. People make a living interpreting them, but most are due to eating sausage and sauerkraut late in the evening or some other dietary indiscretion, or maybe strange images in our sleep come from trials of the day. My dreams are usually centered on frustration at being unable to do something. No matter how hard I try, in my dreams I never succeed. All sorts of obstacles are in my path. I always figured that was the curse of one who is a perfectionist at heart. In daylight hours, in my mind's eye, I see the end result of an operation before I do it. I am flustered if I cannot do what I can visualize. I am my own worst critic.

I had a dream that night, but this dream was different. Arthur Lee spoke as clearly as he spoke in the day. On the next morning, I thought of his words and laughed at how ridiculous they sounded. I had exhausted all possibilities of land for our house. I tried to forget it and went about my work.

Two weeks later, my secretary said Mr. Lee was on the phone. I picked up the phone to hear the words he spoke in the dream. He even quoted the same amount of money, and he was selling all of the land, not just the few acres I asked for. I almost dropped the phone and had trouble finding my voice to accept. A week after I gave Mr. Lee a check, I saw him give the same amount to the church at the Board of Stewards meeting. He sold us the land so we would improve it, and he would have neighbors with children. He drove by almost as often as I did when the house was being built. As soon as we moved in, he gave a standing invitation to use his pool. He liked to see the kids swim. He had none of his own.

Years later several people said, "I wish I'd knowed Mr. Lee wanted to sell that place! I'da bought it."

With no hesitation I told them, "No, you

wouldn't either." I told nobody but Betty about the dream and only after the phone call.

All was not great and wonderful afterward. Betty never told me until years later. A few days after we bought the land, she went to the property and parked at the old house among the weeds near some of the shacks. When N. C. Denton came riding his horse down the rutted road, he found Betty having a major cry. N.C. asked what was wrong. She said, "Gaston paid our money for ... for this ... this mess!"

It has been said that women don't think abstractly like men. Her tears were my fault. I had not explained and painted a vivid picture of what could be done with heavy equipment. She saw the land as it was. I saw it that way too, but I also saw it, as it would be after the redirected branch, grassed waterways, graded pastures, and drainage system along the road. While we were trying to decide where to put the house, we had a 'hundred-year flood' that washed out both bridges, covered roads and put the farm under water except the knoll where the old house and trees were. Now, we knew where we would build our house. Old houses are usually on the best sites. Then a tornado took 50 of the 75 pines and surrounded the house site with desolation. We would still make our last move, but it would be delayed. The only consolation was that the privy was gone. The metal roof is still wrapped around the top of a pine almost a mile away.

The event bothered first-daughter Donna. She said, "Daddy, what will we ever do with all the doo-doo?" As near as I can figure, it's under Betty's kitchen.

The hundred-year-old pines left in front are in clusters framing the house. God was our landscape architect.

Concrete

43

We lived in our house in Golden Springs a year beyond our goal of five. We had the land and began to make plans for our house in the country. We became painfully aware there wasn't enough money to build all we wanted. The bank would lend large amounts for a house in a subdivision, but nothing for one in the country. The children needed space, and they needed a home they could remember before they left for college. The solution was a compromise: the house would be smaller than we would like, and we would build a bedroom wing when finances permitted. I borrowed money from the Bank of Wedowee. Those people understood a house in the country. After the tornado took the pines we planned to keep, we sold the wood and cleaned up most of the mess, but for years our yard had decorator stumps. Before we could build, I hired men with heavy equipment to do grassed waterways, a pond, new drive, and rerouted branch. Eventually, we built our country colonial home, less the south bedroom wing we added after Jeannie was born. We landscaped and planted the yards ourselves.

I chose tree farming and cattle farming for my investment and diversion. Farming took me outside.

And the land? There is a line in *Gone With The Wind*. Scarlet's father said, "Land is the only thing worth fighting for."

I saved enough to begin a barn a year after we moved. We designed and built the barn, by then badly needed for hay and supplies. We were our own contractors. We hired real carpenters to cut the boards, but Owen, Lowell Rohnson, who lived in the little house on the farm, and I drove every nail on the inside walls and the floors. We used rough timbers for the frame, green hardwood for the floor and rough sawn pressure-treated twelve-inch board and batten for the outside walls. It had the expected metal roof. When the green from the treatment faded, we stained the wood red. Is there any other color for a barn? We had a sealed and finished feed room and workroom, two stalls, two sheds, a central hall and a hayloft. It looked big and empty. After the first hay-season, the loft was full. Cows stood on a hard clay mound south of the barn to eat from a hayrack. But when the winter rains came and 35 cows and calves walked back and forth day after day, that hard bank became a sea of mud and manure. Cows struggled to walk anywhere near the hayracks and sank into this mess belly deep in some areas. That startling sound that a cow's hoof makes when it's pulled from deep mud is the standard by which all sucking sounds are measured. Worse still, people found it almost impossible to walk in this sea of mud. Lowell twice lost a boot and watched it slowly sink in the mess. He tried hopping out of the mud with disastrous results. I even got both feet stuck and sat down in this murky mess. The final straw was losing balance and falling into the vile mix from a board floated on this loblolly. Something had to be done!

The hot days of summer dried the sea of mud to a hard red-brown layer. But we knew rain would bring back the sea of mud. We had economized when we built the barn; now we had to have a concrete pad where we fed the cows. Ready-mix plants wouldn't deliver Saturday afternoons, so we asked for the latest possible delivery on Thursday, my afternoon off. We had never spread and finished concrete so I ordered the minimum yard and a half. First son Owen and I could do that, and Lowell would be there late in the day, after work, to help finish. We built forms. We made a float of a one-by-six nailed and braced to a six foot pole. We gathered rakes, hoes, shovels, and hand-finishing tools. We tried to think of everything. We were ready. On the last delivery of the day, the driver would not be rushed. What could go wrong?

The truck came on time and Owen led the driver through the gate at the Rohnson house, and two pastures to the back of the barn. The driver backed the truck close to our work area, unfolded the chute and pointed it toward our forms. The driver stood at the back of the truck and turned the motor up. The fat cylinder in the back turns faster to agitate the mix. The cylinder tilts and as the cement is delivered, there is a rumbling and then a more gentle sliding-scraping sound as the mix comes gliding down the chute.

"Hear it comes! Spread it; smooth it; don't let it pile up!"

We raked, shoveled, pushed and pulled the float, smoothed and filled the whole section inside the forms south of the barn. The sliding, scraping sound stopped.

"Is that about all? We must have figured it just about right."

"Thay's more, Doc ... lots more."

"My gosh, Owen; we have to put it somewhere. Smooth that floor in the stall. I'll get a wheelbarrow." The driver patiently waited and watered the mix a little. We hauled load after load by wheelbarrow and eventually covered the stall floor.

"That has to be it!"

The driver shook his head, "You ain't touched it, Doc. Thay's still more."

More wheelbarrow work. more grunts, groans and sweat and we covered the feed pen. Lowell arrived and was as surprised as we were that we weren't finished.

"Still more?"

"Bunch more, Doc."

So we scraped out the entire area behind the barn and shed and put up more forms and spread that rumbling, scraping, sliding mix as it came down the chute.

"Hold up; it's too stiff to spread."

"I'll wet her down a little, Doc."

We pushed and spread and smoothed and stomped it down and moved the forms three times. We were desperately trying to flatten and smooth concrete, by now too stiff for the float.

The best words I heard that day were, "That's about it, Doc."

The other two were still madly working when I signed the delivery ticket. "I never thought a yard and a half would go so far!"

"Doc, I know ya ast fer a yard and a half, but them commercial jobs early in the day all'us order too much, so I just taken the extre back to the plant and they put the next load on top. Ya got th' leavin's o' the day. I figure ... meby five and a half or six yards. Well, I got to go and ya'all still got lumps to mash."

We stood there totally staggered by the news, covered with cement, not a dry thread on us, sweat dripping off our noses, and trying to catch our breath. We looked around to see Lily Flag, our biggest cow, slowly chewing her cud with that placid sideways motion and blinking her eyes as she slowly sank in our fresh cement. She seemed to be smiling. This was her revenge for sawing off her horns. There is a huge artery in the horns so when we cut them I put a large bandage around the stumps to control bleeding. So there stood a cow looking like she recently had a craniotomy standing in our fresh concrete. Nobody had strength enough to have a fit, so we just said unkind words as we ran her out and smoothed the rough spots. Some were too dry to work, but it was thick. We had done in one afternoon what was planned for four.

Forty years later, the barn still stands--still red, but faded enough to need restaining last year. The green hardwood flooring in the loft dried, shrank, and left cracks over the hall showing the barn-swallow mud nests on the joists below. A thousand baby birds first saw the light of day from these nests in our barn. The children always liked to watch the mothers feed the babies. Lily Flag's bones rest on the farm. Even though she grew old, I would not sell her; I would not let her go. Not so with the children. The gate must be left open, and they do leave. But the gate is still open, and they may come back even for a little while. And the concrete? Experts say it gets harder and harder for the first hundred years. Thirty-five cows couldn't tear it up. It was the only stable footing in the thunder snow of '93. It will outlast us all. It 's still a little lumpy though.

Choccolocco Night Life

44

A strip of gently sloping land running along a range of mountains toward White Plains is called the Choccolocco community. This area was settled and has been farmed since the 1800's. The post office was established in 1878. Some homes are older. Over three quarters of a century ago, the road from Birmingham to Atlanta was near what is now Choccolocco Road in that part of Calhoun County between Highway 78 and Dearmanville to the south and the mountain toward Fort McClellan to the north. The narrow paved road wound through the valley and the community of Choccolocco. The town was on a main road, had a rail line through the middle, and its own station. In the 19th and early 20th century, every available foot of ground was planted in cotton. All this was a basis for a progressive growing community with churches and schools. But after a time, the main route was changed to Highway 78 south of Dearmanville. Few scraps of the old road are left. A half-mile section is still used as a driveway on the Lee Farm. The station was closed, the train didn't stop any more, cotton moved west and Alabama was no longer called "The Cotton State."

After these drastic changes, the valley went back to sleep. The mountains were always covered with hardwoods and a scattering of pines. When cotton was no longer king, 40 years ago few serious farmers were left and trees and brush reclaimed much of the abandoned land.

A drive along Choccolocco Road in these slow years showed small fields, pastures, gardens, a few cattle, several branches and heavily wooded areas. Deer browsed open areas and foxes crossed the road at night. Turkeys were more secretive, but raccoons and 'possums were commonplace. Houses were scattered along the winding road. Some had been deserted for years. Country stores were here and there, but the old gristmill with over-shot wheel on Camp Lee Lake had been torn down. Nothing is left but the stones, which always remain. The top stone is at the Lee farm and the bottom is the base of the fountain in front of our house. Nobody knows how these stones came to be on these two farms.

Life was slow and laid back after the main road, train stops, and cotton fields left. The rumble of wheels and mournful call of the train whistle added to the scene. Others began to see the solitude and beauty of the valley and it began to change. Farms became smaller and more numerous. Some were replaced with clusters of houses on an acre or two. The occupants were not farmers, but those with jobs in the city.

In the midst of new houses, at the western edge of the community of Choccoocco sat a squat two-room never painted house with a tin roof on a two-acre plot. The barn behind the house leaned in different directions depending on which way the wind blew. There was no power or running water and the yard had never known a lawnmower. A crumbling shed covered a hand-dug well in the front yard. The house looked out of step with the changing community, but it had a right to be there. It was there first. Two brothers and a sister lived in the house. It was said the building had wiring when they moved in, but they tore it out because they didn't understand it. The older brother and sister, Milford and Susan, worked for neighbors part time. They sold produce from their garden, but neither had a regular job.

Then there was Binkie, the younger brother. He was ... well ... unique. He was a heavy-set man with a puffy red face. He laughed and smiled a lot, was talkative and jovial even when sober. He wore a faded blue shirt and overalls year round; it looked like the same pair. Sometimes there was a brown stain at the corners of his mouth from yesterday's snuff. Binkie was not known to work ... ever. It was said he bathed when it was warm enough to use the creek. Some claimed each time there was a fish kill downstream. All three wandered the roads and paths. They didn't hesitate to walk three miles west to the grocery store at Golden Springs or seven miles to Anniston. As they walked, they did stick out a thumb for a ride with their more Christian neighbors. Binkie got more rides than his brother and sister because he stood in the middle of the road to thumb.

When people stopped to keep from hitting him, he jumped in their car and said, "Thank ya fer th' ride, I need ta go ta th' store in Choccoloc'. Nise da,y ain't it?"

For whatever reason, Binkie might forget new houses in the community blocked his usual path, and he ended up in a yard surrounded by barking dogs. Several wooded areas had a collection of whiskey bottles and a worn spot by a tree.

Binkie was responsible for getting rid of the garbage at their house. When we moved to our farm at Pinecroft, we hauled away three trailer loads of junk from the southern end of the property. It appeared to have been collected over the years. We put up a fence so we could graze cows. We assumed the dumping would stop. Binkie's path was blocked by our fence so he walked through the woods of his neighbor to the north. He dumped all the tin cans across our new fence, so we would think Mr. Church did it. He never dreamed we would see the worn path from his house. Half of the cans were dog food cans. They had cats, but no dogs.

The most startling experience with Binkie was late at night. About midnight, somebody would hear a bam-bam-bam at the door. When they opened the door, a large gruff man said, "Wanta borry a dollar," or even worse, "Wanta use ya phone," or "Woulya call me a cab?"

Cab drivers wouldn't come unless the caller told them Binkie had the money in his hand. Binkie would ride to a source of booze at any hour. When he woke up, he walked home. He went to new houses and where he had success before.

Binkie went to the Sims' house within a week after they moved in. At midnight, they gave the dollar to be rid of him, so he came back. Everybody knew Binkie shouldn't be given money, but at midnight with a man who fills the doorway, has a gruff voice and breath that would peel wallpaper, the quickest way to be rid of him is to give him the money. Late one night at the Sims' house, the dogs began to bark. Dogs didn't bite Binkie. They never got close downwind. The Sims driveway was a quarter mile long so there was quite a commotion by the time the bam-bam-bam came at the door. It takes several minutes to get from a back bedroom to the door. The bam-bam-bam sounded again. Binkie hadn't been to the Sims' house for some time and never in the daytime. He didn't know they had a new pet--a big spider monkey with long, hairy arms and legs. He roosted, or whatever monkeys do, in the rafters of the front porch over the door where Binkie was banging. When Mr. Sims opened the door, nobody was there.

Binkie was fast fading out of sight, running at a pace nobody knew he had, hollering, "Help me, Mr. Sims, help me, some'n's got me!"

The monkey had dropped down out of the rafters and wrapped those long, hairy arms and legs around Binkie's neck and face. He just managed to see well enough to run, peering between monkey fingers,

The monkey was hanging on for dear life,

making monkey sounds which probably meant, "Help me, Mr. Sims: somethin's got me and it's runnin' away with me!"

Binkie could have gotten a track scholarship that night. Man and monkey were both hollering. The monkey was sober, but he wasn't driving.

Now what was Mr. Sims to do? Call the police? How would it sound to say at midnight, "A fat man just ran away with my monkey?" Should he get in the car and drive around to look for a fat man carrying a monkey? Should he go downtown and fill out a missing monkey report?

By the way Binkie left, he was going overland, so everybody went back to bed saying, "They probably deserve each other. Besides, after his wild ride, the monkey will come home."

The next morning--no monkey. At noon--no monkey, and Binkie was not to be seen around his house. Late in the afternoon, the monkey came walking down the driveway, complaining, panting and at times clutching his chest. Actually, it looked as if he were clutching his chest with one hand and holding his nose with the other. Nobody ever knew how far he walked.

The monkey did not eat well after that day and wouldn't get on his roost. Some thought he had had a heart attack. It's more likely he was depressed over his experience because two days later he stuck his finger in a light socket and committed monkeycide.

After the night of the monkey ride, Binkie didn't drink ... for a while. He never knew what got him and he never again went back to the Sims' house.

Hay
45

Care of livestock is simple in theory. Cows eat grass in the summer and hay in winter. But making of hay is hard work and can be dangerous. It's almost an art form.

One summer when there were many cows to feed and four children to help, we had an ideal crop of maturing hay blessed by sun, rain, and fertilizer. The week was filled with talk of weather, height of grass and dryness of the soil. On our farm, hay takes a day to cut, two days to dry and a day to bale. A mistake in judgment could cost the crop. Toward midweek, we put the hay on the ground with a sickle bar cutter. Hay is made by sun drying grass about knee high when cut. But how dry? It should be about 25 percent moisture. Below 20 percent, the nutritional content is ruined. If moisture is too high, hay will go through a heat and can set fire to the barn.

When hay is cut, there is great anticipation for the next two days. We waited and wondered if we had made the right decision. There is no doubt to passersby that hay has been cut. It's difficult to call what comes from a hay field an odor or smell. The fragrance is said to come from the growth of mold. Whatever the cause, to anybody passing a hay field waves of odors wrap and overwhelm the senses. It can be tasted as well as smelled. To one who has never walked through fresh-cut hay, it cannot be described.

Late Friday, we could almost feel the waves of smells against our faces. But was it ready? An experienced farmer looks at hay, smells it, twists a handful, watches it untwist, and says, "Yup." I discussed this with Lowell Rohnson who lived and worked on the farm and with James Sims, the neighbor with the baler. We didn't have the "Yup" experience, so I did the salt test. I cut the hay to fit, twisted and put it in a quart mason jar, and added a spoon of salt. I shook the jar one hundred times or 'til I got tired, opened it and poured out the salt. I always feel like a witch doctor examining a bag of bones to read the future. If the salt clumps, there is too much moisture. This time there were individual grains. The moisture was right. On the next day when the dew burned off, we windrowed the hay. We were committed. A small rain would not hurt hay in the swath, but in a row it would be ruined. I finished my work at the hospital and Saturday office. I could've found my way blindfolded, the smell was so great. The children, James Sims, Lowell, and Betty had started baling and loading. As the truck driver, Betty already had problems. She ran over a high row of hay or a broken bale and the muffler set fire to the hay field. Then as they were headed to the barn, Betty with her heavy foot, braked suddenly and threw Owen off the stack of hay, across the cab roof, down the windshield and onto the hood where he hung to the windshield wiper. She left in a huff, but did come back later with lemonade.

The baler made a constant chunk, chunk, chunk noise as it picked up and packed hay. Then there was a sharper clicking and sliding sound as a bale was tied and pushed off. As the truck moved down the line of bales, two people picked up bales and one stacked them on the truck. As a stack got taller, Cleo, the smooth collie, with tongue hanging out, rode the top bale, overseeing it all.

The driver can't see the stack so he listens for the tap on the roof and "Head for the barn, Dad." Then I know we have a full load of hay we have grown, cut, baled, and loaded.

We were putting up the best hay we had ever seen. Suddenly the chunk, chunk, click, slide stopped. James was standing to one side staring at his baler and frowning.

"What's wrong?"

"It's broke."

"How soon can you get it fixed?"

"Monday."

James got in his truck and left. He was a man of few words. We were then left with most of our hay on the ground and heavy rain forecast for Monday.

I had recently seen hay put up in the ancient fashion and had talked to the farmers who used the old ways. I sent Lowell and one helper to cut hardwood saplings. I used the long poles to make a square teepee frame with the long crosspieces at the bottom and shorter ones near the top. I held them together with wire. We set the long poles in the ground a few inches.

We loaded loose hay in the truck. Two older children unloaded the hay and the two small ones stomped it. We stacked hay on the bottom cross piece to keep it off the ground. We piled thick layers around and around. As the stack grew taller, we lost Evan. We could hear him, but couldn't see him. A haystack has a hollow center for ventilation. That's why Little Boy Blue could be under the haystack fast asleep. Evan had fallen in the hole and couldn't get out. He was giving excuses as we pulled him up. Standing on the bed of our truck, we built the stack as high as we could reach with pitchforks. We put a thick layer of hay on the top and covered it with a piece of plastic tied on all sides. It was the prettiest haystack in the world--or so we thought.

Nobody had trouble sleeping that night.

Monday's storm blew away the plastic, but we had no need to worry. That haystack shed water like a thatched roof and slowly turned gray then black. We put up an electric fence around the stack. The cows ignored the stack with grass to graze, but as fall turned to winter, cows became very interested. The stack was black and didn't look like hay, but the cows knew it was there.

The cows elect a checker for an electric fence. I've never seen the vote, but they must. The checker is never the bull or a big cow like Lily Flag, but one of the lesser cows in the bovine hierarchy. At least once a day, she eyes the stack and electric fence. Very slowly, the checker cow comes closer and closer to the fence. She covers the last foot by leaning and stretching her neck. Slowly, she pushes her wet nose until zap! The checker recoils not only backwards, but seems to jump up about a foot and goes off licking her wounded nose. At the time of the zap, other cows hear the sound and jump in sympathy.

Winter came, frost killed the summer grass and winter grazing was short. The checker now came several times a day. Winter rain set in and the cows began hanging around the barn with a bad case of mulligrubs. I took down the fence and the cows ate through the black layer and pulled out bright green hay better than any in the barn. It lasted a long time and not a scrap was left.

* * *

Now, years later, few cows are left. The children have gone in different directions. For a few years, we bailed with our own bailer and hired help. I sold the baler and now a crew bails for us on the halves. As I walk the fields and pastures, in my mind I see those children and hear their voices. I think about and regret my inadequacies as a parent. I was too hard on them, as I was on myself. I have left them with a curse of mixed blessings. They have the work ethic. They are hard-working, over-achievers who know the joy of accomplishment, and have the ability to do something and do it well.

One day, they may understand their roots are here and much of who they are, developed here. I wonder about *their* children. In some way, will they learn the joy of knowing a job well done, when somebody hits the cab and says, "Head for the barn, Dad."

"I don't like work--no man ever does--but I like what is in the work, a chance to find yourself. Your own reality--for yourself not for others--what no other man can ever know. They can only see the mere show and never tell what it really means."

Conrad 1857-1924

Intruder

46

No matter how much hay was in the barn, how good the crops were, strong the fences, or fat the cows, there was always something else to do on a farm. As the children knew all too well, if nothing else was pressing, we could always pick up rocks.

Our farm is in a valley between two branches. Over the eons, as the streams changed courses in floods, they dropped loads of rocks that tumbled down the mountains from the north. The streams must have changed many times because most of the farm is covered with rocks. We piled them along the fence lines, filled ditches with them, built walls, made a smokehouse, pillars for a gate, foundations for small buildings and a fountain in the front circle. We were not the first. There is the shell of a stone house on the farm. A pasture would seem clear of rocks, but when the rains came, more appeared. They must breed. I have heard strange clicking sounds in the pasture on a moonless night.

To have free time and not do some sort of work is usually painful to a farmer, especially a workaholic type, even if he is only part time. A farmer's work is never done. Betty always asked me what I was going to do as I went out the door. The standard answer was, "Whatever grabs me first."

Late one summer day when the children were small, nothing grabbed me as I left the house. The loft was full of hay, the garden had been weeded, the fences were intact, the cows were healthy, and I pretended not to see the rocks. Like the poor, they are with us always.

Most of our farm is almost flat. The land ends on a ridge to the south and west. In the distance, there is a mountain to the north, and a low ridge far to the east. The central forty acres are cleared and planted in pasture and hay fields. The house sits on a knoll almost in the center. The garden and vineyard lie to the north, and the barn is by the drive two hundred feet east of the house. From the barn, the house or anywhere in the pasture, there are sweeping views of the mountains and screen of wooded strips at the edge of the farm. Cows graze in pastures surrounding the house.

On this day, mountains and trees at the edge of the farm were shades of green against a brilliant cloudless sky. The open land was covered with pasture grass, rippling with the slightest breeze. A sea of green surrounded me. As I walk the pastures, I always think of the words, *"and in the grass I hear him pass."*

Our cows grazed this green sea. The farm was filled with life. Our family, our cows, chickens, dogs and cats shared this land with of God's wild creatures. Deer browsed in late afternoon; foxes came at night; rabbits, 'possums and field mice were everywhere. Fish and other creatures lived in ponds and branches. Birds filled the air and trees with voices. As I walked to the barn, I saw a coach whip snake, but I didn't see the famous hay snake. When the kids were playing rather than helping with hay work, I always told them to watch for the hay snake: a large snake that lives in the hay and is the same color. The kids never knew if they should believe this or not, but they always became quiet and looked around, just in case. Occasionally, one would "see" the snake to scare the others. I smelled the acrid sweet odor of manure and the musty smell of hay as I walked through the hall of the barn.

The barn swallows were making sweeping circles south of the barn as they caught insects in full flight. I could hardly see them as they swooped in the hall to feed babies in the mud nests. They complained to me when I stood too close. When I saw how hard the birds were working, my conscience bothered me--just a little. But there are days not for work. This was such a day: a time for taking stock, recharging the battery, and renewing the soul. As I walked, more birds surrounded me: bluebirds, redbirds, mockingbirds, and loud-mouth jays. In the distance I could hear the "woody woodpecker" call of the pileated woodpecker in the tall pines on the south ridge and the irritating call of the crows. Above it all, two hawks soared effortlessly in sweeping circles on motionless wings.

I had driven the truck to the southeast corner to check the flood gate at the big bridge, when I heard a sound that didn't belong: a whirring chopping sound like a giant runaway mixer, a harsher sound than a thousand crows over our peaceful farm. We had heard our mountains were like those of the Orient, so this area of the world was used for training helicopter pilots before they were sent overseas. Helicopters of all sizes flew regular patterns over our valley and mountains. They made a turn as they passed overhead. I thought they used our house as a checkpoint. Today's helicopter was a big noisy one coming over the mountain carrying a platform in a sling. At least I thought it did. I glanced away for a second. When I looked back, there was no sling. This intruder to our world came lower, louder, and different from the usual whirring, beating noise. This huge machine was not only low, but landing in our middle pasture to the north. I opened the gate in front of the barn and the one to the north pasture and drove to the helicopter, now quiet with drooping blades. Two men were outside. I suppose they were trying to get the hood up. I considered several astute things to say, but didn't when I saw the lieutenant. He was young, pale and sweating. He was unable to hide the quaver in his voice, when he said the helicopter had motor trouble as they came over the mountain. When the instruments indicated they had a serious problem, they dropped the platform on the mountainside and landed in the first open space.

The sergeant said, "I never saw so many rocks in one place when we came down."

"Sorry about that. I am trying to get the kids to pick them up. At least you didn't hit a cow."

The lieutenant was fuming about being out of communication.

"You don't have a radio?"

"I can't use it. Uh ... you are in a valley ... sort of isolated."

"Yes, we like it that way. We have phones. Would you like to use one?"

I took the lieutenant to the house and he called Camp Rucker. "Yes sir, down. Yes ... well, all the way down ... in a cow pasture. Okay, we'll look for it."

The parade of lookers and sightseers began that afternoon and increased the next day. Early the next morning, a repair helicopter landed, left and came back over and over while men worked on the sick bird. Reporters and sightseers climbed our fences in droves. They never considered asking or using a gate. Our cows were trying to hide in the woods. Pauline, our milk cow, wouldn't even let down her milk. The men working on the helicopter kept sightseers away, but on the afternoon of the second day when the children could stand it no longer, I took them to the downed bird. I told the lieutenant the least he could do was to let the kids look in. They had the whole tour. They walked through the cabin, sat in the seats and moved the controls. Late in the afternoon, the repair crew left, followed by the repaired helicopter. The cows gave a collective sigh of relief. Pauline headed for the barn, but she walked a little funny.

I was certain any day I would get a letter or call from some general thanking me for their being allowed to dominate our farm for two days. The call never came. I may yet send a bill for the day the intruder fell on our farm.

Flights I Would Not Make Again

47

God has given wings to birds, insects, and mammals. At one time reptiles flew. Angels are said to have wings. I don't doubt they are around. I haven't seen one; and hope I don't--for a while. I have never known of a human being sprouting even small wings. I have difficulty convincing myself man was meant to fly. The safety statistics say mile for mile we are safer in a plane than a car. With motor trouble in a car or a flat, we could always pull over to the side of the road and walk to get help. But in a plane at 38,000 feet? Medical meetings are sometimes hundreds or even thousands of miles away demanding time, wear and tear of a bus, train, or car trip. I have flown to get from here to there, but I always feel out of my element. I may fly again when the trauma of the last trip fades.

My first white-knuckle flight was of medical necessity in 1960. As Chief of Surgery at Sandia Base Hospital in Albuquerque, I was treating a retired colonel for severe GI bleeding. We needed at least six units of blood to consider surgery. We were down to two, with no hope of more in our 250-bed hospital. The hospital was well equipped, but AB negative blood was in short supply. I decided to air evacuate him to the hospital at Fort Sam Houston Texas, giving what blood we had as we went.

In the late afternoon, nobody else would go, so I said, "I'll do it myself, cut me some orders."

I managed to locate fatigues and transferred my insignia. Orders and evidence of rank are essential in the army, even when somebody is bleeding to death. The Corpsman and I loaded the colonel, blood, and supplies in the ambulance and headed for the airfield. The plane warming up was a tired old camouflage-painted C47, a military version of a DC3, known as a Gooney Bird. It sat tilted toward the tail wheel. We put the colonel's head on the down side to help his pressure.

As we loaded, the pilot said, "We're gonna fly sorta low. It'll be a little warmer on the colonel that way. Ya know, this ol' bird's not pressurized." Cactus and big rocks were sliding just under the wings as we went through mountain passes. Maybe the copilot's crack about picking needles out of the wings wasn't a joke. I was glad to be occupied in treating the colonel and didn't have to watch all those rocks and cactus. When darkness came, I did wonder how the pilot could see to fly that low.

When we landed, a helicopter was waiting to take us across the city to the hospital. We landed and transferred the colonel to the surgical unit. I turned over his records and the last bottle of blood. The officer thanked me and turned to leave.

"Uh, Major, what about us--our transportation back to the field?"

"Captain, the helicopter certainly can't fly for just two men and we don't run a delivery service at this hour. Sorry, you're on your own. The field is 18 miles due west."

The pilot had said he would wait a short while for us, so we had to act fast. We could have hired a cab, but between the two of us we couldn't pay for more than a mile. We went to the emergency room and bummed a ride in a delivery truck that brought a load of supplies and was going west. Army trucks are not noted for comfort. The driver was in no hurry and it seemed an eternity before we saw the field.

The plane was warming up when we arrived. After waiting over an hour, they had given up on us and were about to leave. The copilot gave us a blanket each and helped us put on a chest parachute.

"How come we didn't wear 'chutes coming down?"

"You wouldn't jump out and leave the colonel, would you?"

"I could have put one on him and pushed him out first."

"Ah ... well, to tell the truth, we wuz too low to jump anyway. If sump'in' happened, we'da just rode 'er down."

That old plane had cracks in the sides and holes where rivets had been. At several thousand feet, wind whistles through any small opening in an unpressurized plane making it unbelievably cold. We needed more than one blanket.

The colonel did survive. He had a duodenal ulcer perforated into the aorta. This needed major vascular surgery our hospital was not equipped for.

I did not again volunteer for air evacuation.

* * *

In 1968, after the memory of the evacuation flight had faded, I made a trip to Springfield, Illinois, to visit a friend in the cattle business and look at calves for sale. The visit was pleasant and the weather good, but on the day I was to leave the wind was high, as it can be in flat country.

Springfield may be the capitol, but it is a small town and has a small airport. We had come into town on a large twin-engine plane in good weather. On the day I left, we were to load by walking across the apron directly to the plane. After they called our flight, I went outside into a wind so severe people were having trouble standing. I couldn't see any plane that remotely looked like something I would fly on. There was a twin motor DeHavelin warming up. Men were holding the wing tips to keep the plane from blowing over. I asked a man who looked like an experienced commuter.

He pointed, "That's our plane right there."

This plane sits on a tail wheel and two front wheels--not tricycle landing gear that makes the cabin floor level. We grabbed a rail and pulled up the few steps at the rear of the plane and walked the aisle uphill. We stooped to walk. The only one upright was the stewardess. She was little over four feet tall and got her job because of her physical qualifications.

There were 18 seats in the same space with the pilots in this commuter plane. We could see them struggle with the controls as the plane bounced down the runway. I always pull up on the armrests to help get the plane off the ground on takeoff. That day I had to try to keep us level also. The pilots were good or we wouldn't have been upright ... well, mostly upright. Wind threw that plane around like a toy. We might as well have been on a big kite. Nobody was allowed out of seat belts. There was no loudspeaker. If the pilot wanted to tell us something, he turned his head and hollered.

The short stewardess worked her way down the aisle seat to seat holding as she went. She carried cabin service in a fishing tackle box. She offered miniatures of liquors and plastic cups. Several passengers fortified themselves this way. There were no napkins; passengers were expected to wipe their mouths on a sleeve. If passengers didn't want straight booze in a cup, they might expect a coke or something. Eighteen cans won't fit in a tackle box. Non-drinkers got a sucker. As the plane lurched about, I couldn't get mine in my mouth.

After what seemed like an eternity, the pilot said, "We're approaching Memphis and will be landing shortly ... I think."

We came fluttering down like a leaf in fall wind,

but miraculously leveled out to make a reasonable landing. After a few minutes, I was able to prize my hands off the armrests. The ride to Birmingham was in a larger more stable plane. I have not since flown, nor will I fly in a light plane or on a kite.

* * *

In 1975 I attended a medical meeting in Anaheim, California. The flight there was uneventful--they always are. The day after the meeting, the bus left in late morning for the nearest airport in a city several miles away. Except for Disneyland, Anaheim is a small town and has no field. After breakfast, I walked in the strawberry fields next to the motel. I would be home in just a few hours so I bought the biggest crate I could fit under the seat of the plane. I didn't want the green ones they shipped out, but the ripe ones just right for strawberry shortcake that night. They fixed a handle for me and taped newspaper over the crate to cover the berries. The crate was heavy, but I could manage it and my small bag.

The first shock was from the lady at the Delta ticket desk, "I see you missed your flight. I'll see when we can get you another one."

The numbers on my ticket were smudged and I had misread it. I couldn't have made the flight anyway. There was no earlier bus. As soon as I was given the new time of arrival, I called Betty. She had already left for Birmingham.

I changed planes in Dallas well after dark. The weather was a little rough as we left and got worse. There were flashes of lightning in black swirling clouds. We changed altitude and direction several times. Each time, the plane pitched, twisted and jerked all the more. The motion on this large airliner was worse than the light plane years ago. At times, the plane suddenly seemed to fall hundreds of feet as we hit air pockets. There was an occasional gasp or muttered curse or prayers, but nobody talked. Passengers were as solemn as a funeral procession listening to sounds of the storm and the groaning of the motors as we struggled through a convulsing sky. Even the stewardesses were strapped in. We were never totally upside down, but it was close.

Suddenly there was a quavering voice on the loudspeaker, "Is…is there a doctor on board? A man thinks he's having a heart attack."

I was glad to have something to do besides worry about the wings staying on. I worked my way along the aisle holding to the seats on both sides. Some passengers reached out to grab my arms and pull me along. Two stewardesses were hovering over a thin man of 17 or 18. He wore a Hawaiian shirt and sharkskin trousers. The stewardesses had pulled down an oxygen mask. He was hyperventilating violently.

The stewardesses were startled when I jerked away the mask. "You don't need this. Now listen to me. Your hands are tingling, drawing and in spasm, aren't they?"

"Well ... yes."

"And your lips are numb?"

"Yesss. ... '

"And your face is hot and you feel like you can't get your breath."

"Yes!"

"All those things are because you are anxious and are huffing and puffing and have blown away too much carbon dioxide and have alkalosis. You have lots of scary symptoms, but it's not dangerous. It's hyperventilation. Look, I am afraid of the storm, too. If the pilots have good sense, they are afraid, but they are trying to get us through. What *are* you looking for in that bag?"

"My grandmother's heart medicine."

"You aren't having a heart attack and you don't

need that medicine. Now, you have two choices. Say a little prayer, talk to me and slow your breathing down to a normal rate, or so help me I will hold a barf bag--even a used one--over your face till your CO2 builds up."

He slowly became convinced that he was not about to die from a heart attack--maybe a plane crash--but not a heart attack. As the violent motion of the plane increased, the pilots spotted a tornado on radar and turned back to Dallas. The kid's breathing was normal and his symptoms cleared by this time, and I made my way back to my seat. I had no trouble finding my place. There was an unmistakable odor of ripe strawberries. The ambulance and paramedics were at the airport when we landed. I had convinced the kid he had no heart trouble, so he wouldn't go to the hospital.

There would be no flights until the next morning when the storm cleared. A Delta representative said they would be glad to get us a room, but with all the cancellations, there were none within thirty miles. They gave us a meal ticket and turned us loose to wander about the building. I called Betty to tell her when I hoped to arrive. She had left again to pick me up. Some people left, saying they would never fly again. Seven of us wandered the entire night, loafed, talked, and had a leisurely meal. As we ate, people in the next booth insisted to the waitress they wanted strawberry jelly. They knew there was some because they could smell it. There were soggy spots and holes in the paper over my crate. Strawberries showed through, and they were ripe. Everywhere I went I had to carry this crate of ever ripening strawberries: the waiting room, the restaurant, even the bathroom.

I tried to leave it once, but couldn't, "Oh sir, you left your box!" Finally, it became a matter of principle. I was determined to get that crate home.

The next day our plane entered a little better weather, but not much. We were flying along a line of storm clouds, but they didn't toss the plane around like the previous flight. Most of the passengers hadn't been on the night flight and weren't as uptight as I was. Suddenly there was a flash of lightning and clap of thunder at the right wingtip. I know that Saint Elmo's Fire is not usually dangerous to a boat or a plane, but I forgot all knowledge at this moment. The rest of the flight was uneventful, except for the increasing aroma of strawberries.

We landed in Birmingham in clear weather. I took my bag and my crate of strawberries and worked my way through the crowd. Betty had made three trips to Birmingham to pick me up, and now I was bringing her a crate of very ripe and some beyond ripe strawberries. She said she was glad to see me. I think that meant that she couldn't have tolerated another trip. All we could do with the strawberries at this stage was make jam--about a five-year supply.

We agreed to not mention the trip and try to forget it. I had repressed the memory until a year later.

I was finishing a local procedure on a patient when he said, "Say, Doc, my brother-in-law from Indiana was telling us last year he was in bad storm on a plane out of Dallas. In the middle of all this, some kid thought he was having a heart attack and a doctor from Anniston worked on him. And ... uh, did I mention them strawberries?"

Medical Politics

48

As years passed and my practice grew, I was drawn into medical politics, for which I had little desire and no preparation. The first major job was organization of the emergency room. As the ER became more active, the administration and medical staff began to see that reorganization was desperately needed. I was asked to do the job.

The ER had never had rules, stated purpose, organization, or stable personnel. The place operated by precedent and tradition at the autocratic whim of the nursing supervisor. She pulled personnel from units thought to have excess staffing and sent them to the ER. Sometimes the nurse had trouble finding the place, much less know about its operation. Nobody seemed to know what the ER was there for. Some doctors used it as an office; some did elective minor surgery there. Basic ER charge was $5.00. The hospital constantly received bad press for poor slow service. I agreed to this job only if demands were met: stable full-time personnel, head nurse status for a nurse in the ER, decent equipment, and a training program for nurses.

The powers that be agreed and I took Jeri Doyle, Sandra Ray (Lindsey,) and Helen Boyd to an ER meeting in Augusta. These were destined to be our first full time ER nurses. Believe it or not, Betty gave permission for me to leave with a carload of girls. When we got back, we organized and wrote the first emergency plan, and I wrote the first statement of purpose of the ER. Strangely enough, none of the other area hospitals had such a document. We wrote basic rules for ER operation, a hospital wide emergency plan and rules for the physicians. Administration and the medical staff and approved the whole package.

I was rewarded by being made president of the county medical society. I thought we needed a good medical meeting or conference. I was told that I couldn't get nationally known authorities to come to a little country town. The most I could lose could was the price of a phone call. I did get turned down a lot, but eventually scheduled men of national reputation and some of international renown. The drug houses funded the two-day event. We had the largest meeting outside of Birmingham two years in a row. A hundred and twelve attended the second year. After my two years as president, a motion was made at our next meeting to never to have an educational medical meeting again. We would have social functions only. Okay, so I lost that one.

* * *

After we moved to the farm and were trying to establish ourselves in a larger house and develop a cattle herd and a garden, more unwanted politics descended. A medical group included an abrasive doctor who smugly told several people their group would control 80% of the medicine in the county within five years. One of the members of the group was vice chief of staff and assumed precedent would be followed and he would be chief at the next election. Sam Singletree came to me the week of the election and said many were afraid the group would control the hospital to the detriment of the rest of us. He wanted to put me up for chief of staff. I had to bite my tongue to keep from telling him I still didn't belong to the country club and couldn't possibly make it in Anniston. The election brought a sharp division in the staff. The man who expected to be elected received only the votes of his group. To this day, he may think I orchestrated my election and his defeat. For years when I passed him in the hall, he looked to the floor. I hope he has forgotten the bitterness. His partners refused to consult me when asked by a patient, saying they couldn't work with me.

The chief of staff job was no prize because the hospital was on probation, and our administrator had left. We had a head nurse as acting administrator. I initially supported her because she said she would stay until a trained person was obtained. That's what she said, but all the while she was cultivating and manipulating other board members. After she gained my support, she announced she had changed her mind and wanted the job on a permanent basis. The hospital then had four problems: 1) we were on probation from Joint Commission of American Hospitals, 2) we had no trained hospital administrator, 3) there was no long-range plan for development, 4) the hospital was under the control of the city and as such was a political football.

Board meetings were unbelievable. Our would-be administrator courted three of the five members. Confidential information was fed to the press. Votes were decided before meetings. I wanted change. Two members agreed, one was wishy-washy, and two agreed to nothing except the appointment of the nurse as administrator.

Radical means were needed to correct deficiencies before inspection. I checked the rulebook and worked on the staff first. We threw some doctors off the staff temporarily for incomplete charts. I threw one off permanently because of chronic failure to do charts. He left over 200 incomplete records. With staff approval, I put one off for drug use. I took a patient from one doctor for a three-day abandonment of care in the hospital. That doc also looked at the floor when he passed me in the hall and never spoke to me as long as he lived.

I was desperate for new equipment in surgery.

Mert Gibson, the OR supervisor, was the only one old enough to remember when the last OR table was bought in the mid 1940's. The board wouldn't agree to a major purchase until we picked a permanent administrator. They wanted the nurse. She was a good nurse, but she had never had a day's training or experience in hospital administration. Hospitals provide treatment, but are also big business. Ours was one of the largest in the county and deserved somebody trained for the job. I lost some battles. I made mistakes and made enemies who remain enemies. I rocked the boat. I was the hatchet man, and nobody likes a hatchet man, especially when he steps on toes and loses battles.

I took two days off from my practice for the board inspection. Through blood, sweat and tears by many people and dumb blind luck, we passed the inspection and became fully accredited. Everybody could have been suddenly inspired to do the dullest work in medicine, but I still think somebody hid a few charts the day before inspection.

As for the administrator; I cheated. I persuaded the board to accept applications for the job through a civil service exam. The plan was to go through the motions and hire the nurse. "A little bird " told me a man, trained and qualified, might be interested in the job. I "accidentally" met him at a meeting in Montgomery and fed him information about our problems before his interview with the board. He made top score on the exam and got the job on a three to two vote. "Wishy-washy" came over. I considered it a landslide vote. We also got our long-range plan and did expand the hospital.

Control of the hospital was another matter. We laid the groundwork for the change in control to occur after I left office. The next chief got his name on the brass plaque. That's okay; hatchet men are necessary, but they don't belong on plaques.

Even as Chief of Staff, I did a lot of ER work, but along with others, I could see times changing. When the sun went down there was no doctor in the hospital unless he was actively treating a patient. Several of us proposed hiring ER docs for weekends. There was an indignant explosion in our staff meeting. Angry doctors claimed this was an invasion of private practice and put the hospital in the practice of medicine. Three times there was a tie vote. As we finished the third vote, Ray Taylor walked in. Somebody said, "Hold your hand up, Ray."

I said, "Hey, I'll take that vote. The measure passes." Six months later when we voted to have ER docs full time, there were no dissenting votes.

The new administrator offered a party for me when I finished my tour as chief. I told him I had made too many enemies and had too many scars. I thought it best to leave quietly.

The Worst Land I Ever Saw

49

After we moved to the farm, I looked for years for more timberland. I knew we needed to plant it soon if there was hope of living to see trees big enough to cut. We also wanted land to the north of our farm. Houses were going up all around. We didn't like the thought of a subdivision next to our garden.

One week, 400 acres near Micaville in Randolph County came on the market. On Thursday, I went to see the land. When I finally found it, I discovered hilly land with a mountain in the center. Mountain is a relative term, depending on where you are. This one was 1,400 feet compared to Cheaha, the highest point in Alabama, at 2,400 feet. The top overlooked houses, barns, fields and roads for miles in every direction. This might have been a little mountain or even a hill in some places, but to me it was a big mountain. Much of the land was steep and some rocky. The north side was strewn with weathered moss-covered rocks big as a car and some big as a house. They were beautiful, but hard to get around and they don't grow trees. Clumps of chestnut oak were scattered across the elevations. With slow mountain growth, they could be harvested in another fifty years. Holes in the ground, some a hundred feet long, marked areas of strip mining. Mica sparkled around the old mines, on the ground along the trails and in the woods. A swamp of a few acres surrounded a branch near the southeast corner. Most of the land was vertical. If I could have flattened it, I could have doubled the acreage. Most of these rolling hills and mountain were covered with blackjack oak and hickory. An occasional long leaf or short leaf pine struggled to survive. Rocky steep land with strip mines and covered with trash trees, this was my kind of land!

I drove home to discover the land north of us had come on the market the same day. I couldn't afford one, much less both. I couldn't bargain with Sam Singletree, owner of the land to the north. He knew I feared the threat of a subdivision. I walked the pastures and woods and brooded for days. I had looked for both for a long time. I wanted the north property to keep from being crowded. Still, 400 acres of sorry land like Micaville doesn't come on the market very often. On the other hand, I didn't want to go into debt any more. I had already hocked a farm to build the house. After days of soul-searching, I bought both, mostly with borrowed money.

After I was committed, I made another trip to Micaville to make plans for site prep and planting. I stopped by a house toward the southwest to get directions to one corner that I hadn't been able to find.

The hollow-cheeked man at the door said, "The road that goes to the corner is right yonder, but won't do you no good to look at the place. They say some crazy doctor from Anniston bought this sorry ol' land. It ain't fitten fer nothin' 'cept to hold the world together."

"Sir, I am that crazy doctor. If you don't mind, I will use your road to go into my sorry old land." He helped my apprehension, just lots.

The sour man was right about the land. There wasn't enough wood on the place to entice anybody to cut it. I couldn't give the wood away for firewood. We built roads into the land and James Fields did mechanical site prep. He was an artist with a 'dozer, but he had never done anything like this. I walked the land with him to explain what I wanted. He bought a special blade and cleared the land so carefully that huckleberries survived. He piled trees and brush in rings around those hills like windrowed hay. It was strange looking land for years. I had to operate in faith that it would look better. My neighbors now knew I was crazy. Our mountain was called Bald Mountain until our seedlings grew.

After 18 years, we cut our first land at Pinehill because of uneven growth. I arranged to have the entire area burned to be rid of weed trees and brush. I didn't watch. I didn't want to see land stripped bare and burning. It was as if I had lost a family member. I had to operate on faith the land would improve through our efforts. As I could afford it, we planted the land in pines except for the swamp. I left it untouched. Forty acres of oak, poplar, big leaf magnolia, gum and a scattering of pine, now over 75 years old, stand with trunks straight as an arrow. The high canopy of branches makes a dense shade in summer. Huge trunks are bare of branches for 30 feet or more. The upland is an unbroken sea of planted loblolly pine. The land has been locked these many years. In the upland and swamp, we have deer, turkeys and unbelievable numbers of birds. It is hard to believe that this land looked like a war zone after the burn. If secrets of the land are learned, and respected, bounty of the land will return. We must learn from the land to know what to do. This planting has been thinned twice according to the years of growth. If we protect and serve the land, it serves us.

We girdled undesirable trees at Swagg and planted all open ground. We have had two major thinnings and salvaged twenty-five acres of tornado damage and clear-cut two areas. We cut and replanted one area I planted forty years ago. The uplands are planted, and the drains by the branches are in hardwood untouched for fifty years. There is even more game than at Pinehill. Deer are everywhere. Turkeys are more elusive, but there are turkey tracks as big as a man's hand. The place has been locked, but poachers are always a problem. I could not be on site for every event. Jim Cleveland helped for years. I now have a long-term contract with a paper company and Trae Bonner supervises site-prep, planting, and cutting, Ms. Pat High, a neighbor at Swagg, walks our roads almost daily and checks for trespassers. She even got our son-in-law for littering.

My problems increased when the lake was flooded at Swagg. I would rather not lose the 90 acres, but I had no choice. I did take the money for the land, but I didn't want to pay the tax. If I reinvested the money within one year, I would pay no tax. I found land before I got the money. Half was adjacent to the sorry land at Micaville and the rest was a mile west beyond Hepesebah Church. It's hard to believe that land could be worse than Bald Mountain, but it was. Much of the area had been strip-mined and there were no trees of value.

The one bright spot was the branch at the foot of our mountain at Micaville. The clear cold water never varies, even in drought. Surrounding the branch was a growth of trees uncut for years. In this heavy growth of timber, the huge roots of the trees had reached over the branch and then been covered with dirt creating a tunnel for the stream to pass through. These suspended shelves of soil were covered with moss flourishing in the dense shade. The timber cutters ignore drains because of difficulty in removing timber. I did not tell the owner. If he didn't want to look at land he had inherited, who am I to tell him about ten acres of heavy timber? If he didn't want it, I did. Except for the drains, this new terrible land at Micaville and at Hepsebah was stripped of salvageable trees, sprayed with herbicides by helicopter and burned. It looked like a nuclear war zone. It is now a forest again. I left the drains in natural hardwood. So, we tend Pinehill, Swagg, Micalille, and Hepsebah for our few years on this earth. I hope those who follow will think the land better for our care.

My conscience began to bother me that we were taking the habitat of game so we kept the loading docks clear on three hilltops at Hepsebah and planted food plots. I don't hunt, but like to see the animals and know they have a home. We began with the worst land I ever saw, but planted trees grow and the forest and animals came back.

The Doctor and The Bear

50

I was stretched thin as I struggled as chief of staff of a troubled hospital, did a surgical practice, tried to run a little cattle farm, look after four tree farms and be a husband and father. Our family was filled with activity on the farm. The kids and I did fencing, plowing, haymaking, bush hogging, gardening and anything else a farm demanded. My surgery still centered around the emergency room, in spite of the new ER physicians. My little office on Eighth Street overflowed if I were late from surgery or in the ER.

One day after the mob cleared, the office crew had gone and I was alone in the deserted office, I noticed I had a headache. That's not unusual for some, but I don't have headaches--ever. I took my blood pressure for the first time since Medical School. I was hypertensive. I made a visit to an internist the next day. He gave me generic advice and told to take diuretics or tranquilizers or both. I took the diuretics.

I called the internist a week later to tell him I took his medicine and it didn't help. He told me to take the medicine and quit complaining. My headaches were daily and at 160/110, my pressure was more than borderline. After the brush-off by the internist, I went to a cardiologist for a workup and was sent to a hypertension expert to Birmingham.

I was like any other patient. I would like for the fairy godmother to wave her wand and make the hypertension disappear or take a pill that made it go away. Instead, the expert told me I had essential hypertension--whatever that means--and gave me a beta-blocker. He admitted treatment of hypertension is a witch's brew: use green pills; if they don't work, use yellow ones; then try white pills; and as a final resort take the green and white striped ones or combine the colors. To a fix-it person, this did sound like witchcraft from the 1600's. If my patient had appendicitis, I took the appendix out. If he had a hernia, I fixed it. Even if the patient had an infection and needed no surgery, an antibiotic rid the patient of the problem.

I was being told that my condition couldn't be cured, but could be controlled. I was to be drug dependent the rest of my life. I took my green pills because I didn't want a stroke, kidney damage, heart attack or even a headache. I couldn't take enough medication to bring my pressure down to normal and still walk. I compromised with the largest dose I could tolerate and function. Even with the pills, my pressure was unacceptable. Most medications have a bundle of effects, one of which is the effect on the disease. Some people have no noticeable side effects. In others, the cure seems worse than the disease. I would have stopped treatment if headaches hadn't come back when my pressure was up.

I examined my work. I could do my surgery as well as ever, but some of the joys of accomplishment were gone. I was just able to struggle through the day and collapse on the couch at night. I was a poor husband and father. I could barely do my work at the hospital and farms. I was still not adequately treated. I had to push myself to do anything. I was miserable. I was not pleasant at the hospital, office or home.

I was angry. I hated my body for doing this thing to me. What had I done to deserve this? Was this all I had to look forward to? Statistically, control of blood pressure prolongs life. I was convinced that life was not longer; it just seemed to be.

I spent months in this state. One day after the last patient left and the office was quiet, I was going through the day's mail and throwing most in the trash. As a brochure fell, I saw the words: *Control of Blood Pressure Without Drugs*. I fished it out of the can.

Sure you can with potions, séances and witchcraft. I scanned the brochure. Then I went back and read every word--twice. They were claiming 89% success rate without drugs, even with severe hypertension. I read the words again. It sounded like a fairy tale. The concept was foreign to any pharmacology and physiology I had been taught. On the other hand, The Meninger Clinic was a reputable group and they were making the claims and teaching the course. I filled out the application and mailed it that night and left a note to the girls to block out time for me to be gone. If 10% of what they said were true, the trip would be worth my time. I didn't believe a word of it, but I would go.

I flew to Kansas City on April 2, 1981. At 8:00 the next day, I found my worst fears justified. I was the only one of 60 students who was not a psychologist, psychiatrist or one working in those fields. They were oriented toward this weird concept and I wasn't. Unaware, I had wandered into the camp of the Philistines. This was a program to teach doctors how to train patients to manage blood pressure. When the others discovered I was a consumer and not a provider, they wanted to know all my impressions and opinions. There *is* no such thing as casual conversation. Every word and event has a meaning.

Everybody knows the story of two psychiatrists standing in the hospital hall. A surgeon walks by and says, "Good morning." The psychiatrists watch as he walks away. One says to the other, "I wonder what he meant by that?"

For a surgeon, this was a weird group studying a weirder concept. I had paid my money and reserved the time so I was determined to listen to these strange ideas and learn what I could. Everybody knew hypertension is treated with drugs. The expert had told me that.

The lectures didn't begin with weird stuff. We talked about standard treatment of hypertension. Those at Meninger would not treat anybody with hypertension unless a physician agreed to follow him with conventional therapy. They agreed with much of standard therapy: exercise, low fat and high fiber diet, reduced salt, proper work habits and adequate rest, but rarely drugs. They were seen as an essential evil to control pressure until the true etiology could be treated. Hypertension drugs, over a lifetime, also represent a huge expense. They asked further why would anyone choose to treat himself with a poison? Anything that made a person feel as bad as it made me feel was a poison.

Our speakers were from the Department of Voluntary Control. They taught control of blood pressure, migraine, seizures, and things too strange for me to remember. The first hours were spent outlining the schedule for introducing the concept of blood pressure control to the patient. The instructor admitted that 50% of the patients never came back after the first session. My worst fears were realized. This stuff was bound to be weird.

We then began a series of lectures on stress. Everybody knows about stress, but it's hard to define. If you ask somebody, you probably get an example and not a definition. The expert, Hans Selye, gives two definitions: "the rate of wear and tear within the body" and "the state manifested by a specific syndrome which consists of all the nonspecifically induced changes within a biologic system." Everything should be clear now.

Stress is not all bad. All living things must have

a fight or flight mechanism to exist and procreate. Life without challenge would be boring. As everybody knows, there is a voluntary nervous system and an involuntary or autonomic system. We will muscles to move and the rest is automatic. Gastrointestinal, vascular, neurological and reproductive functions occur independent of our will. Standard medical knowledge says control of autonomic functions is not possible. Things work this way or we couldn't survive. You don't mess with the clock. It runs on its own schedule.

If we had no involuntary system, when our ancestor came out of his cave to face a bear and said to himself, "Let's see now, I think I better crank up my blood pressure and heart rate, shunt my blood, dilate my pupils then see if my feet can get me out of here," he would have been lunch for the bear and we wouldn't be here at all. Stress cannot and should not be avoided.

The world operates because of stress. Stress goads us to work and react to danger. We identify a problem and deal with it through stress. When the crisis is over, we should go back to the resting state. Animals do this. Two dogs fight, bite and scratch. Then it's over. Ten minutes later they are calm and either friends or have gone separate ways. When our ancestor outran the bear, he relaxed. He returned to his resting state. Man is made to operate this way or we couldn't cope with pressures of life or even survive.

But today, much of our stress can't be solved by fighting or running away. When the source of stress is unclear, unknown, repeated, continuous, or multiple, stress doesn't stop. The stressed person doesn't return his physiology to a resting state. He may not see the bear, but he runs. He may not know why, but he runs. His systems work as if the bear were after him in a lifetime run. The enemies of the stressed man are the pressures of change and the tyranny of time. We understand negative events as stressful, but positive events can bring on stress. A marriage, birth of a child, new job or move, though wished for, brings change and life is never the same. Even a vacation is stressful. The vacationer must follow the rigid schedule of the airline or cruise line. Have you ever told somebody you needed to rest up to recover from your vacation? Retirement is a positive event--for some. Others retire without planning and die within the year. Great change came into their lives. Time and the bear caught them at last.

People respond to stress in different ways. Personalities have been classified as type A or B. Few of us are purely one or the other, but a blend of each. Type A is filled with drive, ambition and overwhelming urge to succeed. Success may come through a stressful way of life. He has "hurry sickness." Type A has controlled hostility, but it can break out at strange times. He is impatient. He has perseverance, but little patience. He must be doing something constructive even in spare time. He must have something to show for any effort or his time is wasted. He sets high standards he can't reach. He counts the number of operations or sales for his own pleasure to measure himself against others and may tell friends of his numbers. Money is only a measure of accomplishment. Type A pushes himself in a race with the clock. According to Friedman and Rosenmen, he has insecurity about his own worth and is always trying to prove himself. He is nearsighted and concerned with the deeds of the moment. He turns conversations to his interests. If a man's security rests on the number of deeds to his credit, then he is under constant threat and stress. Type A must run faster and faster. The bear is just behind and gaining.

Type B can have ambition and drive, but is free

of the pressures of time. He does not count his cases and measure himself. He makes careful decisions before acting. The A person acts in rote fashion because it is quicker. B works for joy of the work and not accomplishment. He is more thoughtful and can spend leisure hours with no worry about wasting time.

A number of illnesses are related to stress. The A and B concept was developed to show that A's had heart disease. This isn't new. In 500 BC, Socrates said, "There is no illness of the body apart from the mind." High blood pressure is the most obvious. Essential hypertension means no reason can be found for the disease. Essentially we don't know what causes it. We don't see our bear. Tumors of the adrenal, stenosis of a renal artery, or arteriosclerosis can be physical causes of hypertension. Most cases are essential. Most of us would agree that heart disease, migraine and some ulcers are related to stress. Our lecturers considered the possibility that others, including cancer, were related. There is laboratory evidence that stress severely reduces function of the immune system, which would allow diseases, including cancer, to develop more easily. In the past, a widow didn't go out in public for a year after the death of her husband. This is the approximate time her immune system is compromised after a major stressful event. The retired man probably has the same deficient immune system. In each of the diseases known to be related to stress, standard medicine treats the symptoms of the disease and not the cause.

In the 1980's, standard treatment began with tranquilizers. This worked for a time, but then hypertension returned. Next, we gave diuretics, which rids the body of water, reduces the volume of circulating fluid and helps for a while. Then come the big guns with the side effects. Some people take the pills with few complaints. I believe they don't remember how much better they felt before the drugs. Standard treatment of hypertension attacks one symptom rather than the true cause. This isn't done in other diseases. When the patient has pneumonia, we don't just give cough syrup. We kill the bacteria. We treat the cause of the problem.

If stress does cause disease processes, how does this happen? There are volumes on this subject. In our course, we covered a fraction of the concepts, and I have forgotten most of that. There is a complex relationship between various parts of the brain and the endocrine system. Whatever I learned has been changed by now anyway. The primary interest for us was the limbic system that may be more theoretical than anatomic. This is composed of parts of the temporal and frontal cortex and centers in the thalamus and hypothalamus. This system is called the visceral brain because it has to do with basic biological functions, as well as emotion and behavior. According to classic neurology, conscious control of the autonomic nervous system is not possible. Then, according to these theories, we make ourselves sick with our mind, but we can't make ourselves well in the same way.

The people at Meninger's had trouble understanding treatment of stress also. They imported a swami or yogi and studied his methods. Under laboratory conditions, he demonstrated control of temperature, respiration, heart rate and pain and even stopped his heart for a brief time.

Now comes the truly weird stuff, like mantras, incense and snakes in a jar. Our lecturer must have read my mind because she said that we can learn from other cultures without embracing their religion. Evidence was presented to show that meditation alone does produce changes, including lowering of the blood pressure. Meditation is one aspect of the changes that should take place in a person's life to aid his ability to cope with stress. It alone is not the answer to all problems.

Meditation is not lethargy or thinking about some concept or chanting a magic phrase. It is a method to gain mastery over attention. Words repeated in unison, in church, at a ball game, or in a closet, gain and direct attention. The use of mantras is one way. In meditation, the rest of the world is shut out and attention fixed on one object, or task. Meditation does cause changes in physiology. In theory, to treat diseases of the limbic system, we must gain entrance to that system. Meditation is an attempt to gain entry and control.

A related concept is visualization or sensual imagery. In one's mind attention is fixed on objects, places, or events or on the disease itself. Biofeedback was a word I had heard, but didn't understand. If we try to abort migraine, change brain waves or make other changes in the autonomic system through relaxation, meditation and imagery, biofeedback is a method to measure effort. It is a mirror to show us processes in our body we can't see. The mirror doesn't show our physical body, but a glimpse of our innermost being, our very soul. We may change the reflection in the mirror and yet not know how we did it. Without realizing, we use a feedback system in much of our learning process.

Progressive muscle relaxation is part of the process. To measure deep relaxation we might measure muscle tension or electrical conduction of the skin, but the easiest way is to measure the skin temperature of the fingers. Temperature is related to relaxation. A stressed person has cold clammy hands, even in a warm room. Warming of the hands indicates that changes have taken place. We cannot have warm hands with a high level of adrenaline. Warm hands show that centers where our emotions live are peaceful, and changes have taken place in our body. Circulating adrenalin is reduced. Without realizing it, we use words telling of stress: 'cold feet, chills up and down my spine, hair stood up on the back of my neck, shaking with fear, dry mouth of fear, knot in my throat, clammy hands, and racing heart.'

I heard all of this stuff and didn't believe a word of it. The autonomic system is just that, automatic. I've never had to tell those parts to work. They run parts of my body without direction.

Then, the therapist came in. Half of the class had training before and were sent out. Our group was a collection of novices and skeptics like me. The therapist explained their concept of this mental exercise. We couldn't truly assume the Shavasana or the corpse pose that is almost the lying down anatomic position and is the best position for relaxation. We approximated the pose as well as possible, sitting at the desks. We taped small thermometers to the index of the non-dominant hand. We began by controlling respiration. Our minds were to focus on the simple act of breathing, to think of nothing but breathing in and out. Slow diaphragmatic breathing slows the heart rate and slightly reduces blood pressure. Most patients in a coronary care unit are thoracic breathers.

All muscle tension was to cease. To identify tension, muscles were tightened and then totally relaxed one extremity at the time. Any tension must be dealt with until arms, legs and neck are so relaxed that there is a feeling of heaviness like the extremity can't be moved. It seems to sink away. All outside thoughts were to be cleared away and we were to fix our mind on some activity, place or event. In our mind, we were to go to a favorite place and see the trees or water or beach or whatever was around. Or we could visually take a journey through our body, carefully inspecting each organ. *Hey, I could do that! I know a little anatomy.*

Our speaker was good. Her voice was almost hypnotic. In fact, what we were being told to do was a type of self-hypnosis. I went the whole route and I didn't believe a word. Deep into the session of controlled respiration, profound relaxation, and sensual imagery, I felt a thousand pins in the palms of my hands. I knew they weren't there, but they felt real. We weren't supposed to look at the thermometer. I cheated. My temperature was rising so fast I could see it move. The little red column went up nine degrees. I almost fell out of the chair. Some of this stuff was **true**, maybe most of it, even all of it!

After the session, a show of hands indicated fewer than half were able to raise the temperature. They picked on me to ask my impression of the event. I told them the experience was weird and frightening because I now knew I had caused my own illness, and I also knew I was responsible for my cure. There was one reassurance. Now I could see a way to do something. Nothing stresses me more than to feel that I am not in control of the situation. No matter how hard an operation is, if I feel that I am in control, there is little stress. The unexpected, the out of control, brings stress.

Even though raising the skin temperature was one small step, I now knew I could control parts of my body I had thought beyond reach. What they had told us was true: the human body can do things that cannot be explained, by methods not understood. I don't understand electricity, but I can turn on the light. My bear was still there, but I had gained a step on him.

As I flew back to Alabama, I read and reread my notes. Time shouldn't be wasted, don't you know. I am still–and always will be--part Type A. Questions filled my mind, questions I couldn't answer. Would this weird program change me into some kind of a mumbling freak wandering in a trance? Would it blow my mind? How long would it take to work? Are there side effects to this treatment of the mind as there are with chemical medication? Where would I go to get help? The instructors recommended two weeks of intensive training. No doctor in Anniston used anything but poison drugs. I certainly couldn't tell anybody. They may have suspected that I was crazy. Now they would know it. Could I still get cranked up for surgery and follow the stress reduction program? Could I even do surgery and do this program? Could I do it alone? What else could I do with this new skill? Would I change my personality? Would I still be me? Could I end up in a dream world? That sounds like catatonic schizophrenia.

I ordered *Mind As Healer, Mind As Slayer* by Pelletier and *Beyond Biofeedback* by Green and Green. My blood pressure showed little change in the first few days. Years brought me to this stage. I couldn't expect overnight results. I had nothing to turn to except my notes and books. I read both books. I ordered a temperature-training monitor. I told nobody but Betty. If she thought I was crazy, she didn't say so. I went back to the same pressures that caused my stress. Some days the relaxation and imagery process was hard to do. I experimented with strange imagery in my mind such as warming my hands by the fire or feeling the sand on a beach. Eventually, I was able to achieve a rise in temperature easily--at night. Daytime was another story. A few minutes sounds so little to ask, but how could I rush to the hospital at 7:30 every morning, do surgery, make rounds, go to the office, make a trip or so to the ER, then make rounds again, and find time to totally relax and put everything out of my mind and focus attention on something else? I was supposed to do the exercise twice a day. According to the experts, my life must be changed in many ways.

Relaxation and imagery may be accomplished at a party, when stopped at a traffic light, or between patients. At odd moments in the day I should consciously attempt to relax. In my office I may go from exam room to exam room and never go to my office until the end of the day. I can't do the trick in surgery or on rounds. My mind has to be focused on the patient and the problem at hand.

That leaves driving. Will I go into a trance and wrap around a tree? The instructor said at a stop sign, not driving. As I gained skill, I was able to relax and as evidence, raise the temperature of my hands while driving. Nobody ever asked why I had a small thermometer in the truck. The only thing I ever hit was a 'possum. It was at night and his fault! I am sure with repetition, controlled respiration and relaxation gave me a conditioned response.

I slowly changed many of my priorities. In my past life, if four problems attacked me at one time, I did as the knights of old. I jumped on my horse and rode off on in all four directions. With multiple problems, I worked as if I were fighting fire. In my new life, I learned to identify stress and stress triggers and respond more appropriately. I had to react to events in the OR and my practice, but other than in patient care, I did not. I avoided simultaneous confrontations and problems. If multiple problems arose and hemmed me in a corner, I learned to put them in my pocket for a while and deal with them one at the time. Some went away after a time and I didn't have to deal with them at all. A pile of papers arose on my desk, which I would deal with later. A smaller pile accumulated in my shirt and coat pocket. From time to time, I do go through them and take care of the matter and throw away the paper, honest! I could still do my surgery and with effort find the time to relax completely twice a day and avoid confrontations that I knew to be stressful until I was able to cope with them.

I experimented with strange phenomena. I tried raising the temperature of my toes, which is harder than hands. If that works, why not the left elbow? That can be done, but is difficult. My worst experiment was trying to control my heart rate. It dropped to forty and was still falling. I stopped the experiment. I found I could stop my migraine variant in five minutes and not have to live through hours of problems. Regulation of autonomic nervous system functions through the will alone involves processes poorly understood. Through experimentation, I saw changes in the mirror and adjusted my methods. I reduced my medication slowly until late summer when my pressure was normal and I stopped the poisons. My approach and management of surgery was the same, but my approach to life was different. Relaxation exercises, meditation and imagery produce a sense of control in life and a positive outlook. I enjoyed work again and my sense of humor returned. A man who is miserable laughs at little, certainly not at himself. I was in control again, not of the whole world, not my entire health, but this one troublesome part of my life.

My trip to Kansas City had been my *véraison*. There is no English translation of this French word used in viticulture. Before bud break in early spring, pruned grapevines look like dead sticks along the cordon. In early spring, shoots come out, then the blooms burst forth so rapidly that if you miss a day, blooms have come and gone. The vines don't wait for bees. They are too slow. Blooms are pollinated by the wind. They are in a race for their lives. They must survive and reproduce! They have hurry sickness—like people. In two weeks, the vines bloom and set fruit. There is rapid growth of canes in this race for life. The vine covers everything in a blanket of green and wraps tendrils around everything within reach. One vine strangles another.

As the blanket thickens, the fruit grows. Then growth slows and the canes harden and thicken. The leaves are coarser and darker. Canes droop from the weight as if they were tired. Berries are near full size, but have little more sugar than leaves. Red grapes began to have color and the whites are a little translucent. In late summer, the rapid growth of fruit and leaves is almost over and ripening begins. The fruit gains sugar and loses acid until it is ripe. This demarcation at the end of rapid growth is called *véraison*. The frantic growth is replaced by slow maturing and ripening of the grapes until they are ready to be picked. The closest English equivalent is "turning point." We all have turning points in our lives. We pass *véraison* without knowing it. We finish years of school, depending on our parents for every need, go into the world and life is never the same. We marry, have children, and life is never the same. We have passed a turning point.

After my turning point and beginning my new attitudes, I found that management became easier as time went by. Except for wintertime, the temperature of my hands was higher even without a conscious effort to raise it. I had reprogrammed my homeostatic systems at a different level. When I took an insurance physical my pressure was 124/76. My bear was gone.

Yet one fall, when early winter gloom filled the sky and cold winds blew with promise of days to come when life ceases, I felt hot breath on the back of my neck. My headaches came back. I thought I had a permanent cure and had neglected my exercises and new attitudes toward life. My bear had not gone. He was in the shadows--hiding--waiting, strong as ever. He appeared in the fall because this season shows us drastic change and reminds us of passage of time and our own mortality. Winter is coming and all the work is not done. Ulcers visit us in the spring and fall because of the stress of change. I chastised myself and returned to my program. This time, I knew what to do and how to do it. Soon, I was in control again.

Old bear, I know you well! I know you're there, though I wish you gone. A man is blessed if he knows his enemies, their tricks and weaknesses. This tells him of himself. Old bear, you are not totally evil. You goad and exhort me to achieve. You are but an apparition, a reflection of a part of me, nothing more. You will never set me free. You will chase me as long as I am on this earth, but I can push you back. Surely, bears don't go to heaven.

'Twas the Day of the King's Castration

51

We were startled by the bang-bang-bang from the front of our house. I got up from the supper table and went to the door. The sound told me who it was. He never used the hard-to-find doorbell and knocked on the door with a pocketknife because it made a sharp noise and saved his knuckles. Each visit faintly dented our door. I opened the door to see Lowell Rohnson, who lived in our little house by the branch at the corner of the property. He stood fidgeting, standing on one foot, then the other and speaking in short jerky phrases as he did when self-conscious. He was a tall man with one leg shorter than the other. With a built-up shoe, he constantly tried to prove he was agile as any other. He stood, solemn as an undertaker. He never smiled when he was intent on a task or wanted something.

"Ya wanta go havers on a hoag?"

"Which half, Lowell?"

"I mean, we'll split it down the middle when we butcher 'im. I wanta raise some little pigs ta sell, so I'm gonna buy me a girl pig, but we have ta breed 'er, so I'm gonna get a boy pig, too. When she has little pigs, I can make my money back, an' then sell the momma."

"And the boy pig?"

"That's what I wanta talk about. We can butcher 'im, and keep the momma to raise the little pigs."

"Lowell, I don't think a boar hog is any good with all of his equipment. The meat is too strong. Folks tell me you can't stand to cook it inside the house, much less eat it. That's why they cut boy pigs."

'Well, what I got in mind is to let him do his ... uh ... his work to the girl, and when we're sure he has, we cut 'im an' jerk 'im. Then after a month or so we can butcher 'im."

I liked Lowell; he was a good worker and I wanted him to stay on the farm. I tried to agree with his wishes when I could. I agreed to pay for half the boy pig and part of the feed until the ex-male made his last journey. I was concerned about one issue.

"Lowell, have you ever castrated a hog?"

"You mean jerked 'im? Well ... no, but I saw my gra'pa do it once, when I was little."

"I bet the pig was little too."

"Well, yes he was. But it's the same thang with a big pig. The ... you know ... the thangs are just bigger."

"And the blood vessels are bigger too. When you cut a little pig, the vessels are just threads. I'm not sure you are strong enough to jerk a grown pig. And if you were, he would bleed to death as big as those vessels are."

"I can't afford no vet bill. Besides, I never heared of doin' nothin' but jerkin' 'em."

"Lowell, a big pig has to have the testicles taken out and vessels tied off so they don't bleed. I can do it for you when the time comes. Shouldn't be different from people. I've done that." Lowell smiled as he left. I always wondered if he knew more than he let on.

I sat at the supper table and tried to explain to Betty and the kids I had just bought half a hog at the front door. Betty was almost accustomed to my frantic efforts at country life. When we had built our house, moved, our furniture semi-settled in place, children assigned rooms, our new house settled in place with creaks and pops in the night, we began to turn our eyes toward all things countrified. With cows grazing on all four sides, we did live in a pastoral setting. We wanted to have everything that went with a country life: a garden, chickens, ducks, hay-fields, and milk-cows. We wanted to satisfy the pent-up desires and frustrations brought on by life in Fairfield Highlands, an Army post, and a subdivision in Golden Springs.

The Rohnsons moved into the little house before we built our house and Lowell started building the fences and planting pastures. Both of us wanted these evidences of rural life immediately. He had lived in town, too. I knew the line about fools rushing in, but we knew what we wanted and besides, that warning is for other people. We delayed some projects, but we could not live without a garden. When the rains came and put all the rows of our new garden under water, we began to see that we should move the garden and go slower. When our first pasture fence fell down after a rain, we knew there were lessons we should learn. Knowledge learned though experience is expensive, but we never seem to remember. We settled into a slower haste to do the farm things, until Lowell had the hog idea.

He bought his pigs and he stored the feed in a leaning garage behind his house. He put the pigs in an enclosure of the most disreputable used fencing imaginable. Most of the posts were so rusty they broke with the slightest pressure. By then, we had figured out how to put in corner posts, but he didn't brace these corners because it was a temporary pen. Whole sides fell at times. When the pigs were small, catching them was easy for Lowell and his children. They tucked them under one arm, and took them back and repaired yet another defect in or under the fence. Over the late spring, the pigs grew. No longer could they fit under one arm. When they rooted a hole, it was quite an opening.

Lowell appeared banging at our door one day almost at dark. "Them dang pigs is out agin, an' we can't get 'em back."

The Rohnsons, Owen, and I managed to herd the wayward pigs back to the pen. When we left, the Rohnsons were weaving more wire and sticks together to repair the fence.

Over the next few weeks, I dreaded to hear those words, "Them dang pigs is out again."

Each time they were harder to get back to the pen. They usually crossed the branch and headed for the south ridge on one of the trails in the heavy woods. And they didn't run together. Once you think a pig is headed in the right direction and is moving well, he will see his pen and double back and run under you. To have such short legs, they are fast and are the world's best blockers. They will put a grown man on his back in a heartbeat. I had heard of people calling pigs. I tried, "Soo pig-pig-pig." Pigs can laugh, or at least they look like they are as they run up the ridge. I can call cows, but not pigs.

One especially hot day, we ran the pigs down the ridge by the stone house, across the branch and finally into the decrepit pen for the third time. After repairing the fence, Lowell wanted me to walk back across the branch to talk. He wanted to look at the stone house. The house had been abandoned years ago, but was still sound externally. Rafters and metal roof were intact. The floor was an elevated concrete slab and the walls were solid stone collected from the farm. They looked as if they would turn away everything but a direct bomb blast. Openings in the wall had wood framing where windows and doors had been. Two stone partitions divided the rooms. The house was surrounded by sand and gravel from floods of the branch, but the floor of house was well above water level.

Lowell stammered and fidgeted. He was not smiling. He wanted to put the pigs in the house.

"I could put some boards 'cross the doors to keep 'em in, an' they would still have light from the windows. They wouldn't get out through solid rock walls an' they couldn't root out through cement floor an' th' windows are high"

"Lowell, that's a solid house. I know it doesn't have running water or power, but it looks like it would last forever and we could add those things if we wanted to use it for people instead of pigs."

"Well, I promise I will clean it out after we use it. I can scrub it down an' it won't stink. Queenie needs some place to stay."

"Queenie?"

"That's 'er name."

If you have lots of pigs, they are just pigs, but if you have two. they have names. Her consort had to be named King, I reluctantly agreed to the use of the stone house for a pigpen. I don't know how he got the pigs up to the waist high floor, but they lived a contented pigs' life for a time. Surgery is directly related to the temperature, so I was busy for the next few months and welcomed the absence of the complaints about "Them dang pigs."

Just after supper one night there was a knock on the door. I knew the sound.

"Yes Lowell?" He was somber, fidgeting and stammering again.

"Ya remember, ya promised to do the job on that boy pig? Well, he's done his thang an' he ... uh ... needs his operation so we can butcher 'em 'fore winter."

I must have looked puzzled.

"You know, you promised to cut 'im like a real operation--with anesthesia an' ever'thang."

"Are you sure he's done the job?" You can say a cow is "safe in calf." I never heard anybody say "safe in piglet"; somehow it just doesn't sound right. I didn't know how to ask the question.

"Oh yes, Lieutenant looked at 'er yesterday. He said she was uh...in a family way--an' he knows lots about hoags. He will help us do the job. You just let me know when."

I regretted my promise, but I had no choice. "When I am off next Thursday afternoon, about one. I will have to get some things together."

On Thursday, I drove the pickup to Lowell's house and carried my supplies across the branch to the boarded-up stone house. Wives were left at home and children forbidden to cross the branch. Our smooth collie, Cleo, came with me, but saw the pigs, sniffed the air and left. This was to be a man's job.

I could hear grunts and splashes from the house and from the aroma downwind, there was no doubt about where the pigs were. Occasionally a snout appeared at a window, probably to get a whiff of fresh air. I held my breath and looked in the doorway of the hog house. I saw shadows moving in the light from the windows. Compared to the last time I had seen them, the shadows were huge. Other than what had spilled over the doorway, the dark silhouettes walked in a sea of every bit of pig doo and pee they had put out in the last three months. Rain had blown in the windows, but water just thinned the dismal slurry. Lieutenant was standing at the far side of the building looking in a window. Lowell explained that he was going to help for the parts.

"The what?"

"You know, what you cut out. He don't want no other pay."

"What's he going to do with those things?"

"Says he's gonna eat 'em."

Lieutenant walked over to talk. He was a lean muscular black man with white hair and a big smile showing lots of white teeth. His agile and smooth walk didn't match the face and hair. He worked with Lowell at Lee Brothers Brass Foundry. He looked to be beyond retirement age, but according to Lowell his birth date couldn't be established.

He said, "Yassah, I eats em. They good. Old as I is, they better'n *****."

Just then, I knew that I had a real professional crew. I turned to speak to Lowell and found him looking skyward.

"Now, what is the plan, Lowell?"

"We gonna get King hemmed up an' drag 'im to th' light at th' doorway where you can see, an' then hold 'im for ya. You stand on th' ground right in front of the door, an' the floor will be about the right height to work. It won't take long, will it?"

"Lowell, on people it would take 15 minutes. I've never worked between the hooves on a hog. Just where do you plan for me to work? That mess is running out the doorway."

"Oh, we got this pasteboard to cover it with. We'll put the pig on that." The cardboard did cover, but not for long. I laid out my surgical tools and solutions on a wooden crate to the side of the doorway. I had some retired instruments, gloves, prep solution and zylocaine for local anesthesia. Everything was sterile, just like for people. This was to be a pig orchidectomy in style. I had one pack of catgut suture. That was enough for a people. I reasoned that it should be enough for a hog with the same number of parts. I opened and arranged the sterile tools and drew up a syringe of local. I discovered I had forgotten one item. I should have thought to bring a fly swatter as a surgical tool.

After Lowell and Lieutenant knocked down the boards across the doorway, they disappeared in the depths of the stone pig house. I replaced the boards as a precaution. There were a few quizzical grunts followed by squealing, running, splashing, frantic grunts, falling bodies, screams and curses. And then it got worse. Unimaginable, indescribable sounds came from the black pools in the stone house. I saw pigs run by the doorway chased by figures that soon took on the same color as the pigs and they were the color of the black mess on the floor. Sometimes they seemed to come from the left twice before they came from the right. King had the advantage of weeks of practice on the slick floor. He knew his territory and raced around the partitions several feet ahead of the pursuers. Once, as they passed by, the people figures shouted for me to not let the hogs jump over the boards. I added a stick to my collection of instruments. From the racing back and forth, I would have thought there were no less than five pigs and eight people. I knew when a pig fell because they don't curse.

Eventually, the men threw a pig with grunts, squeals, and splashes. One end of a pig was slowly pushed toward the light of the doorway. I looked at the three forms beyond the opening--one horizontal and struggling and one squatting at each end in the slick pool holding the four hooves. And their hold wasn't very secure. All were covered with a thick black mostly liquid, best not further described. One squatting form held one end in the doorway as still as he could by holding the two legs and leaning across his back. He covered the end of the pig. I could see neither snout nor tail under the muck.

"Lowell, are you sure we have the right end of the right pig?"

The form at the back opened his mouth to show the only clean part of his body, "I ain't Mista Lowell, but dis here th' right end. The otha end bites."

Lieutenant no longer had white hair and he didn't smile much. As they pushed the back end of the pig out over the cardboard, I couldn't believe my eyes. I had not seen the pigs since the last time they escaped. They were now enormous. This wouldn't be like operating on a man. I went to the branch to get water to try to wash off the black muck so I could prep with iodine and pretend to be sterile. I washed the appropriate area and still couldn't find the expected anatomy.

Lieutenant saw my concern, "This here th' right pig, and thas the butt end."

It suddenly occurred to me, as a child, I had never seen a pig that wasn't cut when small. I had never seen an adult boar hog. Pigs don't have their parts hanging down like cows or people; the testicles are in the abdominal wall. I should have known as low as pigs are, their parts would drag in the briers if they hung down. I had nothing but scissors, clamps, a knife and one pack of suture. Even if I had a retractor, I had nobody to hold it. If I chickened out, I would fear for my life after the splashing in the pig pool. I prepped the site of the testicles between kicking episodes. I injected the local. I warned King about the stick but he kicked anyway. I reprepped and put on gloves. I laughed at my sterile technique, made an incision over both testicles and exposed them. Nobody warned me about the size of those things. They were like two oval softballs and I had one pack of suture. I dug one out and held it in my hand while I ligated the cord twice and cut the cord.

Lieutenant said, " Now, you be careful wi' them balls. Don't drop 'em in this here mess."

I carefully dropped it in the pan he brought. The second side went as well--for a time. I had more difficulty trying to dig the testicle out of the wall. As I was about to tie the cord with my very short, and only gut tie, the King got away and left with one testicle gone and one hanging out white, shining, and flopping in a sea of black. This time I shouted with the others. They managed to get him back with only a spot or two on the white anatomy. So much for sterile technique. I set surgery back a hundred years that day. I did a single ligation of the second cord, cut it and put a single suture to loosely close the incisions and we turned him loose. I tied the last knot with two hemostats. I had less than half an inch of suture left. When Lowell and Lieutenant turned King loose, he went back to the feed trough as if nothing had happened. He was less disturbed than we were. He was resigned to living in a sea of black goo. Lowell nailed the boards back and we walked toward his house.

Lowell and Lieutenant were dripping black slime and sloshed their shoes in the water as we crossed the branch. As the cleanest of the three, I carried the pan of parts. The other two washed faces and hands with a hose. Lowell brought out another pasteboard for Lieutenant to sit on to drive home. After he washed his hands, I handed Lieutenant the bowl holding the two testicles. As he stood there looking at his prize, the pan was the cleanest thing about him, and that wasn't totally clean.

"I can't believe you would go through all that for a pair of used pig balls. You're not going to eat both of them at one time, are you?"

"Oh nosuh, some of the mens where I stays at come ova an' hep me eat 'em. What's left we put in th' frigilator fo' later."

"And you just eat that and nothing else?"

"Oh Doc, they good! They strong! When you eat 'em, you ken feel 'em wukin'. I does have to cook 'em outside, though. Wife say they stink too bad in th' house. Cou'se she prob'ly be gone, time I cook 'em. She go to her suster's house. She leave cause she know when I eat 'em cods, I be dangerous an' I come lookin' fa 'er."

Even the most calloused person must feel pity for a woman fleeing a grinning man with a gleam in his eye who has just eaten a serving of something so disgusting it has to be cooked outside, even if he did take a bath after a romp in the pig house.

Lieutenant sat on the doubled cardboard in his car and watched the stain slowly creep out from his overalls.

He looked down at pan on the floor and smiled. "Guess I betta go fo' I soak through this little ol' pase'board."

On the following Monday, Lowell asked Lieutenant about his feast. He did cook and eat them. When Lowell asked if they worked, Lieutenant gave his biggest smile ever and said nothing.

I took my half of King and cured the ham, bacon, and loin in an old refrigerator and cooked them in a stone smoker I built from a retired pie cooker. I took the shoulder and scraps to a shop in Ohatchee. I bought a sausage horn, cured casings, and cotton string. I had to learn another farm job. There is an art to gathering ten feet of cured hog casings onto the horn, tying one end, and releasing it slowly as ground sausage comes out of the horn. The casings fill to make a huge cluster of coils of meat. If done improperly, the casing explodes and blows meat all over the room. We made an enormous amount of hot sausage and summer sausage. I cooked it and gave much of it away. I never told the people at the hospital the sausage was stuffed in hog guts. The ham and loins were good, but I did ask Betty to never serve brown gravy with any pork product. I gave my half of the head to Lowell. Souse meat didn't interest me.

Lowell never mentioned pigs again. Lieutenant had to look elsewhere for his rejuvenating feast. Cholesterol was discovered about that time--or at least it was by me--and mine was high. Hog meat was not a big part of our diet in the following years. It has been said that nobody would ever eat pork if they saw where pigs live. My appetite for pork chops was less after the episode with King.

* * *

Many years later, after a non-pork supper on a summer day, I walked out to our front porch and noticed faint dents in the door, now almost hidden by coats of paint. Before all light was lost as the sun went down, I walked to the corner of the property, crossed the branch and strip of sand and gravel by the old stone house. Weeds and bushes had grown up around the building. After thirty years, rafters had given way and the roof of the stone house had fallen. Evening shadows showed a jumble of broken wood and twisted roof on the floor. Withered weeds grew in the ruin. One piece of rusty metal above the wall creaked as it swung back and forth in the wind. The stone walls still looked solid enough to last a hundred years. I stood at the doorway, pulled the bushes apart and looked at the floor where I operated on the King. Thick sheets of black material were curled up on the floor like old linoleum. Lowell never did clean it. I knew he wouldn't. I thought about that day of the King's castration. Three men had gathered for a strange job, a dirty job--each for a different reason. Lowell has departed the farm. Lieutenant has departed the earth and our children are spread to the winds.

My hair is as white as Lieutenant's was when I first saw him by the corner of the stone house. I remembered that day so long ago. In my mind, I heard the sounds again, saw the faces and wondered. I wondered if I did eat some of those mountain oysters; reckon how long would I be dangerous?

Departures

Jimmy
52

Projects on the farm called for my labor, forced labor from the family and coerced help from friends. After we moved, there were projects I wanted to do, but couldn't because of scarcity of daylight hours in those days. As the years passed, after long hours in surgery, my ability to do heavy work after five in the afternoon, weekends and Thursday afternoons became harder.

Our first major project was a barn. Even with the help of Lowell Rohnson and first-son Owen, I didn't think we could attempt something that big. I called the contractor who built our house, Hughes Martin, and asked to borrow a carpenter or two when they were between jobs. The real carpenters cut the boards and we rat-carpenters drove the nails. We worked until we got to the rafters and roof. Novices belong closer to the ground.

After the barn was finished, the real carpenters left and the three of us attempted other projects. We put up fences, built catch-pens, planted pastures and gardens. Work on a farm is never finished. Farmers live longer than city folks because they never get their work done well enough to leave. There is in farmers the hidden feeling if all work was finished on every project and nothing left to do, they would be gone in a flash. For this reason, one part of a project is left unfinished or another project is begun before the first is finished. This work ethic keeps them going. In spite of all efforts, the farmer does depart one day leaving unfinished enterprises and visions of future work. They might complete those projects even though gone. There must be work for farmers in Heaven. Having nothing to do would be Hell.

Other projects remained undone on our farm and in our house. I called Hughes to borrow another carpenter.

"We are a little slack right now. Call Jimmy Clayburn. He grew up on a farm, is young and has a family. He probably needs the work."

Jimmy did need the work, but I had to learn to work around his regular job. I never knew when we would tackle our next project. Jimmy grew up on a farm and deep down loved farm life and all the animals, although he would never say so. In the years to come, we made lists of things to be built, projects to be started, and repairs to be made. Sometimes we waited months to begin. When he was laid off from his regular job as carpenter, we could do everything on our list. If there was an emergency, he found the time. He would come to build a table or a stand if Betty needed it right away. He might come quicker if Jeannie needed something. He always was a softie with girls, either his or mine. He was available when the waterline blew out, when the cows got out, and when the five-year drought came.

Jimmy had a personal disaster when his wife died. He recovered enough to begin a major project. We reworked the little house at the southeast corner and put a new roof on it. He must have liked his work. He remarried and moved into the house. He was happy in the country, but had troubles with damage to his own house by renters and had to move back. He promised he would not desert us when he left. He drove from Coldwater to help after his regular job or in between his other jobs. Our list of things for Jimmy to do was never really caught up. The current project was whatever had the highest priority. Some were such crazy things, I would not tell him until I was ready to push to begin. Work with the cows and in the hayfields was constant. Cows always recognized Jimmy no matter what car he drove and came running when he came down the driveway. Jimmy did the repair work and maintenance on three houses, two offices and a barn and some repairs on the baler, tractor, and truck. Construction of two well houses, a thirty-eight-foot-long storage shed at the garden, a ramp and sheltered pier on the lake at Swagg, workshop behind the house, and hayracks at the barn were all straightforward. There are still two boards left off the pier. A small part of the roof of the shed is yet unfinished. That's the farmer way.

Then we began the weird stuff. Whenever we finished a job, I always waited a while to spring the newest wild idea on Jimmy, but there was always something else left to do, to build, repair, or replace. Jimmy didn't do these things free of charge. His meter was running when he was here, but he worked for less than he made as a union carpenter, and he was willing. I talked with him once about a raise. He didn't want it. He used me as a savings account. The hours piled up for months and then he asked for his pay for something special like a vacation or Christmas. He kept a key to our house, my office and the farm on the lake and knew the code on the gate. He had freedom to buy materials for these strange projects and charge them to me. He seemed to appreciate the trust we placed in him. Jimmy did not waste materials. Sometimes, there would be only a few short sticks left after a construction project. We saved the sticks and used them later. Jimmy was perfectly happy building or fixing something by himself. If he could drive his car to the work-site, he turned the radio up to a country music station and sang along in a whining off-key voice. He had rather work with somebody. He would not let me do certain things for fear I would be injured. I could not lift something heavy or use certain tools.

Whenever we took a break, he would tell me about events and problems in his family or his regular job. He did small construction jobs for others if he were not on his regular job or working for me. At times he gave contract prices to people and had problems in dealing with them. They wanted the work done cheaper or in some strange way or in half the time.

He told me of one couple, "Doc, they got in to such a rip-it I jus' had ta leave; told 'em I'd be back after they settled it one way or th' other. She wanted it built one way and he wanted it a whole differ't way. So I'll go back after a spell, maybe couple of weeks."

"Well, Jimmy, which way do you think you will build it, his way or hers?"

"Ain't no doubt about it, Doc, after he thanks on it a spell. She's got half the money and all the tootie. No doubt about it, we'll do it her way."

This was not just an employee relationship. Jimmy was a friend, a part of our family. Some might think this a strange friendship. Jimmy considered himself illiterate. He always said that he didn't "have no education." He was not as illiterate as he claimed; he just never wanted to read the instructions on anything. He always called his Makita saw a "Chiquita." You can learn from anybody no matter what his educational level is. Jimmy's loyalty, work ethic and personal philosophy had much to teach, though he would deny a fancy word like philosophy.

I saw him angry once. His stepson climbed down off a ladder when we were trying to repair something and said, "It can't be done. There's nothing we can do."

Jimmy said, "Don't *never* say that! Thay's always something that can be done. If we can't do nothin' else, we'll tear it down and start over agin." We fixed it.

He was a small man without an ounce of fat, but unbelievably strong. His brown hair was his most orderly part because of his beautician wife. Tight waves and curls told of yesterday's permanent. This was crowned by a Billy-Bob hat with some strange saying on it like: "Thanks for holding your breath while I smoke." In summer, his face was deeply tanned. There was a small sinus tract in the center of his nose he would never have fixed. He said that he didn't like doctors. A medium-sized mustache partially camouflaged the fact that he had no teeth. He had false teeth; his wife made him wear them for vacations and photographs. In summer, he worked in a tee shirt that had seen better days and a pair of ragged shorts showing scarecrow, slightly bowed legs, and tennis shoes. They were clean when he came and dirty when he left. He shivered in winter with little more clothes than in the summer. Several years at Christmas we gave him a new pair of insulated coveralls.

He had a sly constant sense of humor. "Doc, we sure do need to cut hay. Be sure to listen to the weather forecast. I would myself, but I got a cheap radio so I just get a cheap report. Durn! I cut that board twicet an' it's still too short."

Jimmy did have his down side. He prided himself on being able to do most everything in construction, electrical work, plumbing, or mechanic work. There were things he could not do, but he didn't want to admit it. He kept making a rough finish with an old broom on concrete slabs. I finally insisted that I wanted a glass-like finish on the new greenhouse floor. He mumbled something I never really understood and made arrangements for somebody else to do it. He did very little for his health. He was a heavy smoker, though he never let it interfere with his work and made special efforts to never offend me with the smoke. He never smoked in our house or my truck. Whenever he had respiratory illness in the winter, he took vitamin C. When he felt better, he quit. I gave him antibiotics and other medicines when he was sick because he wouldn't go to another doctor. One reason was probably his experience with his first wife. She died while having chemotherapy for breast cancer. He helped me in the garden and vineyard, but on his own was not a great gardener. I gave him tomato plants every year. He always had some excuse why they didn't do well. When Betty finished canning, Jimmy and his family picked gallons of whatever was left. He did have a problem with alcohol at least once. He was a closet drinker, only at night and only beer. He talked with me and told me about praying for help when trying to quit.

Tools came up missing at times. Jimmy would take something to the pasture and forget to bring it back. I have sets of wrenches with several members missing. Sometimes I asked him to check his truck, and he had forgotten to bring something back. Sometimes he borrowed tools to take home and they were lost. I am sure he meant to bring them back. He borrowed tools from others to use on our farm. Several are still here. I have no idea who they belong to. But what are a few tools between friends?

The first strange project was a ground-level cellar.

"A whut?"

"A building cool and damp like a cellar to store and ferment the wine, and a shed next door for the stemmer and press."

After a few simple drawings, I got the standard reply, "I ken do that far ya." With the air conditioner on for three hours, the three layers of insulation hold the temperature at sixty-eight in summer.

The next strange project I proposed was a fiberglass greenhouse. "Doc, I ain't never built a greenhouse."

"Hey, don't worry about it. I never have had one like this either. Besides, things like that have never stopped us before." We sat and talked and figured and then built a greenhouse more efficient than the fancy bought one at the house. Then I told him that I wanted a thermal chimney on the greenhouse.

"A whut?"

"It's to suck out the hot air if the power goes off. The plants would burn up without ventilation."

"Well, ken you draw me a pitcher?"

When he put the turbine on the top of the eighteen-foot structure and it began spinning like a top, he just shook his head. By then he had learned to never sell short my crazy projects. He seemed to feel he could build anything I could dream up and draw a picture of.

Sometimes Jimmy did work on his own initiative. I arrived one day to find that the storage shed at the garden had been wired. Jimmy said, "You needed some lights. I g'rantee th' work. If th' lights don't burn, th' building will." He needed the work, but he never made work.

A five-year drought almost destroyed my young vineyard. We built a dam across the branch and put a pump in the pool. This kept our plants going, but we were losing our pond. I proposed an underground pipe to siphon water, since the branch was higher than the pond.

Jimmy said, "Won't never work." He put it in anyway. When the water gushed into the pond, he shook his head and said, "Ya know, just lookin' at ya, you wouldn't think you'd be smart enough to figger that out."

The mustache almost hid the sly grin and there was a bare twinkle in the squinted eyes. Jimmy was not much on compliments, but I took that as one--in a left-handed way.

The next crazy project drew the same response, "A whut?"

Jimmy had already put up the posts and helped with the wire around the vineyard. Now we had to get ready for the Blessing of the Vineyard. I needed a pulpit or platform for the speakers. Jimmy built the pulpit, but he wouldn't come to the party, though he was invited as always. I knew he had dress clothes, but he wouldn't come. Other tradesmen who were important to us did come to events at our house. Confusion was evident in eyes of other visitors. They just couldn't place that man, never dreaming he had wired their house or drained their septic tank.

Jimmy would never eat at our table when we offered to share our food. Sometimes we might sit in the vineyard or pasture and eat a bite. Jimmy actually ate very little through the day

As time passed, Jimmy began to show the effects of heavy work. Jimmy's regular job was usually the building of forms for concrete walls and columns. He worked when he shouldn't have. He prided himself on being able to do anything and besides, as he said, he didn't get paid if he didn't work. When I got the call from the emergency room, I knew Jimmy was badly injured. He had threatened personnel in the ER with bodily harm if they called anybody but me. He didn't like or trust doctors. I was an exception, but barely. Jimmy's left index finger was crushed like a stepped-on cracker. The bones were crumbs, and it was short, thick, and pointed in a strange direction. Jimmy was proud that he had all of his fingers. Most longtime carpenters are missing one or two. His work was always careful and neat.

"Jimmy, what on earth happened to you?"

"Well, I was holdin' this stake fer a feller to drive, an' he missed the stake and hit ma' finger with a sledge."

"Sounds like a dumb thing to do. I can't believe you did that."

"Had to, Doc. It was ma' boss's son."

I groaned and looked at the X-rays again. The book says with a crushing injury put in a metal pin and apply traction. Crumbs will not hold a pin. I stared at the X-rays for several minutes, and called the nurse.

"Now listen carefully, because this is not a standard request. I want a cast setup, a coat hanger, a pair of pliers, some rubber bands, a finger-splint, a tube of super glue and a dress hook--like on the back of your dress. I don't need the eye part."

The nurse thought I was crazy, but she disappeared to get the stuff so she could be rid of me. Jimmy may have had the same opinion, but he had seen my other ideas work, so he grinned and said nothing. I put on a short arm cast. At the base of the index, I incorporated a padded aluminum splint bent in the position of function for the crushed finger. I cut the coat hanger to the proper length and bent it to a loop around the fingers and incorporated the ends in the sides of the cast. I glued dress hook to the index fingernail. By then a small crowd had gathered, probably in preparation for the sanity hearing. We now had a cast that held a splint to support the injured index in proper position. It was still collapsed, shortened and twisted to one side. If healed in this position, the finger would have been worse than useless. The wire loop based on the cast stuck out like the loop on a bucket. I put a crimp in the wire and stretched a rubber band from the crimp to the dress hook and put the finger in traction over the splint. While we watched, the finger length increased along the splint and the position became more normal. X-ray showed the crumbs to be gathered together. The crowd thinned. We've never had the sanity hearing.

I gave instruction on care and wrote a prescription for pain as Jimmy was looking at this strange contraption. I told him one more thing, "Now Jimmy, when you get home, get a piece of wire . . ."

"Wire? What kind of wire?"

"Copper wire--any kind--and hook up one end to the loop on that cast and run the other to the antenna wire of the TV and you can pick up Channel 40 real good."

As soon as the crumbs were stable in near-perfect position, he insisted on going back to work with the dress hook in place. I convinced him to tell his friends the hook was the newest thing for carpenters: a special hook to pick up finishing nails. My crazy rig must have worked. In a few weeks, he never knew which finger had been hurt.

Our two biggest projects were almost, but not quite too much for us. We had always wanted a gate for the farm, especially after things were stolen from the barn. The gate was easy to understand. Then I proposed the next item.

"A whut?"

"I want a dungeon, where I can store and work on my wine. My upstairs cellar is kinda full now. It can also be a storm cellar, and on top of it we can put a greenhouse connected to the house. I know that's a lot to ask, so I will hire an architect or an engineer to design it."

After he shook his head and groaned, he said, "Doc, we don't need no engineer and no arch-e-tec. We can do it ourselves. I been buildin' forms for years." We sat and talked, argued, planned, and the next time Jimmy was between jobs a large structure began to take shape next to our bedroom. We hired the excavation, brickwork and greenhouse construction, but the rest was Jimmy's. My first requirement was it must not leak, even though underground. We planned drainage, plumbing, ventilation and wiring. He put up plywood forms and filled them with reinforcement bars and then with six to eight inches of high strength concrete in four walls, floor and ceiling. There was waterproofing on all sides and a gravel bed underneath with a connecting pipe for drainage. We had power, hot and cold water, a worktable, shelves and one wall covered with racks for wine bottles. It does not leak. Jimmy claimed that we could run a bulldozer over it. He had no knowledge of stresses on structures. I am sure he overbuilt it to make sure that it was safe.

The other project took much longer because of me. Jimmy made his position clear about rockwork for the gate. He would do brick or concrete block work, but not rocks. "Don't you remember, Doc, how you got the wall crooked on that smoker firebox? You ain't gonna be able to do the gate either."

"Yes, we will Jimmy. I've got it figured out."

With some grumbling and muttering, we began with an outline drawing of what I had in mind. Jimmy borrowed a transit and laid out sites for six pillars. The curved wall was a little more complicated. We cut a pattern of plywood for the shape. Jimmy poured deep reinforced concrete footings. He drove a square steel tube on each side, filled and surrounded it with concrete. I asked Jimmy to raise a single stack of small concrete blocks in the center of each proposed column. He cut plywood the exact size of the column to be and fixed it in place at the top of the blocks. I attached strings to the four corners, plumbed and fixed them to a stake in the ground. I would lay rocks within the strings. Jimmy assured me again he would help, but could not lay rocks. I asked him and his brother to take the trailer and pick up rocks for the project. If a hundred rocks are used, then five hundred are needed to choose from. We needed a huge number for six columns and two curved walls. When I arrived on Thursday afternoon expecting to work, I found broken rocks, almost round rocks, rocks with jagged sides, rocks with no straight surface, and rocks I couldn't lift.

I complained, "Jimmy, that's the ugliest bunch of rocks I have ever seen. I can't use them for anything but the inside of the pillars where they won't show."

"Now, Doc, I don't know when a rock is ugly or purdy. Far's I'm concerned, rocks is rocks. You wanted rocks--we got rocks. You gonna cut 'em anyway, aren't you?"

"No Jimmy, I'm going to build this gate scripturally. Stones will not be worked with iron tools; we have to find rocks with flat surfaces, straight sides and straight ends for corners. We're even going to find curved rocks for the wall."

"Rocks that curve?"

"We have two choices: we can find crooked rocks or get flat ones, steam 'em and bend 'em."

I walked the pastures and along the branches and picked every rock myself and collected huge piles which I marked with a flag so Jimmy could pick them up and haul them on the trailer to the gate area. There is still one pile that he missed. To this day I still see rocks along the pastures and say to myself, *Now this would be good for a corner or on the curved wall.* We collected thousands of curved rocks, rocks for corners, for top edges and for flat sides. Jimmy mixed the mud, and I laid the rocks. I used two of the ugly rocks. They weighed 100 to 150 pounds. Jimmy had to lift them shoulder high for me. The work was unbelievably slow, complicated by my broken shoulder and hernia operation. The job took three years in fits and jerks. Jimmy had long since completed a drainage system of his invention. An ugly ditch was beside our new gate. Jimmy built a storm sewer with a steel grate for drainage and ran a pipe under the wrought iron portion of our gate. The water now drains through the pipe and the ditch is gone. Jimmy was right; we didn't need an engineer. Jimmy cast the capitals for the columns with forms of molding. A friend with the phone company volunteered a bucket truck to place the pineapples as symbols of welcome. All the while, there was hay work, garden work and vineyard work to do.

One hot August Sunday in 1994, I visited my father in Birmingham. When I got back, there was a note on the front door. I went straight to the intensive care at Stringfellow. Jimmy had severe chest pains at home. In his usual stubborn way, he said he wouldn't go if they called 911. He wanted to go in a car like regular folks. He was given an anticoagulant and had a hemorrhage and stroke. He was on life support. The monitors showed function, but I knew Jimmy was gone. He never did trust doctors.

Jeannie came from Nashville for the funeral. She never remembered the day Jimmy was not working on the farm or available if needed to make her a stand for a school project or a tabletop for her room. I was one of many pallbearers at the funeral. I knew he kept other households going, but I never realized how many there were.

As we were leaving the church with the casket, a fat man even older than I was said, "Let some of them young folks tote 'im."

"Not likely. I will do my part. He would have done the same for me." I held the corner handle every step of the way.

Jimmy never expected to see old age. He said none of his family ever had. Jimmy lived fifty-three years. He worked for us twenty-five of those years. I am sorry for those who are left, but I cannot be sorry for Jimmy. He did not suffer the anguish of disability.

He did not languish in a nursing home. He said he had no education, but he was wise in many ways. He was built for work. He loved to work, and worked until he died. He lived until he died. Is there a better way?

I have no doubts about the last words Jimmy said to me on a bright summer Saturday in the vineyard. He always said the same thing when he left.

"Well, I'm gonna get up ma tools and go. If you need me, just call. Ya know wher I'm at."

There are few places on the farm I can go and not see things Jimmy and I worked on together. When I go to the supply store where we bought our materials all these years and ask for help and advice about a project, sometimes Danny shakes his head and says, "I don't know. We just need to get ol' Jimmy back."

Ol' Joe
53

I have always been a solo practitioner, but I needed an assistant on major surgery and a consultant for problems. I had seen the results of those who work totally alone and didn't want to make their mistakes. If a doctor is close to a problem, he may lose perspective. Another may see what he does not. When I came to Anniston, rules required a second surgeon for major cases. There were surgeons so secretive and possessive about patients, they wanted no other doctor to see their patient on the unit, and if possible, no other doctor in the room when they operated. When they made errors in diagnosis or in surgery because they are human, those errors might not be seen. There are a few of these lone-wolf types who think if they can't diagnose the case and do the surgery, nobody can. Some of these doctors do outmoded or unorthodox surgery. A few never attend any postgraduate training. They see no need. Surgeons have been accused of a God-like stance--sometimes with justification.

I knew days would come when I needed help, so I approached Joe Henry when I first came to Anniston. I got a smug brush-off. He was a well-established surgeon and didn't need help from a brash young guy. After a little reflection, he changed his mind, and we established a working relationship lasting many years. At first, our work together in the OR was almost constant because he was assigned as my monitor. We had a rule about new surgeons being observed by another surgeon for six months before they were allowed to operate alone. I have no idea if the rule was enforced before I got here, but nobody has been proctored in such fashion since, except by a partner in a group. Joe was there for every case, with his lower lip poked out, checking the chart, probably to see if I had stolen one of his patients. I had not done anything crazy or wild in two months, so Joe said don't call unless I needed him. He must have thought I was moderately competent because he went on a long vacation for the first time in his practice. This was the first of many vacations. He was the number one surgeon in Anniston and could take the time off. When he was gone, my office was crowded. When his patients had a new problem I tried to play it straight. If it was acute, such as appendicitis, I operated. If the problem were chronic and long-standing, I didn't. I told the man with a hernia of two years with no complications, if he waited that long he could hold on for two weeks until his doctor got back. He smiled and agreed. There were many of these visits. Joe had a big practice. They took up a lot of time, but that was part of the deal.

Joe got back from his vacation in October, a dead month for surgeons. True to his personality, the first thing he did was check the OR and office appointment schedule. He was livid when he came to my office. He had almost no surgery scheduled. The most obvious answer was I had stripped the practice while he was gone. We reviewed my books and the OR schedule for the past weeks. The man who agreed to wait two weeks for Dr. Henry had gone down the street and found somebody to do the surgery the next day. I had seen his new cases, but another surgeon did the operation.

"Tells you just how loyal your patients are, doesn't it, Joe? They have a hernia for twenty years, but when they decide they want it operated on, they want it fixed now, by somebody, even if it's a strange doctor."

Joe stuck his lip out, scowled, huffed, puffed and pondered the situation, "Okay, let's do it a little different next time. If anyone *wants* to wait for me, they can. You operate on the rest. I had rather you do it than those other guys."

Joe could take the time off. He did go to medical meetings, but his only interest outside of medicine was travel. He made many trips, usually by trailer or van, sometimes weeks at the time. I did take care of his practice and save patients for him when I could. Some became my patients. As big as his practice was, he didn't have to be possessive, but he was. His answering machine said, "Dr. McGinnis is taking my calls" and then added, "But remember, when I get back you will *still* be my patient!" He always checked the OR schedule to see if somebody had operated on one of his patients. I heard about it if I had done the surgery.

"Sorry Joe, I didn't see a label on that guy. You should tag your patients, so I would know."

We covered each other on off-days and on out-of-town trips and we assisted each other in surgery on major cases. Joe never wanted his patients to know another doctor was in the OR, so I never sent in a claim or charged the patient. Joe was always there if I needed somebody in the middle of the night for a bad case or for a consult. I helped him more in surgery than he helped me at first.

Joe was a morose man, six feet tall with black hair streaked with gray. He was a few years older than I was. His features were a little heavy, and he had a recessive chin. One night, Joe called a doctor who referred patients to him. A child answered and called to his father to answer the phone.

The doctor said, "Is it anybody important?"

The honest child answered, "Nah, it's just Ol' Joe." Thereafter he was known as "Ol' Joe."

He was stuffy and pompous at times and a worrier. He worried about his patients. He worried about the results of his surgery. He worried about his home. He worried about himself. When he lost weight, he worried that he had cancer; when he gained, he worried about a heart attack. He complained that his feet hurt and sometimes stood with bare feet on pillows to operate. He whined and complained in the OR and was so self-righteous some called him "Holy Joe." When he came to the ER at night, he always wore bedroom slippers so everybody would know his rest had been disturbed, but he came when I needed him. He was a good technician and had excellent surgical judgment. In the early days when I was so fearful of missing a diagnosis, I consulted him a lot--sometimes just to reinforce my own diagnosis.

When we worked together in the OR, after the main part of surgery was finished and we were closing, there was time for conversation about his patients or mine, our problems and difficulties or even something totally unrelated to medicine. Once around Easter, we began a conversation about the ridiculous use of eggs and rabbits in the Easter celebration. After all, does anyone really think the Easter bunny lays those colored eggs he brings in the basket? Rabbits don't lay eggs. Joe and I were in total agreement on the issue. He added that the situation was almost as bad as that business about Santa Claus at Christmas. This was more than our anesthetist, Martha Honaker, could stand. Martha was a young, not obese, but just a large women. She was a congenial pleasant person whose most striking feature was a major smile showing the biggest white teeth you ever saw. Even in surgery with a mask on, though we couldn't see it, we could hear the smile in her voice. Martha tried to reason with us without success.

On the next afternoon a strange letter was on my desk in the office. Envelopes are not usually saved after my secretary opens the mail. This one was. The handwritten return address was:

Harrington Herkimer Hare, Esq.
Easterville, U.S.A., 1234

This letter was addressed to:

Ms. Martha Honaker
for Dr. Gaston McGinnis

The cancellation stamp was dated April 1980. The words around the edge of the stamp said: *Have a blessed Eastertide!!* The stamp was a smiling bunny with a bow tie. I did read this letter before I saw any patients. It's not every day you get a letter from a rabbit. The letter to *Dr. Gaston McGinnis, ET. Al* read as follows:

It has come to my attention that there are a number of misconceptions circulating concerning the various roles and job descriptions of the assorted (smear-smear) Easter creature-personnel. I am delighted to have the opportunity to resolve some of this confusion. The major Easter preparatory chores are shared by chickens and bunnies, but many people are unaware of the fact that rapid population growth in recent centuries has necessitated (smear-smear) recruiting help from several other sources, as you shall see. (Please pardon the errors in penmanship-- they are due to the fact that in rushing about gathering eggs before daybreak, I tripped on a rock and got a "stone bruise" on my right front paw!!)

But to continue--The traditional role of egg production continues to belong to the chickens, whose special talents suit them well to that assignment. Gathering eggs is accomplished by young bunny trainees--with supervision, of course. In great rushes we are sometimes assisted by squirrel-types and raccoons. ***Then****--due to the vast population explosion --the job of coloring and decorating is now being done by the elves from Santa's workshop, North Pole. This arrangement works well for us and for them; it lessens the pressure for us, and it breaks the long lull after Christmas. Also, it gives the Santa people a rare chance to work in warmer climates.*

That bit of information should be reassuring to one among you who has been given the distressing impression that "there is no Santa Claus." Horsefeathers!! The dear fellow would help us himself except that he and Mrs. C. take advantage of this quiet time to visit grandchildren.

I do hope that this little "essay" will correct some of the misinformation that has been circulating. All of us here at

Easterville wish all of you a most **Blessed Eastertide**!

Sincerely,
Harrington Herkimer Hare

I brought the letter for Joe to read the next day. He frowned as he read it, He handed it back and said, "Humph!"

"Be careful saying 'hump' like that, Joe. Remember, that's how the camel got his!"

"What?"

"Sorry. I forgot who I was talking to there for a minute. You might like to read *Just So Stories* some time. Then you could be a Best Beloved."

"What *are* you talking about?"

I am sure he never read the book, or if he tried, he quit before he got to the part about the camel.

Martha Honaker would become an Episcopal priest or, as I called her, a high priestess. I always wondered about her first Easter sermon.

Pompous people have little sense of humor. Joe thought few things were funny, mostly silly things. To my discredit, I can't resist the chance to needle such people.

Once during surgery Joe was telling me that he had seen my patient on rounds, "Yes, I saw her laying on the bed there."

" Joe, that wasn't my patient."

"What do you mean? It was supposed to be your patient?"

"It wasn't. My patients don't lay--they lie on their bed." It was worth all the righteous indignation. The nurses couldn't laugh. The circulator made some excuse and stepped out into the hall.

We worked together many years, never with any financial relationship. I tried to be there when he needed help. He complained, but he came when I needed him. This was a friendship, but it didn't extend to our social lives. He casually visited our home once, but never came to any social event. Ours was a medical friendship. If we had not seen each other for a while, he would call and say, "Well, whatd'ya know?" Loosely translated, do you know any new medical gossip?

Joe and his wife Lucile went on a mission trip to Africa. She was a nurse, but had not worked in many years. Lucile spoke in an affected voice characteristic of the very Deep South that sounds almost like baby talk to one of red-neck persuasion. It has been said that the longer two people live together, the more they are alike. Joe and Lucile were not. She was so arrogant and overbearing they could never keep domestic help and had difficulty hiring painters and plumbers. Joe did much of the housework and some of the cooking. He was protective of his wife and devoted to her. She came to the OR to learn to function as a scrub nurse for Ol' Joe on an African trip. When they came back, she decided to continue to work so Joe wouldn't have to hire anybody else. She was so pompous the nurses in the OR called her "Uncle Joe." So we had Ol' Joe and Uncle Joe--a self-righteous pair. On the first day back from Africa, Joe was doing a colonoscopy in the OR. These patients are now heavily sedated because of severe discomfort. At that time, they got essentially nothing. The patient was complaining loudly.

Lucile was patting his arm and saying in that high-pitched sugary voice, "Thaah- thaah--it will be all right."

The patient raised up off the pillow and said, "Shut up old woman! I wish them cannibals in Africa had eat you!"

I was surprised she made it back for a major case that night.

In the late afternoon, before I came in for Joe's case, one of the OR nurses called me at home and said, "When you come, bring us somethin'. We're tired and hungry."

What do you mean bring something? Bring what?"

"Just something." In the past, I had brought sacks of lettuce, watermelons, smoked meats, honey in the comb and other farm treasures, but this was short notice.

I gave the paper sack to Martha as I came into the OR. She grinned. Neither of us spoke. We began the abdominal surgery. As we placed the retractors after opening the abdomen, I noticed a hand toward the head of the table. I suddenly realized it had no glove. There was a quick motion and an unsoiled surgical pack well above the incision disappeared. The three of us looked up, speechless.

Martha Honaker said, "I had to move it. I couldn't see the operation! I was very careful not to touch anything."

After Ol' Joe and Uncle Joe chastised her, she sat and pouted. The OR was quiet while Joe removed the gallbladder. I began to notice strange noises so faint I was not sure they were real. Then the others noticed. The sounds came from the head of the table: slurp--grunch--pitooie. They came at regular intervals over and over: slurp--grunch--pitooie.

Finally Uncle Joe looked over the ether screen and said, "Miss Honaker, what evah *ah* you doing?"

With wide innocent eyes Martha looked up, "Eatin' muscadines. I'm being very careful. See my mask is still on and ... and the machine is on automatic!"

She was taking muscadines from the sack I brought, pushing them one at the time under her mask on the left side. After she ate them, she pushed the hulls and seeds from the right side. Her mask was in place, though a little damp. Uncle Joe never came back to surgery. Nobody cried.

Joe's worries were justified. He did have heart trouble, and over the years had a bypass and an angioplasty. He had surgery for blocked femoral arteries, carotid arteries, a pulmonary embolus and prostate surgery. Each time he went to Birmingham for surgery, he said I was to stay home and take care of the practice rather than to come to see him. He wanted none of his patients to know he was having troubles. I did operate on him in Anniston once under a fake name so nobody would know.

He began to do much of his surgery at Stringfellow. Some thought they petted and pampered him more, so he liked it better. He became even more of a worrier. Sometimes he came by the office to talk about cases I hadn't helped him with. He admitted he lost sleep worrying that someone might sue him, though nobody ever did. He developed a tremor. I have seen surgeons with an intention tremor, which stops when the knife hits the skin. His didn't. Joe tried to compensate by making sudden motions so the tremors didn't show. I advised him to stop all caffeine to see if it would help. He cut a ureter once. It can happen to the best. He asked me to scrub with the urologist to fix it.

One day, I got a panic call from Joe. As soon as I finished my case, I scrubbed in to help. All surgeons live in horror of injuring the common duct in a gallbladder case. Joe had cut the common duct *and* the hepatic ducts. Part of the hepatic ducts and entire common duct were gone. Three hepatic stumps protruded from the liver dripping bile. He thought this happened because of a congenital anomaly, in which hepatics empty directly into the gallbladder and not the common duct. Whatever the cause, we had the problem of what to do.

"Joe, there's only one way I know of; build a Roux-Y loop of small intestine and anastomose all three of those ducts. We've got to drain the bile some way. Cut the small bowel, close the end, swing it over sew it to the liver bed, and then we can hook up the ducts."

The procedure progressed with agonizing slowness. We built and attached the loop of small bowel to the liver. As he began the first and easiest anastomosis, I could see Joe was having problems. I debated with myself about what to do. I didn't want to wound his pride, but there was the matter of the patient.

Joe finally said," Why don't you finish this?" I did the anastomosis of each duct and we closed. I was there nine hours and Joe eleven. Nobody even took a bathroom break. My kidneys go into shutdown in the OR. Just don't stand between me and the bathroom when it's over.

Joe never relaxed until the patient fully recovered. Our anastomosis has worked for years.

One day Joe quit, with notices in the paper and transfer of records and the other formalities. He had talked about what he would do in the future, but had never named a time. He wanted to stop major cases and do minor surgery in his office. I think he knew he was not good enough at skin surgery, so there was nothing to do but quit something he done for a lifetime. He worried about events in his practice even more now. He was not happy in practice, but was more unhappy having to stop.

I didn't see Joe much after that. I did go by the house a time or two. He and his wife still traveled a lot in their Airstream, but if at home, each day he dressed in his suit as he had for forty years and sat in the back room. He was by the phone if I called.

He came back from a trip and was telling me about it at the office. He couldn't remember the name of the place he had been. He still dressed in a suit every day and looked as he always did.

Months later, he was in the office to talk about his wife. He said, "You know she's got that ... that stuff ... you know ... that women have." He couldn't remember fibrocystic disease, something he had operated on a thousand times.

The next time he was in the office, his wife drove the car. Joe had always driven for her. I did some minor procedure on a toe. He continued to complain about his feet as he had for forty years. He had trouble remembering words he wanted to use and had hesitation of speech. The next visit was another trip for his feet. He showed me a rash on his toes and the medicine he was using.

"Joe, you have simple athletes foot. This is Whitfield's Ointment. I didn't know they still made it."

Lucile said, "Oh, he remembered it from his father's drug store when he was a boy."

"Joe, that was fifty years ago." I gave him samples of a fungicide cream. He had increasing trouble communicating. He couldn't remember words and at times jabbered nothing but gibberish.

His wife cried during the last visit. Joe never noticed. She said, "I sure wish somebody would straighten him out. I am tired of taking care of him."

I had to bite my tongue to keep from saying, "He probably felt the same way about you for forty years."

Joe wanted surgery on his foot. His circulation was so poor I advised against it. I watched him as he left; he was dressed in his suit as if he were going to his office. He carried on social amenities like nodding to people as he passed and shaking hands. He opened the car door for his wife as he had for forty years. From a distance he looked fine. Changes at each visit were painful to watch.

Some months later, I went to a birthday party at his house. His family was there and twenty or so friends. As I entered the front door, I saw him come in the room. He looked like the Joe of old. He was well dressed and had a slight smile, which was unusual for him. He looked as if he would come up to me and say, "Well, whatd'ya know?" Somebody gave him a plate of food. With no comprehension and a silly grin on his face, he showed it to his son as a child would show a new toy. I couldn't hear, but I saw his son explain to him that the food was his to eat. They looked toward me. There was no recognition on Joe's face. His son pointed to me and explained who I was. Joe nodded. With his son guiding him, he came to shake my hand. He did not speak. He could not speak. This person standing two feet away looked like my friend of years and dressed like him. As he shook my hand, I looked in his eyes and saw nothing. He had no comprehension and no awareness--of anything. This had been a man who had done intricate surgery for years and had held thousands of lives in his hand.

Does this dysfunctional prison of flesh hold captive a being struggling to communicate, screaming to be free? Or has the man we had known, his essence, his being, his very soul already gone, and what we see now is a cruel shadow of what has been? Is this form like a shell on the beach? To the eye, it's a thing of beauty. But from within, there is the sound of emptiness. The living being has gone. Is there a cause and effect? Did Joe cause these changes through diet, activity, or moody nature? Was he unalterably destined from birth for this ending or could he have changed his destiny by manner of life or magic potion?

There is an appointed time for everything. *And there is a time for every event under heaven* (Ecc.3:1) Nothing happens without cause. Yet, what is the purpose of all this? I don't know the answer to any of these questions. I am not sure I want to know. As far as I could tell, when I looked into mirrors of his soul, there was emptiness in those eyes. Ol' Joe was gone.

My Trip
54

The end of a matter is better than its beginning; Patience of spirit is better than haughtiness of spirit.
Ecclesiastes 7:8

In thin light of early morning, I looked to the east from the bathroom window. Rays burst from clumps of clouds in a slate-colored sky. The hidden sun colored edges gold and amber. I shaved, dressed, ate, and left the silent house into drifting mists, wet against my face as if I stepped into a cloud. My nurse, Shirley, arrived. We considered the fog, but were due for surgery. I drove slowly down the driveway. Rain on warm earth had turned to fog, changing common to uncommon. Yesterday, fences were old and drab. Now they looked new, wet, and glistening. The spider's works of art sagged with droplets of dew sparkling like diamonds. Cows stood in mist layered on the ground, making then floating bodies in a milky sea.

The fog was less on the interstate. After a few miles on I-20, we turned south on 46 across the Tallapoosa toward Ranburne. As the road dropped into Trickum Valley, almost impenetrable fog lay along the ground flowing across fields, hiding bushes and fences, growing thicker toward the woods. Buildings near the road glistened in the mist. Leaves on trees showed colors of early fall, brighter in wetness.

The slightest breeze rolled pillows of fog across the road. Trees and ridges on either side hid the sun from this valley. Shafts of light came through openings in the trees making the fog glow as if there were a light within. The fog was not dismal, but alive with motion and glowing from the sun we could not see. Stripes on the road were just visible. There was no traffic. Strangely, I had no apprehension and felt secure crawling along in the fog. We saw not another human on the roadside, as if all had fled this strange mist. There was no sound other than the rumble of the motor and slap of the windshield wipers. My usually talkative nurse said not a word. I drove slowly and deliberately. I had the sensation of floating on a cloud that billowed and swirled, bathed by light from a world we couldn't see. For no reason, great swirls came from the deepest fog as if they were living things.

In this magic land of changing mists, strange shapes approached the car. Ghosts of the past came and beckoned. These phantoms showed me things from the past. They reminded me of changes I have seen in my short lifetime, all the turns I have made and even changes that brought me on this trip and on this road.

It is hard to believe now, but when I went to medical school, civilians of this nation had penicillin only five years. Organ transplants were an impossibility and heart surgery a dream. Patients with severe heart or kidney disease were made comfortable until they died. When I began practice, the general surgeon did generally everything. I elected to eliminate urology and major orthopedics and concentrate on what I knew and could do best. After a few months, I knew the truth about surgery in Anniston. Surgeons were well qualified for major cases, but some needs were poorly served. Some surgeons continued as they were taught in medical school and residency. Change frightens us all, even surgeons who see fear every day. With change there is fear of failure. Nature hates a vacuum. Empty space will be filled, if not by those nearby, others will come.

When I came to Anniston, workmen's compensation injuries were thought a plague. Nobody wanted them. Hand injuries and trauma to the face were not always treated well. Windshields of the old type broke into shards causing unbelievable damage. I liked reconstructive surgery, but I had little experience with the type of job injuries I was being sent. When I could afford to go, I took weeklong courses on hand surgery, plastic surgery, job injuries and general surgery. Even the experts didn't have all the answers. Nobody knew about brass fever. As company doctor for Lee Brothers Brass Foundry, I saw cases most weeks. I didn't know what it was or how to treat it. I thought my first patient with the fever was going to die. He thought so, too. I read all seven of the articles in the world's literature and learned treatment from older employees. Smoke was so thick in the foundry, I could see only a few feet. Now, exhaust fans clear the smoke and there is no brass fever. It was due to inhalation of the white zinc smoke from molten brass. Brass fever caused shaking chills, fever, chest pain, shortness of breath and cough. Patients who looked to be near death were well the next day, whether treated or not. The old hands' treatment of hot lemonade and a wrap around sheet or blanket worked as well as some wonder drug. I am an authority on something that no longer exists. Is this an omen?

There were no seatbelts. Most car wrecks caused facial injuries. Nobody wanted to treat facial fractures. Dentists wouldn't come into the hospital. The two ENT guys did a few. Some of these patients were drunks from a Saturday night melee, but some were injured through no fault of their own. I had done facial fractures in the Army. I went to courses and bought books. At one time I did 75 % of the facial fractures in the city.

With gall bladders, thyroids, colons and other general surgery added to the trauma to the face, hand surgery and job injuries, I was busy. One year by official count, I was the number one visitor to the ER. No matter how hard some of us tried to cover the ER, there were times that no doctor was in the hospital, and some took an hour or more to come when called. When I was chief of staff, I pushed for ER doctors. The new ER coverage brought change I did not anticipate.

A new doc came to town and did what nobody had done: he convinced ER doctors, large companies and other doctors that he was an expert in industrial injuries. He solicited these patients--effectively. Somewhere along the way ethics had died. He had been trained as a family practice doctor and had some industrial medicine as a part of that program. He lasted a few months, but patterns were broken and never returned. The ER doctors treated hand injuries, and sent orthopedic injuries to the orthopedist on call, even if a general surgeon were requested. My own secretary was told she would have to see the ER doctor; I could not be called. Who am I to stand in the way of progress? I had plenty to do so I didn't pursue the matter.

Oral surgeons came to town eager to do facial fractures. The ER referred all facial fractures to them, but I still had plenty to do.

New general surgeons came to town and diluted the practice. One day, I came to realize I had taken calls for twenty-nine years without a break except for medical meetings and a few short vacations. Enough is enough. I asked to be placed in the senior active status. I would come to the ER for my own patients, but I no longer had to come for the patients without a doctor. I wrote letters explaining the circumstances to the ER doctors, but I wasted paper. My patients were told I no longer came to the ER and another surgeon was called.

A few not so passive patients called me themselves or demanded that the ER call me. Much of my practice disappeared. The surgeon on call did all acute abdomens.

I tried reason. I documented events. I saw much of the same things happen to older surgeons. These were men who wanted to stay in the mainstream of life. They weren't ready for the nursing home. Even though they couldn't do the big surgery of the past, they wanted to do something productive and not disappear. But they did fade away in a cloud of bitterness. Some I never saw again after they retired. Some family practice doctors or internists yearn for the day they can quit. Surgeons are different. I am sure it's not their ego!

I did much soul searching. I did not want to join the ranks of the bitter. I was blessed by not having major disability. At this stage in life I could not stand long hours and physically do the big surgery as in the past. I could do appendectomies and hernias as well as twenty years ago, but the flow of these had been cut off. I returned to the logic I had used when I came to Anniston. What surgical conditions were poorly served? What did nobody else want to do? What could I do and do better than others? A degree of egotism is essential for a surgeon. To take apart a human being and put him back together demands a degree of confidence, but not overconfidence or arrogance. Egotism must be tempered in a delicate balance with humility. The two do not cancel each other and can coexist.

I was unhappy with my management of breast disease. Other surgeons managed their patients much the same as I did. Breast cancer is devastating to a woman and her husband. While the breast is not essential for life, it is a sexual organ and symbol of motherhood and womanhood. Loss of a breast is necessary at times, but the loss is a psychological blow. Two episodes became deciding factors for me. I followed the traditional procedure and used large dressings for mastectomies. In the office two weeks after surgery, I told a patient she could leave the dressing off. She wanted the heavy dressing. She said she was not yet ready to look at the scar. Another patient tolerated her surgery well, but her husband left her bedroom and never came back. He never saw her scar or the other breast. Several patients refused to exercise and had limited motion. One could barely get her arm away from her side to dress. The standard mastectomy operation was long and tedious. A surgical text said if the surgeon spent less than five hours, the operation was inadequate. There had to be a better way. If I were to continue breast surgery, I would change my management.

I made two trips to Louisiana to work with a man who did nothing but breast surgery. I attended training programs. I bought books. I put all these things together in my mind and asked the hospital to spend $28,000 for new equipment so I could do better breast surgery. I asked for new programs. A large conference resulted. Change breeds fear and fear breeds resistance. Changes were opposed, not only by some of the radiologists, but some surgeons. The gynecologists supported me. After a few harsh words, I got the equipment and began my new program. When I laid out the new program for the crew in surgery and central supply, they thought I was crazy.

The supervisor of central supply said, "You want what?"

"I want a complete supply of sizes from ittie bittie to gee whiz, maybe six each, of Mary Jane brassieres." Their worst fears were confirmed.

The gynecologists installed the first good dedicated mammography X-ray unit. Eventually the hospital bought a new machine. With these units, we began to see tumors we could not feel. The radiologist localized these obscure lesions just before surgery, and I did the biopsy. Confirmation X-rays of the biopsy specimen with our new machine were made to make sure the proper area had been removed. Tiny cancers were removed years before they could be felt on physical examination. The procedures were new and confusing to the staff at times. After the first biopsy, I told the nurses to put the bra on before moving the patient to the recovery room. The bra supports the breast for comfort and prevents the patient's own bra from being soiled. There is an IV in one arm, which confuses the procedure, especially for one young male nurse. I could see he was perplexed.

I handed him the bra, "You can do this. It's just like taking one off, except backwards, and you don't breathe as hard." He became the brassiere expert that day.

I did the modified radicals with a Shaw hot knife to prevent bleeding. I made incisions transversely if possible and closed a smooth line, or a flap was rotated so that a graft was not needed. I couldn't prevent loss of a breast, but I could give them a thin scar. I used no dressings. I left catheters under the flaps to draw out any drainage. I worked out a system to place them and fix them and even wrote a paper on the procedure. The nurses on the unit were horrified to find a patient from surgery with no dressing. I had to do a lot of reassuring and show them the incision line was sealed with collodion; the operative area could be touched to make sure that there was no fluid collection. Sooner or later, the patient would look at the area and accept the loss. The nurses taught me another reason to leave the area open: the patients took less than half the narcotics that others did. Some took no narcotics and went home the day after surgery. With the old method some stayed ten days. Operating room time for a mastectomy with the new procedure was about two hours and could be as short as one hour, and I am a slow surgeon. The old mastectomy not only took longer, but required several units of blood. We used no blood for a breast case for years. I brought physical therapy personnel into the OR to see an open mastectomy so that they could understand the problem. We began physiotherapy the day after surgery. Patients complained about soreness, but after the recovery phase had essentially normal motion. The hospital recovered its money for equipment in a few months. Other surgeons began changing routines.

In the early days, the patient was put to sleep for her surgery, not knowing if she would have a breast when she woke up. Now, the patient did have options. She could have the one stage as in the past, but with a modified mastectomy with preservation of muscle, or biopsy alone. The next day after the simple biopsy, I sat down with her and her husband and talked about options. If the cancer was small, she might elect a limited resection, node dissection and X-ray therapy. If the husband didn't show up, I sent for him. I gave him a short direct talk. His job was as important as mine. His wife was about to lose one of the symbols of motherhood and womanhood. If he did not make her feel she was as much a mother, a wife and a woman as ever, then she would not do well. He must say and do the right thing at the right time.

When I talk with a woman and her husband about her biopsy report, that she has cancer and needs more surgery, after all these years, I know of no easy way. The husband's presence may create a problem. Sometimes he sits in a chair across the room for the bad news and says nothing. We had one husband faint. His wife was not happy, but she was well enough to drive her pale husband home. And women are the weaker sex? I tell the woman directly and without delay. In this day, we are never supposed to touch the patients except for examination. As I tell the bad news, I hold her hand or her wrist. I cannot truly feel her pain, but by touching I can show I identify with her in her time of trouble. My nurse sometimes puts an arm around her.

Some of this management has changed my patient's and their husband's attitudes toward this surgery. With no dressings, the patient will see the operative site from the first day. Once, early in this new program of management a patient was well healed and was discharged for three months. She felt that her husband should see her scar. That night in their bedroom her husband watched as she removed her upper garments. The left breast was gone, replaced by a thin red line. She looked to see his reaction.

He said, "Weell, 'at ain't too bad. Sorta looks like one o' them cars with disappearin' headlights an' one of 'em got stuck." She had her answer. If we can laugh at disaster, the battle is half over.

* * *

The phantoms of the fog told me of yet another part of surgery not fully served. I had always liked skin surgery and reconstructive surgery after cancer surgery. The Southeast has a large Celtic population and we have our share of sunshine. Our lifestyles have changed so there is much more sun-exposure. All of these things cause an increase in skin cancer. When I came to Anniston, I rarely saw skin cancers; now I was seeing them in a flood. The small lesions were no problem, but neglected tumors required removing great parts of a nose, cheek or ear. Then there was a huge defect on the face needing a flap or graft. If the reconstruction were poorly done, the patient was permanently disfigured. The otolaryngologist and general surgeons did some of this surgery. If it was too complicated, they sent it to Birmingham. My problem was where to go for more training. The plastic surgeons have meetings, but I would be considered an infidel and couldn't get beyond the front door. General surgical attitudes were the same as in training; skin surgery is not life threatening, and is considered trivial. It is not trivial if half of your own nose is involved with cancer. Most of the meetings I went to offered little help. I discovered in the years since medical school, management of skin surgery had changed. Some dermatologists were now doing big-time skin surgery. When I was in medical school, they did surgery only if it didn't need sutures. There were now organizations to train dermatologists in surgery of major reconstruction. Would they accept a non-believer? I read their constitution, rules and by-laws. I qualified, or at least I wasn't disqualified. But was it a closed club? I went to a symposium on skin surgery held by the American Society for Dermatologic Surgery. I took a weeklong course held by the founder of the organization. I talked with him and told him of my needs. Fellowship in the organization required two endorsements by members, one must be within the state. One dermatologist from Birmingham agreed to endorse me, not once but twice, and did not. He must have considered his organization a closed club. I would have never known if the secretary from the ASDS hadn't called to say they hadn't received my second endorsement. It probably didn't hurt that my one endorsement was the founder. A local dermatologist gave me the recommendation. I had not called him first, thinking that he would see me as a competitor. I became a Fellow of ASDS and the International Society for Dermatologic Surgery. Because of this membership, I get invitations to the Moes Surgery meetings and receive journals and publications. Over the years we have been to weeklong meetings from San Francisco to Florence, Italy. I am not the only general surgeon in the group, but almost. There are a few plastic and ENT types also. I have a source for techniques and training.

What do I do with all this desire and some knowledge? Breast cases are referred by gynecologists. How do I get the patients with skin tumors? Do I run a full-page ad in the paper? Do I have a talk show on the radio or TV? Maybe I could give out coupons on the street corner. All of these systems might be used, just like a grocery store. I don't judge others. For me, such methods would be in poor taste. My skin surgery increased slowly by word of mouth. Some were referred, most are either long-time patients who see something on their face and refer themselves or a neighbor sends them. After several years, I put together a slide show for the nurses showing before, during and after photographs of our cancer surgery. Some of the nurses have sent us patients after seeing the results of our surgery.

For years during the reconstruction stage of this type of surgery I noticed whispering behind me. I may remove a huge cancer from full thickness of the nose leaving the septum in full view. I then make a bad situation worse by freeing a large flap from the adjacent cheek to move over to reconstruct the nose. Then there is a hole in the cheek and the nose.

One day the truth finally came out, "Doctor McGinnis we look at all those places and say to each other, 'He's really done it now. He'll never get that back together'--but you always do."

"Girls, I have news for you; sometimes I think the same thing. If you will notice, I draw pictures and measure several times before cutting. Then when we raise the flap, it may not go into position right away. There are a thousand little tricks to move the flap just a little closer until it fits in place, but I too wonder sometimes if it will fit."

There are now new ENT types and plastic surgeons in Anniston. Others noticed fields poorly served. Breast surgery and skin surgery don't produce many calls at night and represent something I can do till one of the three Ds gets me. I'm still alive and I don't have the shakes. The third and most treacherous is: Discouraged. Our government and third parties are working on that one every day. There are health organizations that severely limit the choice of surgeon to a select few. If I am not on that list, the patient may go to Birmingham or another local surgeon. The patient might not even be allowed by the system to have the surgery.

* * *

We crept through the fog-shrouded sleeping city of Ranburne and east toward the Georgia line, disturbing swirling mists. The sun was up enough to burn away most of the strange fog and the magic was gone as we neared the Bowden Hospital. Small hospitals have a hard time surviving. We agreed to operate there two days a month to help them. Some days we work all day and some days are not so busy. We do essentially the same surgery we do in Anniston. Bowden is a different world, like Anniston once was. Everybody knows everybody. The nurses are always glad to see us because they wanted to work--to survive. I can identify with that.

Before the last of the magic mist and specters of the past faded, I thought about the road I had traveled these years. I came from a family who had never had a college graduate and were low on the economic scale. I had a poor educational background before college. I struggled in college and medical school. I chose the wrong place to practice and was forced to move. My type of practice changed, not once but several times over the years. The world about us changes, and if we don't adapt, we die. We arrived in Anniston almost as paupers and now are rich. Betty and I are rich because we have a home and a life together, which has lasted many years. We are rich because we have four children who are working and like to work. We are rich because we have work to do. Every day, there are things that wouldn't be done if we didn't do them, and we like to do these things. A man is blessed if he is surrounded by those he loves and has work to do, that he loves. Possessions don't insure happiness, and don't indicate riches. If a man works hard, and if possessions are meant to be, they come. Nobody should strive to amass money and possessions. If he does, he fixes his eyes on rewards and is consumed by means to get them. The trip up the mountain is the reward, not the view from the top.

As the mists cleared, I saw an old farmer feeding his cows. If I were to stop and tell him this story of how I came from modest means and strove for a education in spite of adversity--if I told him of struggles in medical school and the Army and the wrong choice to practice and of the conflicts with some of my own colleagues--if I told him all these things and then told him I had persevered; I had not only survived many years after medical school, but am still able to provide a service, even though modest, to yet accomplish something in this world.

If I told him all these things, I know his answer. He would shake his head and say, "Ya know, ya just can't hardly do that sorta thing no more."

As we made the last turn toward Bowden, the mists faded. Before they did, there was the promise of ghosts from a time to come, from mists yet to be. They may wait in Trickum. Whether they be many or few, good or evil, they will come. My trip is not yet over.

How Many?

55

The telephone rang at the house at the foot of the hill. In 1931, few people went out at night, but Doug Trammell did. As dusk changed to night, he walked a block and beyond the corner where the sidewalk ends under the last streetlight and knocked on a neighbor's door. He walked back home with Luther Lafayette Owen. They placed a call to Goldsboro, North Carolina. As the connections got farther and farther, they shouted louder and louder. Neighbors walked out on the porch or in the yard to hear the words. After several minutes, L. L. Owen heard his only daughter say his only grandchild lay in a hospital bed packed in ice with a temperature of 106. The doctors could drain no more eardrums. Infection had spread to bone. There was little hope, but they would try to do a mastoidectomy to drain the pus.

There was no hesitation. "Fate" Owen called two friends who had phones and knocked on doors of others on the way. Neighbors were startled to see lights come on in the little church at an odd time on a strange day. The church was never locked, but the neighbors couldn't resist looking in the door to see who was there. They saw a gathering of men at the front of the church, some with gray hair and some snow-white. Their heads were bowed and they spoke in turn. Some wept. The neighbors tiptoed out and gently closed the door. After the men in the circle were sure the operation was over, each went his own way, walking in the stillness of dark stretches between the glare of lights at the corners of the deserted streets of Boaz, Alabama--500 miles from the sick child.

The next day, the doctor told the young mother infection still raged even after surgery. Her son might not live, but if he did, he would certainly be deaf in the right ear. Shock from the surgery was being treated in the usual fashion: a spoon of bottled-in-bond Bourbon every fifteen minutes.

One year later to the day, my hearing returned. My right ear is now the only one I have.

* * *

January 7 in the year 2000, I finished my usual Friday office hours. A vague abdominal pain had visited me for short periods of time over the past few days and chose to return in a more insistent way. I had a few cramps and a "cold sweat." I dictated my charts and drove home.

I made a trip to the bathroom. I lay down with a heating-pad to the vague discomfort in my back. None of these things helped and my sweats came back. I felt unusually weak, even for a Friday. Betty was surprised to find me in bed at 5:00.

Doctors, especially surgeons, are not stubborn, but they are reluctant to admit that they need help. I finally did. I refused the ambulance, which would have been slower for our seven-mile drive, but would have gained us a little respect.

When Betty stopped in the ambulance ramp and ran in to get help, the guard came up shouting, "You can't park there. You'll have to move right now!" He followed her into the ER, still shouting.

As she rounded the corner, I heard her say, "You just watch me." Betty didn't know the urologist just inside the door. When Terry Phillis asked if he could help. She said, "Sure, you can park my car and get that guard off my back."

With all the fuss, I opened the door and walked into the Emergency Room. I was very careful. I lined up the door straight ahead and looked down to concentrate on each step, because I seemed to float through a doorway that was unusually bright. I sat in the wheel chair the nurse offered.

Nobody wanted to accept my only significant symptom. I said it over and over, "Yes, I have a little discomfort in the back--on the right side--but not bad. Mostly ... I have impending syncope."

A patient might come in and say, " I'm 'bout to let a faint." They don't say, "I have impending syncope."

When they found my blood pressure to be 60/40, they understood. After sonogram and a cat scan, I was sent to Interventional Radiology. At 5:30 on a Friday night there were physically present in the ER: an Emergency Room doctor I respect and helped train, an Interventional Radiologist who wasn't even on call, and a Urologist who parks cars. They took over my care and stayed with me until I went to ICU. The Specials Technician who runs the computer for the procedures had just left and was called back. Donna did not expect to see her daddy come into the procedure-room on a stretcher and did well until the nurse brought in the crash-cart.

I lost an estimated six units of blood internally--about three quarters of a gallon--a near death event by any definition. Through the magic of Interventional Radiology, Bob Bain put in a platinum coil and particles in the uppermost of my four right renal arteries. The vessel was blocked and bleeding from the burst aneurysm stopped.

Some would say that all those people just happened to be in the ER on a Friday night, and all those years ago a child just happened to survive a raging infection without antibiotics. I don't believe it. God hears prayers of an anguished young mother, of old men gathered in a circle in a little church in the gloom of night, prayers of a frightened wife and daughter, the wife of the radiologist and a frightened surgeon. Nothing terrifies a surgeon more than feeling he is not in control of a situation. I don't know why He honors some prayers and not others. Who can know the mind of God? I was thankful to see the sun come up on January the eighth.

In those two days, thoughts of wife and family filled my mind, but I was a child again and heard my grandfather's voice say words I didn't understand then, "God has a job for you to do, or you wouldn't have lived to see this day."

For a time, I thought my work was finished, but there must be more for me to do. My first life was three years. My second was much longer. I could not know the length of my third, but I knew each day was a gift. All past days were gifts, but not as cherished then. I knew I had blessed with three lives, but on this earth I might not see a fourth.

And yet, in my third life on April 11, 2006, I did my usual one case in Mini-surgery, ate in the Doctor's Lounge, saw a few office patients and went home a little early. I walked out to the greenhouse in the pasture and potted a grape cross from the year before. On the way back I began sweating. Betty wanted me to come across the yard to look at something. My sweats were worse and I had to rest halfway across the yard. When I sat down to eat, I checked my pressure. It was fine. I had a little tachicardia, but it was a warm day. I ate little and declined dessert. A trip to the bathroom gave me the answer for the sweats: a large tarry stool. I had no pain and was on a proton pump inhibitor for reflux. I had not missed a day's work in six years. I had no reason to bleed, but long ago I learned to believe what I see. We went to the hospital. I told them what I had when we drove up, but there is protocol to follow. Our oldest daughter came and called a surgeon. I indicated a family doctor. Both were there within minutes. The ER physician came later, did a rectal and made a profound announcement of what I had told him when he walked in the door. At one time there were four doctors in my room. I lived through the night with a Levin tube that did little more than confirm the diagnoses. After four units of blood, on the following morning Jim Hixson, my gastroenterologist, cleared the stomach, found the arterial bleeding site and cooked it with a laser. I never heard of a Dieulofoy's ulcer. After days in intensive care and a regular unit, Betty took me and somebody else's blood home.

I recovered enough to do office surgery and had plans for bigger cases the next week. Wednesday April 28, I finished the office went home, ate, and went to bed at an early hour. About midnight, I felt the urge and headed for the bathroom. I did not realize how weak I was. I wiped off a table of framed pictures and fell in the floor. The tarry stool told me the laser patch was gone.

I bled more this time and the laser couldn't hold it. Dewayne Clark did a limited gastrectomy and I had more blood–now almost an exchange transfusion. All the blood came from tired people.

I only have weird things. This was the first Dieulofoy's done in our hospital. A second was done the next week. The stress of blood loss caused a heart attack and he died. He was five years younger. In recent years, I have had three near death experiences, but am blessed in many ways. I am a little unstable and wobble when I walk, but my hands are as sure as when I was thirty-five.

I was humbled by what has taken place. I was humbled by the numbers of people who prayed for me. I was grateful for the medical care I received, using tools unheard of twenty years ago. I was grateful for the love and devotion of my wife, family and friends. Most of all, I was humbled to know that God loves me or I wouldn't be here. If we consider recent events as one, I entered my fourth life.

One Sunday in my fourth life, I forgot a pair of rarely worn shoes tended to hang on rugs. I fell against the wood frame of a couch. I didn't break my neck and I didn't have brain damage. I broke my right maxilla and orbit. The orbit was decompressed within an hour to an hour and a half, but it was too late. I lost sight in the right eye. I was sent to UAB in Birmingham glad to be alive, but depressed. When I talked with the doctors there, I felt no better. I was admitted to a unit for observation. Personnel observed me and I observed the ceiling.

On the second night, I woke in a dark room with a sliver of light shining through a doorway to my right. In the corner near the door, I saw a cluster of desks covered with a piece of wrinkled fabric. As I walked toward the light, something pulled at my left hand and wrist, holding me back. I jerked it off and walked on. I opened the door and stepped into a brightly lit hall--empty and quiet. I turned left. I passed closed doors--all with a big white hand in the center. There were handrails along the sides of the hall, but I walked in the middle. I turned right. More rooms--with closed doors and white hands. I turned right again. There was a smaller hall to the left--dark and empty. I walked on. I came to a large opening to the right--even brighter.

A woman looked up from a desk, "May I help you?"

"Yes, you can tell me were I am."

"UAB Hospital. May I see your wrist band?"

Another woman stood at the far desk and I recognized her as the night shift nurse and remembered where I was. A nurse on each side steered me down the hall, as if I might get away again. They put me to bed and started another IV. They put intermittent pressure cuffs on my legs. If I tried to leave again, they might slow me a little. Betty, sleeping in a chair by my bed, woke almost as confused as I had been.

I had been given Demerol 25 mg IV and 5 mg Ambien at ten P.M. The drugs had given sleep, but had worn off. I was also given Flomax for the first time about nine. At three AM, I woke in a dark room, avoided the side rails, got out of bed for the first time in two days and walked the hall in slick stocking feet. With my progressive loss of sense of balance, I walk by sight and use a stick in strange places or stabilize myself by touching a rail, the wall or piece of furniture. I walked the circular hall of the Unit touching nothing but the floor wearing slick elastic stockings. There was no visual defect. Both sides of the hall were bright and clear. I walked as easily as I did at twenty-five. When the nurse turned on the light in my room, the desks were gone, but everything in the hall *was* real. There *were* white hands on the doors. The pictures reminded people to wash. There *had* been something on my wrist holding me back. There was no pain when I tore away the taped down IV.

I lay there, looked at the ceiling and thought about my strange walk. I woke in darkness where there was no knowledge. My mind was filled with one thought.

Go to the light and discover where you are.

I pulled away from what held me. When I went to the light, there was silence, no one there, and nothing familiar, so I walked. I went left because I saw no end to the hall to the right. In my dreams, I run or skate like I did as a child, but I am in a phantom body. In my hospital trip, I used my real body, but my disabilities were gone, as if I were fifty years younger. If this altered state were drug induced or if I were sleepwalking, why do I have such vivid memory of the emptiness of that hall and every closed door? If I can walk well in that state, why can't I walk well when I am oriented in time and place?

I went home glad to be alive, but dejected because of the loss of yet another sense. The first time I put on a coat and put in my little book of notes and phone numbers, a page fell out. It was frayed and worn at the folds from the years I had carried it.

Have you ever been out for a late afternoon walk in the closing part of the afternoon, and suddenly looked up to realize that the leaves have practically all gone? And the sun has set and the day has gone before you knew it—and with that a cold wind blows across the landscape?

That's retirement.

Stephen Leacock

After days of soul searching, trials of simple tasks with my hands and consultation with my nurse, I put a notice in the paper.

To my patients

How different life would be--
without a single event of a single day.
Thank you those who cared
and those who prayed.
I will continue to practice
as before the injury.

Gaston Owen McGinnis, MD, FACS

We live in a small town. Everybody knew of my injury. I had no idea what would happen. Most of what comes through my door, I have seen hundreds or thousands before. My mind is still clear and my hands sure. I have always used magnification for skin surgery. It is harder for me to do my skin surgery. I am even slower now. I can sit and do skin lesions. I would not attempt deep surgery. There are increasing numbers of skin cancers in our town. I am further blessed with a loyal office crew who has been with me almost as long as I have been in practice.

I am amazed at how many people trust an old guy with one eye, one ear, 3/4 of a stomach, 1 1/2 kidneys and no sense of balance. The surgery I do is equal to what I did before, but slower. And I am my worst critic.

My grandfather would say the same words he did so many years ago, "God has something for you to do, or you wouldn't have lived to see this day."

In my fifth life, I may be the last corn stalk. I hope this life is longer or more lives are waiting. Though bitter winds blow and I do fall, I have had a glimpse, a preview of the easy walk and bright view of a time to be. When Winter passes, Spring will come.

How many lives does one man get? The number is not for me to know. As many as God chooses ... until my earthly journey is done.

www.ingramcontent.com/pod-product-compliance
Lightning Source LLC
Chambersburg PA
CBHW071827270326
41929CB00013B/1914
9780788451683